BEHIND THE BARS —
EXPERIENCES IN CRIME

D0743853

FREDERICK J. DESROCHES
ST. JEROME'S COLLEGE
UNIVERSITY OF WATERLOO

Canadian Scholars' Press   Toronto   1996

Behind the Bars: Experiences in Crime
Frederick J. Desroches

First Published in 1996 by
Canadian Scholars' Press Inc.
180 Bloor Street West, Ste. 402
Toronto, Ontario
M5S 2V6

Canadian Cataloguing in Publication Data
Desroches, Frederick John
        Behind the bars: experiences in crime

Includes bibliographical references.
ISBN 1-55130-089-3

1. Thieves — Canada — Biography.   2. Thieves —
United States — Biography.   3. Bank robberies — Canada.
4. Bank robberies — United States.   I. Title

HV6665.C3D46   1996   364.1'552'092271   C96-931398-5

Page layout and cover design by Brad Horning

Second printing October 1999

This book is dedicated
to my wife Lisa.

TABLE OF CONTENTS

INTRODUCTION

BEHIND THE BARS — EXPERIENCES IN CRIME IS BASED ON EIGHT YEARS of research with Hold-Up Squad detectives and convicted bank robbers in Canada and the United States. Each of the ten chapters in this book provides thematic and theoretical overviews of specific issues followed by excerpts of interviews with individual offenders. The interviews give readers insight into criminal value systems, rationalizations, thinking processes, and the vast range of situations these men have encountered. The news media constantly report on criminal activities in part because of public interest and fascination with crime. Crime itself often involves high drama: conflict, confrontation, courage, danger, desperation, skill, tragedy, morality play, heroes and villains, escape and capture, chases, guns, and shootouts. The interviews that make up this book document the tragedy and sadness these criminals have brought upon themselves and others. There is also excitement, adventure, comedy, and passion. The reader will discover bravery and cowardice, good luck and bad, competence and incompetence, initiative and inertia, trust and betrayal, love and hate — generally more of the latter than the former. The stories are funny, quirky, pathetic, and violent.

But they are all fascinating to read and to question "Why?". The interview materials will evoke sorrow, admiration, disgust, bewilderment, and a whole range of emotions we experience when we look closely at the human condition. This book is about crime and criminals, but the detailed analysis and the varied stories within help to shed light on human social behaviour in general. Interview materials have been selected to expose the reader to both common and unusual circumstances that guide the lives and decision-making of men who commit serious crimes.

Almost all the men in this study were serving time in Canadian or U.S. prisons. Why should convicts agree to discuss their lives and criminal experiences with a university researcher? One might expect them to be embittered by their incarceration and view with suspicion anyone wishing to question them on sensitive issues. Fortunately, most bandits cooperated for reasons that range from altruistic and idealistic to self-serving and mundane: they enjoyed talking about their "work"; this was an opportunity to be released from institutional work obligations; it was a break from the boring mundane life of prison; they wished to "straighten the record" regarding what has been said about them in court and/or the media; they recognized the value of research and wished to help; and, since they were retired and their crimes a part of the public record, they had nothing to hide. Inmates also wished to be viewed as cooperative by the parole board and correctional personnel: "It makes 'them' happy." "This might help me with my parole." "It's something to put on my file." Although they don't mention it, some are flattered to be included in the study and are excited by the possibility of their escapades being published. Most promise to purchase a copy of the book so that they can read all about themselves. Most respondents were forthright, detailed, and animated in their depiction of events. Many described their criminal adventures as the most significant and exciting moments in their lives. Information received from the police helped stimulate discussions and corroborate inmate accounts of incidents.

Interviews averaged two and one-half to three hours, took place in prison, and were tape recorded. Five men who agreed to be interviewed refused to be taped because they were worried that information might be obtained by the police and/or the parole board. On occasion, bandits would ask that the tape recorder be turned off so that they could answer the question honestly. Topics discussed "off the record" include: the number of robberies committed; the number of months or years the offender has robbed banks; specific incidents that occurred in holdups; the involvement of one's wife/girlfriend or family members; the assistance of a girlfriend who worked as a bank teller; the discharge of a gun in the bank; the fabrication of a false name for parties who escaped; and the planning of crimes that had not been attempted. Despite such cooperation, certain problems exist in conducting criminological research. Cases are sometimes before the courts for long periods and offenders are unavailable for interviews. Similarly, whenever a case is under appeal, inmates are advised by their attorneys not to discuss criminal matters with anyone. Time was often a constraint and 30 inmates were re-interviewed at later dates to take advantage of their extensive experience.

The purpose of this book is to apply theory and research to the cases presented in order to illustrate the diverse and complex factors and processes that influence criminal behaviour and lifestyle. Each chapter begins with a theoretical overview followed by synopses of relevant interview materials that illustrate particular theories and provide readers with an opportunity to see for themselves the life histories of serious offenders. Chapter One, *Need and Greed — The Motivation to Bank Robbery*, focuses on motivational components that lead someone to initially commit a holdup and lifestyle and spending habits that motivate them to continue. Discussed in this section are anomie, opportunity, and rational choice theories. Chapter Two, *Learning From Others — The Tricks of the Trade*, analyzes the manner in which criminal skills, values, and techniques of neutralization are learned from other criminals both in prison and on the street. Also discussed are cultural transmission, differential association, and illegitimate opportunity theories. Chapter 3, *From Bonnie and Clyde to Kojak — The Influence of the Mass Media*, deals with the manner in which offenders are inspired to crime through media portrayals and dramatizations. Learning theories, differential identification, and imitation theories are discussed. Chapter 4, *Nothing to Lose — The Tragic*, focuses on social control theory and the down-and-out life and situations of people who engage in crime. Chapter 5, *Feeding the Need — The Addicts*, explores the relationship between addiction, substance abuse and criminal conduct. Chapter 6, *Taking the Short-Cut — From Respectability to Crime*, analyzes the sudden involvement of previously law-abiding persons into serious criminal activity. Chapter 7, *A Dangerous Breed — Career and Professional Criminals*, presents the case histories of men who are clearly committed to crime as a way of life and who exhibit superior skill and planning in their chosen career. Chapter 8, *Violators of the Code — The Informants*, examines the inmate/criminal prohibition against informing and instances in which the code has been broken. Chapter 9, *In the Arms of the Law — Encounters with the Police*, discusses how bandits are caught, the dangers of arrest situations, and the often harsh response of the police to violent offenders. Chapter 10, *Deals and Appeals — Sentencing and the Courts*, focuses on the theory of deterrence in sentencing and the lengthy prison terms imposed on men who rob banks.

This research would not have been possible without the financial support of the Social Sciences and Humanities Research Council of Canada.

CHAPTER ONE

NEED AND GREED —

THE MOTIVATION TO BANK ROBBERY

- SENIOR CITIZEN
- WHEN NEED TURNS TO GREED
- PLANNING TO GET MARRIED
- EXOTIC DANCER

ROBBERY IS A CRIME THAT IS PRIMARILY MOTIVATED BY THE NEED OR DESIRE for money. Anomie, opportunity, and rational choice theories all emphasize the rational and utilitarian components of criminal motives and behaviour. Robert Merton's theory of anomie (1938; 1968) argues that North American society holds out as available and desirable the goal of financial success. At the same time, however, there is much less emphasis on the means of acquiring money. Merton suggests that this cultural phenomenon will tempt individuals to take the most efficient means to reach their goals even if that involves criminal conduct. He also argues that the legitimate means to obtain financial gain for most lower-class persons are blocked since they have few educational and job opportunities. People in a situation of anomie — aspiring to cultural goals but finding the legitimate opportunities blocked — are likely to experience strain and choose illegitimate means by which to obtain money. Anomie theory best explains utilitarian and instrumental crimes such as robbery and implicitly suggests that offenders think, plan, calculate, and choose their courses of action.

Richard Cloward (1959; Cloward and Ohlin, 1960) expands on anomie theory by pointing out that crime is not simply a matter of will, it also requires illegitimate opportunity. This includes knowledge about the techniques needed to commit the crime and target vulnerability. As will be seen in this and subsequent chapters, robbery is an easy crime to commit and knowledge of techniques are learned in large part from others and through media presentations.

Rational choice theory (Clark and Cornish, 1985) is based on the idea that offenders do indeed think and make choices. From this perspective, property offences are the result of rational decision-making reached by men and women who confront a problem faced by many others — a need or a desire for money. The would-be criminal thus views theft as a rational and productive activity despite the fact that capture, imprisonment, and death may be part of the equation.

Since robbery is an economic crime, it might be expected that would-be robbers mentally calculate possible financial gain, what actions are required, the risks involved, and how he or she feels about undertaking these actions. If there appears to be an acceptable chance at not getting caught and a desirable amount to gain, then the individual should decide in favour of committing the crime. On the other hand, if the perceived risk of capture is high and the expected penalty is great, the would-be criminal should be deterred.

Because robbery is a serious crime with severe penalties and significant possibilities for getting hurt, would-be robbers might be expected to give careful thought to the choice of target and the development of a plan for reducing the chances of arrest. Research indicates, however, that most do little planning, use minimal disguise, and give little thought to being caught (Desroches, 1995; Feeney, 1986; Camp, 1968; Conklin, 1972; Ciale and Leroux, 1983; Haran and Martin, 1984; Gabor et al., 1987; Ballard, 1992). Rational choice theory does not make an objective evaluation of the offender's decision-making processes, rather it attempts to understand behaviour from his or her perspective and assumes that decisions exhibit limited or bounded rationality (Simon, 1957). In other words, behaviour may be planned and premeditated but not fully rational. Decisions are made under time and other constraints and even though objectively it may be true that the gains are small and the risks high, there are nonetheless elements of rational thought behind the crime. At the time the offender feels that the risk is worth the potential gain even though in retrospect he or she may (and often does) view his or her rationality as deficient.

Most culprits intend to rob only one bank, but soon become hooked on the lifestyle and the friends and partying that accompany it. Early success increases confidence and contributes to the offender engaging in a pattern of successive holdups which, for the men in this study, eventually result in their arrest and imprisonment. Even after they have robbed several banks, most offenders intend to quit "after this next robbery." If need convinces men to rob banks in the first place, then greed motivates them to continue. The small amounts of cash available from individual tellers combined with the lavish spending habits robbers quickly acquire lead them to commit a series of robberies in rapid succession to support their escalating lifestyle. Because of the ever increasing probability of arrest, the career of most bank robbers normally ends after several weeks of robbing, spending, and partying. Partying typically involves frequenting bars, purchasing drinks and drugs for themselves and others, staying up late, sleeping in, and doing more of the same the following day. Having no responsibilities or money worries is described as fun and the bar scene is the focus of much of their time and energies. Offenders also spend money on clothing, gifts, taxis, and expensive hotels. The fact that most squander the money indicates that they are unlikely to retire from bank robbery because they have no alternative income. The value of money appears to diminish the more one has and the easier it is to obtain. Many become addicted to the money and the corresponding lifestyle that easy wealth brings and are reluctant to give it up. Most express a "live for today and to hell with tomorrow" philosophy or fall into this pattern without admitting or realizing it. The fact that few men purchase expensive material goods indicates perhaps an awareness that they will not be around long enough to enjoy them. Most prefer instead transitory pleasures — drugs, alcohol, sex, companionship, and attention or status. Their attitude towards money is "easy come, easy go" and they spend freely and foolishly because "there's always more where that came from." It is their continuous return to the bank for more that is their eventual undoing.

The interview synopses that follow in this and subsequent chapters illustrate several motivational components — a need for money, the assessment of banks as easy and opportunistic targets, and a degree of rationality in selecting their target and *modus operandi*. Interview data allow the student of crime to examine the offender's perspective in order to understand which factors are taken into account when planning a crime. The following cases illustrate how rational thought and calculations are clearly evident in robbers' decision to rob. All bandits interviewed needed or wanted money and all believed that bank robbery was a low risk crime that provided fast, plentiful, and easily accessible funds.

Senior Citizen is a 68-year-old man who robbed the same bank twice. His motive was to obtain sufficient funds to purchase new furniture and a camper van so he could better enjoy his retirement. The story behind *When Need Turns to Greed* is that of a 29-year-old married man who loses his job and decides to rob a bank to pay his bills. Like others, he finds that bank robbery is "easy" and that need changes to greed and propels him to commit an estimated 40 bank holdups. In *Planning to Get Married*, the motive behind the robbery is to obtain enough money for two of the culprits to get married and receive their landed immigrant status in Canada. Events take a terrible turn for the four youthful robbers leading to the death of one and the arrest of the other three. The final interview in this chapter represents the partying lifestyle that is a partial motivation to most young bank robbers. *Exotic Dancer* moved from stripping in nightclubs to bank robbery after becoming infected with venereal warts. Depressed over losing his employment and missing the lavish lifestyle and bar scene that went along with it, he robbed banks in order to maintain his previous spending habits. He also reveals that he learned about robbery from a brief prison stint and that coming from an inner city neighbourhood provided additional criminal learning opportunities.

Senior Citizen

Age 68, this offender was arrested when he attempted to rob the same bank a second time in the same week. Sentenced to four years imprisonment on three armed robberies, he expresses no regret for his crimes.

"I did three offences within the same block, which is my big foul-up. I tried a drug store two hours earlier and the cashier refused to hand over the money. There were a couple of stupid things I did, I accept this now. Like going back to the same bank a second time. It was the same bloody teller! My sister-in-law works for a bank and I had been told many times that if a girl is robbed, she automatically gets two weeks off. Maybe it depends on how many people are there because if people are on holiday, maybe they can't give her the time off. This was in August and she was there. I wasn't very observant. She left her counter to tell the manager and apparently she left a second time to phone the police to tell them to hurry up.

"I was reading the papers and it seemed that everybody was doing them and nobody was being caught. It entered my mind and I dismissed it. I read up a little on it, cased the bank, and it just came together slowly. I lived right across from the bank so I could case the thing from my living room.

"It was around five o'clock and the street is one of the most travelled in the city. After robbing the bank, I just walked out and crossed the street to my apartment. No problem. I was going to do it again but I didn't count on being spotted. This girl who fingered me was Vietnamese and I would give her around 35 years. She was a marvel. The first time in there, I handed her a note, 'This is a bank robbery. Hand over the money quick.' I had my gun in my jacket and brought it out of the pocket so she could see it. She wasn't impressed with it. She wasn't shattered. Her composure wasn't ripped down at all. She was good, perfect.

"I could have done it without a gun but the availability came up to have a gun for fifty dollars and I wasn't going to rob a bank without one. It's the bona fide way to do it. I sure wasn't going to rob a bank without the tools. I'm familiar with guns because I was in the military and fought in World War II. Guns don't intimidate me unless someone points one at my head. The thing is, if some goof from the police force comes into the line-up and says, 'I'm a policeman,' see how much of a hero he is with a .32 in his face. See if he's a smart guy then. That was the only reason. There was a ten percent chance I was eliminating — the hero factor. It was loaded, but I had absolute control.

"I had five gentlemen with revolvers arrive at the scene. 'Gentlemen,' I use the term loosely. Stupid cops. I actually laugh about this occasionally. They had five guys in uniform come in with guns pointed out. One cop came straight at me and I assumed I could do one of two things — shoot it out or hand over my gun. I handed him my gun as soon as he arrived. He took my revolver immediately. He put his gun to my head and was shaking like he was a leaf. I told him, 'For goodness sake, put the gun down!' He scared me and I dropped my teeth as they pushed me out the door. I tried to bend down to pick them up but couldn't. Later, somebody brought them to the police station. I wasn't wearing a disguise, but I took my teeth out for the first one.

"I had just been approved for a senior citizen's apartment and I wanted new furniture. I had a ten-year-old Chevy van and I wanted a new van too. I have a piece of property up north on a river with good fishing and I use the van for camping. Like a dummy, I couldn't wait so I robbed a bank. I have no patience. I have a bit of a background of boozing and my record at work is not great. Even when I worked as an electrician, I had a lot of difficulty.

"I blame the government for a lot of my troubles. I was in the navy fourteen years before getting a misconduct discharge. It doesn't really matter how it happened, punching some officer in the beak. At any rate, I don't get any pension. I should have fought it and I could have come out of it with something. We have access to lawyers in prison and I'm looking into it.

"After my discharge. I've done time before for uttering. I used to do frauds by picking open mailboxes and cashing government cheques. It was getting tougher to utter and after I got nicked they were on to me. Computers have thrown a lot of people in my particular field out of business. They're a lot faster at detecting us. That's why I moved to armed robbery. I have known other people into it and it's fairly clean. It's fast — 25-30 seconds — you can't make 2500 dollars any faster. I needed money. It was logic with me. If you want bread, you go to a bread store, and if you want money, you go to a money store.

"I don't care for bank robbery because it's so out-and-out. As soon as you commit an armed robbery, you've definitely said to yourself, 'It's not outsmarting anyone, you've gone to violent crime.' With fraud, you're playing a game and it's like doing business. You've outsmarted someone, and for me this is being a shrewd businessman. You're not an out-and-out thief. That's my thinking on the matter. There's more professional pride to fraud because you have to dress nicely, present yourself, be friendly with the tellers. It's an art.

"I used to be married and I have three children. My daughter is a school teacher and my two sons are lawyers. I was a dummy when I was in the navy and didn't pay attention to my home affairs. I still thought I was single and spent my time chasing women. It was all stupid and selfish. It's okay for me to say so now, but 30 years ago I didn't think that way. My wife and I eventually split up and she died a few years ago. I've remained on good terms with my family. My kids were amazed when I first went to jail, but little did they know that three-quarters of their education was paid through various criminal escapades.

"Drinking was a problem for me, but I was always trying to make money and impress everybody. I always wanted to have a nice car and enjoy going away — fishing or whatever. Do things for my family like put the boys through university. Quite frankly, I don't regret for a moment what I did. This doesn't degrade me personally by being in prison. Four years for three armed robberies, it's a kiss. The food and accommodations are better than we had in the navy fighting for our country. I even have a private room.

"In future, if worse came to worse, I would do the same thing, but I wouldn't do it as easy as I did before. I would have a lot more patience in the future. I still get my old age pension and it's gone into a bank account while I'm in prison. I have that waiting for me when I get out and I also have some loot in a safety deposit box. Quite frankly, this wasn't something new for me and I didn't spend a cent of it."

When Need Turns to Greed

Age 29, this offender is serving ten years on 14 counts of bank robbery. He admits robbing two to three banks a week over a six-month period and estimates that his final tally amounts to more than 40 holdups. His *modus operandi* never changed: he wore no disguise, operated solo, drove his own car, robbed banks that were empty of customers and that did not have cameras, would not rob male tellers or central tellers, passed a note demanding money, was unarmed, and chose the teller closest to the door whenever possible. Married for seven years, he has three children and comes from a middle-class background. He also has a criminal record and served two years in prison at the age of 17 for the robbery of a variety store.

"The newspapers named me the 'Cheque Bandit' because I always made out a deposit slip stating: 'I Have Gun. Hand Over Money.' I started robbing banks out of stupidity. Most of all it was the publicity from T.V., radio, and newspapers — everyday there's something. This bank being hit and this bank being hit. They always told me how they did it. Like passing holdup notes.

"I was down and out and I had to support my wife and kids. I was just laid off and had to go to court because the rent was three months behind and the landlord was evicting us. The sheriff gave us 48 hours to move. I needed the money and I had to do something. My wife wasn't working. I was down and out so I decided to get some money. I was reading about all these bank robberies. I tried it and after that it just rocketed. I guess when you get desperate like that you'll do anything. I did it for my family.

"The first bank was across from the unemployment office [chuckle]. I was sitting in my car and seen the bank and I decided this is it! It was a spur of the moment thing and I wasn't wearing nothing to disguise myself. I drove around the bank looking for a spot to park the car. I wrote the note on a piece of paper bag I ripped up. I walked in and waited for my turn. Afterwards, I shook all the way home. I stopped in a donut shop for an hour and drank coffee. It just happened so fast, like in 30 or 40 seconds, and then I was gone.

"I told my wife that my lottery ticket had come up. I had never lied to her before so she had no reason to doubt me. The next day we found a nice condominium, put first and last month's rent down, bought groceries, and moved in. I did another bank the very next day [laughs].

"After the first, she didn't know we had the money. I'd rob a bank and then go to my bank and make a deposit the same day. I ended up purchasing this television rental franchise. I invested about $50,000.

About two months before I got caught the business was booming. I was making $800 a day. I was happy, everyone was happy. I had to do one more. The mortgage on the business was coming up, $2500, and I thought one more bank score would cover that. I had stopped for two months and the business was going well. My wife thought I had a silent partner who was doing the financing. My luck was going good so I had to do one more and that's when I got caught. I did so many that I didn't think I was ever going to get caught.

"Everytime I did one, I'd say this is my last one. But it was never my last one. I wish I had been caught on the first one. I wanted to quit but I couldn't, something inside telling me it was easy, 'Do another one, you can do one more.' Greed, greed and stupidity. There was a point there where I didn't even need the money. I had $5000 in the trunk of my car in a paper bag under my spare tire and I still robbed a bank! Greed. I was spending foolishly. I passed a panhandler after I did one and gave him a $50 bill. I never seen a guy so happy in my life. One Sunday, I chartered a plane and flew off to a resort with my wife. Another time, I went to a carnival and took the whole family, brothers and sisters and ten kids too. Had a ball. I spent $600 there. Good day!

"Then on my last one, a bank manager followed me out and took down my licence plate. I was parked in the back alley. I seen somebody with a suit on and I assumed it was the bank manager. I drove home and sat around and waited. Then the police came. They all came! They were rough. One fella was nice and one was a hard core. The one gives you cigarettes and coffee and the other choked me and threw me against the wall.

"They had a file full of robberies they wanted cleared. I didn't admit to any of them, not even the one I got caught for, until about midnight. There were six of them and they took turns questioning me. I phoned my lawyer and he told me to shut up. I didn't though. They forced it out of me. They threatened to harass my wife and confiscate all that was new in our apartment. I didn't want my wife hassled and everything in the apartment is brand new. Finally, I made a statement and signed it. I lost the business after I was arrested, but my wife is still with me even though I put her through a lot. She told me I have one more chance [laughs]. I just had another daughter since I've been in here."

Planning to Get Married

Four men in their early twenties commit an ill-fated bank robbery in which one of them dies. This offender, age 24, was described in the newspapers as the mastermind behind the robbery and is serving a ten-year sentence. Three men masked and armed themselves before entering the bank while another accomplice waited nearby in their getaway vehicle. The newspaper article indicated that they were under police surveillance and that the bandits opened fire at officers as they emerged from the bank. This man was shot in his ankle shortly afterwards. He was originally charged with attempted murder but pled guilty to robbery and a firearms offence.

"My partners tried to make it look as if I'm the one who did everything. But that's not the way it is! They're saying that I'm the mastermind behind all this. One guy got three years for everything and the other got five years. They gave me ten years, but that was reduced to eight on appeal. They tried to give me ten years for something I didn't even do, fire that gun.

"My partners got a break to say things to make it look that I was all behind the thing. It was my sister's car. So I have problems. I swear on my mom, my dad, I didn't do nothing what these guys said I did. I went in the bank, I jumped the counter, I took some money, and put it in the bag. I didn't even have a gun. Porter had the gun and he's the one who fired it. I didn't do nothing. It's just that they said that I fired on the officer. So the judge is going to figure this guy's not a soften criminal, he's a hardened criminal 'cause he's shooting at cops. I didn't do it, but they charged me with attempted murder.

"You see, I was taken to the hospital. Porter's dead so he's taken to the morgue. Walker and Johnson are brought to the police station. They're there and Walker said he was influenced by me to participate in a bank robbery. Johnson said that he didn't know nothing about it. He said that he asked for a drive and the next thing he knew he was on the highway. Well these guys never worked. Johnson's got landed immigrant status and so am I. But I'm here quite awhile before him. Since I came to this country, I went to school, I been working, I contribute to this society of yours. These guys never worked. Porter and Walker don't even have work visas. They just have visitors' visas. I've been here 11 years and I worked in furniture repair ever since. Like I used to do it after school. I'm trying to help myself by way of working. Then I become friends with three idiots. They turn around and make it look like I'm the one who's telling them to be crooked.

"Porter wanted to get married so he could stay in the country. He and Walker only have visitors' visas. So they asked me if I could assist them with the car while they were doing it. And they had the necessary things that it takes to hold up a bank. I was laid off in April and this happened in July. I had my sister's car 'cause she was in Jamaica then.

"Porter talked to me about it. Johnson came out of jail at this time and he decided to be the driver and we explained everything and told him that I could help with the holdup. So we go ahead with it. This is what happened. I was trying to help these guys 'cause they can't stay in the country unless they're married. They're not even in the country legal because their visitors' visas have expired. I know what it's like to be in a difficult position. I realize you could be walking down the road and a cop pull you over and grab you and you're back on a plane to Jamaica, and that's not what he wants. He wants a future. He's trying to make himself somebody by being here 'cause there's not much in Jamaica he can achieve.

"So these are the things why I even took part in it. Johnson did it because he does not work. He's just like that. I've known him for five years and he hasn't worked. He was the one who caused me to meet Porter and Walker. I don't think it would have happened if I hadn't gone along 'cause they didn't have a car and I couldn't just trust them with the key and say, 'Okay, go ahead use this car.' I would rather be there. So that's how I really got involved 'cause this wasn't even my car. It was my sister's car and these guys don't have a licence. I don't feel like saying no to these guys because I sort of felt compassionate for them.

"Porter wanted to get married the most because he was the one pushing the issue. Walker wanted to get married too. They asked these girls who said yes, but they had no money and they were sort of concerned about doing the wedding the proper way. These girls are going to think, 'Okay, where is he going to get the money to marry me? He hasn't got a job. He hasn't got a work permit.' Maybe she knows that he's doing it because he wants to be in the country. I don't know. Porter wants the money so he can say to her, 'Okay, I got three thousand dollars, we can get married.' He wanted to get on with it, to get himself straightened out, get a place to live. These guys wanted a chance and they asked me and told me I got nothing to worry about. Everything was going to be okay.

"But I really didn't have a need for it. Sure I was laid off my job, but I was getting unemployment cheques. I was living comfortable with my girlfriend. I'm pretty sure my job would be there as soon as the business picks up because Christmas is coming up. Things are starting to pick up and I'll be back at my job soon. Porter and Johnson had got some guns somehow. They told me about this bank so we drove up one night and they said, 'This is it.' Porter explained everything. Johnson wasn't there. It was just the three of us. We planned it at home. Porter said he would stay at the door with the shotgun. Walker had a little handgun and he said he would jump the counter with me and take the money from the tills. It sounded easy.

"We drove to the bank and parked the car. Johnson stayed behind to watch the car. We walked up to the bank and pulled on our masks. I had a tam I pulled down over my face. I just cut some holes in it for eyes. Walker and I went in first and he went over to the counter and he started yelling. I went over the counter and looked back to see Porter at the door. I was worried he wouldn't be there. I was taking money out of the tills and I was sort of eager 'cause it was my first time. Everytime I took money I had to go down to Walker because we only had one bag [laughs]. I was shaky but not frightened. I kept my eyes opened because I didn't want to get pinched. I was eager to prove myself to these guys.

"One lady in there was kind of scared. She was helping Walker and she backed away from the till. One of them picked up something and Walker slapped it out of her hand [snaps fingers]. I don't know why but he must have figured it was some sort of alarm. He pointed the gun at her too. That's when he said, 'Let's go.' He jumped the counter and I was behind him. We get out of the bank and Porter is ahead of us 'cause he had said, 'Let's go' and I didn't hear him.

"Porter is running back towards the car and I see him raise the shotgun and the gun went off. I was wondering why he fired it, but then I see this guy behind a wall bending down. Porter fired the gun in the air to scare the guy but I guess the police don't take it that way. I was the last guy out of the bank and I followed these guys across a soccer field. Johnson was at the car and I yelled at him to pick us up. Johnson drove back towards our direction and he continued driving by us and he drove past us! So Walker started running the car down and I was looking at Porter and thinking this is crazy! He's totally left us! Johnson is driving away and Walker is running behind the car waving the bag of money. I'm standing there and I was saying to Porter, 'This guy's crazy! He drove off and left us!' He says to me, 'Can you believe this guy?' Then I see Johnson stop the car, reverse, pick Walker up, and they take off. I talked to him in jail and he told me he saw a car down the road. He didn't trust the car so he didn't want to pick us up.

"Porter and I went and hid in this back yard under a tree. We were hiding because we knew the cops were going to be looking for us. We were only about 100 to 130 yards away from the bank sitting under a tree. Then I heard, 'Hold it! Don't move! Freeze! Police!' Our backs were turned so I look and six officers are pointing their guns at us. Porter started running and I started running too. As I turned my back, that's when the shots started firing. They were firing at us! I didn't make it to the fence. I was shot in the ankle, my right ankle.

"I never seen Porter ever since. I just heard that he died. Johnson and Walker got caught a couple of blocks down the road. I heard they were driving at full speed and the police had blocked the road and Johnson didn't want to stop the car so the police fired and he stopped.

"They took me right to the hospital because I was shot. My bones weren't broken but I'm still feeling pain. I wear soft shoes. This was my first experience at getting shot and at the time I couldn't put my mind to the pain. I was too concerned with asking myself how I could let this happen to myself. How could I get involved in this robbery in the first place? This is not like me. A lot of people were surprised, my boss, my family.

"I got a good family. They didn't give up on me. They knew it was because of these friends I keep. My mom has always said, 'You've got enough brothers, just keep them as your friends.' My parents think this is the worst thing that can ever happen to me. That's what I think too. My family visits and so does my girlfriend. She has a kid from me. None of my family has been in trouble before.

"I was never in jail before and this is a maximum security place. When I came here I met one guy, he was from Jamaica. You talk to a guy socially, the next thing you know some guy's telling me don't talk to him because if I do I'm going to get killed just like him. When I came here I was friendly. I wanted to know exactly how to get around and he's the one who filled me in. So I don't want to show the guy a bad face 'cause he was helpful to me. Then he got beat up and was in the hospital for an operation. Then I hear that the same guys want to drop me. And I said, 'But I haven't done anything. Why should people want to drop me?'

"I saw them when they beat him. It was after supper and we were standing near the gate and I saw one guy grab him and started choking him. But I couldn't really participate in defending him 'cause I don't know the reason this guy struck him. There's all these big guys and they're choking him. I got scared because one of these guys came up to me and said he was going to shank me in the back when I turned my back. I got scared so I checked into P.C. [protective custody]. I asked to go because I was being intimidated by these people. There were a few people who knew me and that I mind my own business. They talk to these guys and say the dude is cool so I'm back out now. It's just me. I'm alone anyhow. I'm not bothering nobody.

"Walker is going to be deported after he serves his time. A lady from immigration came here to see me. We talked for an hour and I may be sent back too. I don't want to go, but if I have to I guess I have no choice. So like I'm on my way out of the country for my first mistake, my first real mistake. This is my mistake and I paid for it. As long as I live this ain't never going to happen to me again 'cause this is not me. I'm telling you."

Exotic Dancer

Age 24, this offender was convicted of nine bank robberies over a three-month period. He operated armed, entered the bank alone, and handed tellers a Crown Royal whisky bag demanding they

> fill it with money. He explains that part of his motive for robbery was to maintain the lavish lifestyle that his previous employment as an exotic dancer had provided. He was caught when someone took down the licence plate number of his getaway vehicle.

"I was an exotic dancer and that brings a lot of fame. I was dancing in some of the finest clubs in North America: the West coast, the East coast, Montreal, Chippendales in Beverly Hills, California. And it's the fame and the free money. I say it's free because I'm not actually working for it. And when you get paid you say, 'What did I really do for this? Take my clothes off and show them some of my talents, that's all.' The money's coming in and it's tax free cash — $1200-$1500 a week and I was only 21 and 22.

"It does something to your values. I had to be the king of hell. My father didn't approve of me dancing, but I was enjoying it and I was making good money so he left it at that. My mother was really amazed, 'My son the exotic dancer.' Oh, she liked it. It was a good conversational piece at work for her lady friends. And I'm always looking sharp on the street, the image, clothes. It's not just a job, it's a lifestyle. It only lasts so long, but at the time when you're at your peak it means so much to you. Working in bars and always partying. Everything was sex with me. That's all I was doing all day just about. I'd meet girls everywhere.

"But I worked at it too. I'd be training, learning new steps, and rehearsing different acts. In some places you have to wear a G-string; in other places it all comes off but it's illegal to have a hard-on. The cops can arrest you if you have it pointing in the air. In some cities, you have to be a waiter, dance on tables, and do a stage show. Weird. Some nights you'll have 300 rabid women and they want to see a dancer. Like it's a little encore before anyone goes on. They hit their glasses on the tables. They want a dancer and he gets up on the stage and they just go crazy. Then you get off the stage and they all want a piece of you.

"I started a relationship with a woman who I'm going to marry in prison in two months. That's when I went downhill, but not because I met her. It's pretty personal. I grabbed a venereal disease through one of the clubs and I passed it on to her and at that time I thought it was incurable. It was venereal warts. They got very serious because at first I was very shocked and thought they'd go away on their own. I didn't know what the hell was going on. They didn't go away; they got worse. I went to see a doctor and he was a really bad doctor. He said there was no cure for this, this is a virus. It's like trying to cure the common cold, can't cure that. I've been treated with liquid nitrogen in here and they're going away. There is no pain. I had one on my finger too. I caught the warts before I did the banks, way before I did the banks, and I couldn't dance any more because I had the warts.

"My girlfriend noticed them first and she went for a check and she had them too. When she found out I gave them to her, she freaked out on me and I freaked out on her. We didn't deal with it like we should have and we split up. That's when I said, 'Fuck it,' and I was thinking of different ways of killing myself. The state of mind I had was suicidal. I'd sit over a bottle of rye, Crown Royal, and drink my problems away — boo hoo hoo. I couldn't open myself up to anybody. I couldn't tell anybody I had a dose. Even my close friends. I was keeping it inside. Couldn't confide in anyone. I'd always see the same people I party with and with the ladies it's not the same. There was no way I could sleep with them, no way to fool around at all. Just a mere fact. I had a real close friend I took a chance with. I slept with her and she found out I had them. She found them and she asked, 'What's this?' and that just blew my lights. I was fucked from there in. It was my fault and I should have told her in the first place and I felt really bad about this. I'd lay awake at night thinking of ways of killing myself.

"Robbing a bank has always been in my mind. I got nine months one time for selling cocaine to an undercover officer. I was dancing at a club and this guy came to my dressing room and I had some coke for sale. He looked really cool, a beard and everything. I can feel the vibes off cops, but for some reason I didn't with him. I give him a line and he did it. I thought cops weren't supposed to do it but he did. I sell him a gram and he leaves. Then somebody approached me and asked if I saw a guy with a beard walking around because we think he's a cop. 'Holy fuck! I just sold him a gram of coke.' They said, 'Fuck off out of here of he'll come back and bust your ass.' Then somebody else says, 'He didn't look like a cop to me.' So I stayed and was going to do my set when they cut the music and come up on the stage and grabbed me. Everybody's screaming, 'Hey, what are you doing?' and they take me away in handcuffs. So I met a lot of guys in the can who talked about robbery and that's how I learned how to do it. In prison, you make a lot of contacts and learn a lot about crime. I also learned a lot about crime from the people I grew up with. It was a rough neighbourhood and there was plenty going on.

"I've always had this abnormal get-up-and-go power. Not just anyone can dance. Anyone can make a fool of himself, but not anyone can do it and please 200 women at the same time. It takes a lot of balls to do that. I used different stage names, but I liked 'Gangster' and used that a lot. As I was doing my time I talked to these guys, bank robbers, and they told me how they did it. Even when I was dancing and things were going good it was there, the idea, 'I can do that' or 'Right on, just to try one.'

"I was drinking a lot and I was really depressed. I couldn't see her any more. I went to crime because I didn't care. I couldn't dance and I couldn't face the people that I knew because 70 percent of my friends were women and you're marked with a disease. Basically why you see these women is just to have a good time and there is no more of that because they don't want that disease. So my mind started working towards banks. I regret what I've done and I'm doing eight years, but it was fascinating. Incredible! If you want a high out of life, rob a bank.

"The first one freaked me out. Each one is different and the hardest part for me is walking from the car to the front door. Once I got inside the bank it relieved the pressure. Once I walk through the doors it's my bank. I own that bank. The second hardest part would be from the door to the car again. I'd have a jogging outfit on and I'd jog. While I'm in that bank, I'm in control. In one bank the whole place caught the play and nobody moved. If anyone blinks I catch them blink. I see the bank manager's feet get up and I see them walking over to the end of the divider. He takes a peek around the divider and catches the play. Now I've got the chunk here in my coat and I open my coat and look at him and just with my lips I tell him, 'Sit down!' and he sat. It's a very serious feeling. The vibes are there. 'He's going to kill me if I make the wrong move.' If you don't make those vibes, some hero will try to tackle you. I've never had that problem. The impression I give them is, 'Don't fuck up and I won't fuck up.' The whole mood of the performance is very serious. But it's an act because you're not going to shoot anyone. So in that way it's not serious.

"This one time, I'm standing in line and I see this teller. She looks really nice. She looks at me, I look at her, we smile at each other. She's doing her work and looking at me. What the hell am I doing? Walking into the bank to rob the damn place and here I am flirting with the teller [laughs]. I walk up to her and she smiles, 'Yes, can I help you?' I give her this note and this bag and I thought she was going to faint. She steps back about two feet, gives me this smart little look, and goes, 'Really?' I look at her and said, 'Move it.' I changed my mood, changed my face. I showed her the butt of the gun and she said, 'Okay sir.' They always address you as sir. They amaze me, tellers. They do their job and they do it well.

"I was always calm. The teller would hit her alarm button and I'd say, 'Okay you fucking idiot, I saw what you did so move it.' That would get them off guard and they'd say, 'Yes sir.' And then they take their time, give you five and tens and I'd say, 'Gimme the $100s and $50s.' I'd have to tell 'em to lift up the drawer and sure enough there are the fifties and one hundreds. They were smart. Some would say, 'Do you really have a gun?' or 'If you don't have a gun, I'm not giving it to you. Show me your gun.'

"There is one incident where I flipped out and ran out of the bank without the money. I walked up to the head teller because I intended to ask for the foreign currency too. She's giving me all these notes, putting them in the bag when this other teller comes over, looks at me, and catches the play. She just freezes and her hand goes under the counter and she presses the alarm. I saw her do this and she was a snotty bitch. Next thing I know I hear this heavy duty noise that sounded like an alarm. Everybody's twisting their heads and they're all looking at me. I get paranoid and I think they're thinking, 'You cocksucker, you're robbing our bank.' So I grabbed the bag, but there's a string on it which I usually put around my wrist and it gets caught behind the till. Already a minute's gone by so I run out and tell my driver, 'Let's go, we got no money.' He said, 'What's wrong?' And I said, 'They set off an alarm.' But when I get outside I still hear the alarm. It wasn't an alarm at all, just someone outside drilling into the concrete.

"I used a getaway driver because I couldn't handle driving. I don't like driving at any time. I owned two cars and if I'm going out for the evening, either my girlfriend drives or I get a buddy to drive because I can't stand all the stupid people on the road. And coming out of the bank I'm paranoid as hell. I couldn't handle the getaway car. I always felt it was better to get yourself a driver, somebody you can really trust. I'd park them a block, two blocks away. He'd be sitting waiting, see me coming, flip the back seat, I'd get on the floor of the back seat, and he would just drive calmly. He looks nothing like me. Even drive right by the bank sometimes. I'd give him a cut, a flat rate, say $800.

"I did one a week and the way I was doing them I was getting $3000 to $4000 each time. I got $9000 in one. I'd know where they kept the money and I'd know when I didn't get enough and send them to the next teller for more. I'd do them on a Thursday or Friday when there was lots of money in the tills, and I did them in industrial areas where a lot of guys come to cash their cheques. And I'd do it at the time they cash their cheques, lunch hour. Friday night I'd grab my ounce of hash, my supply of coke, and go from party to party. I've got a bad smoking habit. Pick up people, go here, go there, and have a really good time. I was king of the hill. Lots of friends, lots of money to spend, a partier. When I was dancing, I was making lots of money so there was never a change of image. I had a big reputation as a dancer and I did the banks to maintain the lifestyle.

"My stupidity at being caught — my stupidity was doing them to begin with — but my stupidity of being caught was I got greedy. You get greedy very fast. It becomes like a game. The next day you pick up the papers, 'I wonder what they have to say today?' They're always describing you, how much money, what you did, how you left. I was doing stuff for the papers because they'd make it big if there was anything interesting to print. They called me the 'Crown Royal Bandit' because in two or three banks I handed the teller a Crown Royal bag to fill with money. This was part of the game. And greed. I would do a bank and spend it in three or four days. About a thousand dollars a day. Living like a king as long as it lasts. I'd buy clothing, partying, most of it was given away. A lot of the women I met were on welfare, single mothers, on welfare or mother's allowance. Everytime I'd drop by, I'd shoot them a couple of hundred. A lot went like that. Robin Hood.

"It worked out good at first and then you get lazy, you drop your guard. You leave clues behind and the cops eventually catch up to you. Obviously the Crown Royal bag; when you do get caught they bring up each one of those. Eventually somebody took down a licence plate number and I was arrested."

CHAPTER TWO

Learning from Others —

The Tricks of the Trade

- Young Offender
- Native Indian
- Papa was a Rolling Stone
- Travelling Bandit

Two of the earliest sociological theories of crime are cultural transmission (Shaw and McKay, 1942) and differential association theory (Sutherland, 1947). Both models argue that crime is learned behaviour and that high crime rate areas of the city expose residents to criminal values, norms, attitudes, and role models. A tradition of crime and delinquency is culturally transmitted from one generation to the next within specific neighbourhoods. Differential association theory further contends that interaction with delinquent or criminal peers is particularly significant in the learning process and that both techniques of committing the crime as well as the vocubulary of motives are learned. The principle of differential association states that a person becomes delinquent because of an excess of definitions favourable to violations of law over definitions unfavourable to violations of law. From this perspective, older criminals act as role models for younger ones who learn from them and emulate their behaviour.

Cloward and Ohlin (1960) suggest that contact with experienced criminals represents illegitimate opportunities to learn new types of criminal conduct. Robbers have to learn how to execute the crime, control tellers and customers, prevent identification, and make their escape before the police arrive. Knowledge of bank policies and police capabilities is frequently learned through interaction with more experienced criminals. Sykes and Matza use a version of differential association and social control theory to argue that offenders also learn techniques of neutralization to justify their actions. Criminals do not necessarily reject conventional, law-abiding values but render them partially and temporarily ineffective by using techniques of neutralization. These techniques are rationalizations that allow people to justify deviant conduct, protect their self-concepts, and help release individuals from the social controls imposed by the internalization of societal values. Common techniques used for bank robbery include the denial of responsibility, the denial of injury, and the denial of the victim. Robbers may partially diminish responsibility by blaming drug or gambling addiction or other forces beyond their control. They will also emphasize that no one was hurt in the crime, banks can afford the loss, and any fear experienced by tellers is transitory and not really harmful. Robbers also argue that banks deserve to be robbed because they exploit their customers and make such obscene profits. In addition, any harm that should befall someone who plays hero and interferes is justifiable since the robber must act in self-defence. Offenders may also justify robbery as an attempt to gain justice or seek revenge against their own perceived unjust social and economic situation. Sykes and Matza (1957; Matza, 1964) argue that techniques of neutralization are culturally available and learned in interaction with others.

In over one-half of the cases in this study, offenders originate the idea to rob banks through other criminals — offering support for learning theories of crime. Most of these bandits are introduced to robbery through family members, friends, acquaintances, or fellow inmates. *Young Offender* was 16 years old when he was arrested on two counts of bank robbery. This young man was separated from his parents as a child and spent his youth shunted from foster home to foster home eventually arriving in a youth detention centre. He is the fifth youngest male in a family of eight boys and his four older brothers have all served time for bank and armoured vehicle robberies. He speaks highly of his brothers who appear to be role models for him. His case illustrates how the learning process takes place within correctional institutions and with older experienced partners.

Native Indian describes a man who has a low-paying job, is tired of being broke, and learns from his cousin how to rob banks. *Papa Was a Rolling Stone* details the manner in which a criminal father influenced his two sons and nephew to engage in serious crime. The story is told by one of the sons whose emotions are clearly ambivalent: anger for the trouble his father caused him mixed with love despite the latter's failings. *Travelling Bandit* is introduced to bank robbery from a prison acquaintance who provides him with justifications for the act and shows him how to commit the crime.

Young Offender

Age 17, Jules comes from a family of eight brothers and eight sisters. His five older brothers have all been convicted of robbing banks and armoured vehicles. He is serving 18 months for two counts of bank robbery. He was friendly and cooperative in the interview and spoke matter-of-factly about his extensive experiences in robbing banks. At the suggestion of the prison superintendent, I took Jules and his partner Warren out of prison on day and weekend temporary absences and learned a great deal about his life. I later travelled to Montreal with him and met several of his brothers and sisters.

"I started robbing banks when I was only 15 while I was on the run from the detention centre. I escaped from there many times since I was ten years old. It took me three days to bend those sucker bars and the only one who could fit out was me. Not too many escaped from that area of the prison — it was really quite scary. Every door was locked and you couldn't go anywhere. Warren was there and so was my brother. In Montreal I'd have to say I'm just a beginner. Maybe I did a lot of banks — I would guess about 20 and a lot more corner stores — but I'm still a beginner. I know that robbing banks isn't exactly the right thing to do, but I have to admit I loved it.

"I first got involved in bank robbery through Warren. I had already heard from someone else that he was into banks. I've known him since

I was a kid. We grew up together and understood each other. I was in detention with him so I knew him pretty good. He didn't want to go back to banks. He was reluctant but I knew I could convince him. He used to rob banks with a Paki until he got ripped off. The Paki said he threw the money away because the cops were chasing him down the street. Warren didn't believe him because it's a rule that you don't throw what you've just earned by putting your life in danger. It's only common sense, you stake your life on something, you stake your life on stealing these pieces of paper, you stake your whole life on it man! Would you let it go? No! You put both hands onto it.

"I learned to rob banks through experience. The first time you don't do it so good. The next time it is a little better, then a little better still. I knew a teller and that helped me to learn the processes in the bank. I learned a lot from my other partner, Augie. He had a partner who was blown away in a bank so he was extra careful. His partner got blown away by a security guard — splattered all over the bank window. This guy had a shotgun and was holding it on the security guard. He made a mistake by not telling him to hit the floor or drop his gun and he made another mistake by looking away. The guard drew his gun and blew his head off and then started shooting at Augie. He put his hands up right away because he was unarmed. Because he saw his friend get blown away he's twice as terrified when he goes in. Instead of standing still and being really quiet and watching them, he'd be jumping up and down from one foot to the other like a jackrabbit. How he used to do it was like skipping — always in motion. That really freaked some people out because they probably thought, 'We've got a maniac on our hands.' It's too much. It even freaked me out a couple of times [laughs]. It looks dangerous.

"Augie was lucky because he threw up his hands and didn't get shot. He was still a juvenile when that happened so he got away almost scott free — eight months for five robberies. I know only a few guys my age doing it. That was about two years ago. They were 15 and we were in an institution together. One got shot and killed. There were four of them who would get a three-day pass for the weekend and rob a bank. They would get out on Friday and do it Friday afternoon and blow the money on the weekend. Then they would bring drugs into the institution when they came back Sunday night. The institution teaches you how to do crime. I was in there five years. That's where I learned how to steal cars and do B & Es and bank robberies. I thought about robbing banks ever since I was small. All my older brothers are bank robbers. There's a guy in here who tries to get information off of me, how I did it, because he wants to go rob a bank.

"As soon as we go through the first set of doors everything is out — the mask, the bag, the gun. Warren showed me how to pull the nylon stocking up so it won't get in your eyes. My partner takes five steps inside and yells. The guy with the gun is pretty convincing. My partner has the gun and I have the bag. As soon as he's in I would go over the counter. A couple of times he went in and I jumped over the counter so fast he hadn't even started yelling yet. Speed! You have to rifle the drawers yourself because it's too slow if they handle the money. Besides, they'll hand you a bandit pack. As I'm doing that, he watches the staff and customers. He backs up to near the door but off to the side so he can also watch the people come in. Anybody who comes in stays in. You'd swear you're in there forever. It's only seconds, but it feels like hours. I'm not nervous in the bank, but I get nervous after I realize what could have happened. I don't want anything to happen to people. We'll scare the fuck out of them, but that's as far as I would go.

"In Montreal we would sometimes use a ten-speed bike to get away. There are lots of alleys with cement blocks and steel posts in the street to prevent cars from going through. Mostly we used a taxi. Warren learned this from the Paki. I thought it was right on. We would get a couple of chicks and pay them $100 or $200 to hail a cab and sit in it. If caught, they would just say they had nothing to do with it and they didn't even know what was going on. We knew the girls from detention. They were reliable. We knew them a long time. The youth centre was co-ed. We watch them hail the cab and walk up the side street and go in and do the bank. You come out of the bank and your mask comes off about ten feet away. You pull it off and turn down the alley or side street and jump into your taxi. When we turn onto the street the cab is waiting. We may be only 30 feet away, but it's a panic situation and you have to act cool. You tell yourself not to run when all your instincts are screaming, 'Run, run!' You want to get there as fast as you can and you're walking and your knees are wobbling. Then you drive away as all the cop cars drive by with their sirens and lights going.

"We slow down and walk to the cab and take a second to catch our breath. Then we talk to the driver. We go about five miles from our destination and get another cab. Make sure no one is following us.

Sometimes we wouldn't have any money and we'd pay the taxi driver with the bank's money. Sometimes we'd change our minds about robbing the bank but we wouldn't have any money to pay the cab. Then we'd get in the taxi and jump without paying. One taxi driver chased us around the block. It was a real drag and I was glad when he quit. One time me and my partner did a store. There was a chick holding the cab and she whispered to me, 'I think he phoned someone.' At the end of the trip she tells me! He radioed a message and there are 15 taxis after us. No police cars but taxis everywhere. There were four or five taxis behind us. Some beside us, some in front of us too. Too much. We jumped on the subway. Once you're on the metro you're gone. They can't stop all the metros.

"Sometimes the cab would only have to wait 30 to 40 seconds while we're in there and 10 to 15 seconds to get to the cab. Sometimes 10 minutes, sometimes half hour. That would be if we're contemplating, thinking about it. Sometimes we had to get up our nerve. I had a guy hold the cab one time and the driver — a coloured dude — he got all excited. He's waiting and all of a sudden he sees two guys jogging up to the car and we jump in. He pulls out in traffic then he sees these cops whizzing by. And we just came from that spot and we're puffing out of breath. He's looking around. He is suspicious. He's looking in his rear view mirror. Here we are breathing heavy. He was all excited. It's usually me paying so I give him a big tip. He said, 'Where did you get this money? Hey, wow man, thanks. Anytime you want to go anywhere, just phone me. Here's my card. Here's my card.' Too much. Some people.

"I had fear the first time I did it, but I like fear. It's a challenge. I like to fight my fear to see how much I can take. I knew I could rob a bank, but was I nervous. The first time was probably the most I was nervous in my life. I wasn't even near the bank and my heart was beating. I thought it was going to come right through my chest. I was trying to be calm, but my heart was pounding so hard that I thought everyone could hear it. I kept looking at my chest to see if it was all right. But once you get there, you go in. It's like parachuting, you have to push your own self. You can't change your mind when you're in there. Customers are usually shocked. Tellers will freak out and cry, especially when they see me come over the counter at them. Some try to hide under a rug or under their desk. Too much! I don't touch customers. I don't say, 'Give me your purse.' I don't do that.

"The first thing that goes if you're really scared are your knees. Once on the subway — an hour after we had done a bank — we were sitting on a bench when two cops approached. We had the nylon stockings wrapped around our ankles. Warren's girlfriend stood up in front of me and I stuffed the gun and the money down my pants. I had been smoking a joint and they wanted to see some I.D. I acted cool and calm, but I was really scared. The gun began to slide down my pants so I kept sitting down and they kept telling me to stand up. They wanted me to empty my pockets and I did, then I would sit down and he would tell me to stand up. I had cigarettes and a bus pass but no I.D. because I don't carry I.D. when I'm on a job. You never know what might happen, it could fall out of your pockets when you jump the counter. Warren and his girlfriend waited at the next stop until they finally let me go.

"I've been in institutions all my life. I was only five when my parents split up and I was put in a foster home. I thought I was kidnapped and kept running away so they put me in a reformatory. I've been in institutions since I was seven years old so I can adjust to prison. I just finished a month in solitary — that was new. I made an escape attempt and they put me in the hole for a month. I don't mind an experience if I learn from it. Right now I'm teaching myself to read. I like to learn. I used to like school, but I didn't work very hard. I liked it because everyone was there.

"I rob banks for the money. I like the excitement and thrills, but I do it for the money. The danger is exciting, but I don't do it for that. I spend my money on drugs — a lot on coke. It really does fly. I don't know where half of it goes. I had an apartment when I was 16 and I was really proud of it. I bought a bed, a T.V., a 13-foot-long couch worth $1600. I was proud of myself. I was doing well. I was living with a chick who was 18, but she was just a friend. I'd also spend a lot of money on my family. I'd give some to my sisters. I spend a lot on taxis. I'd take them everywhere. On movies and amusement parks. Money is important to me. I never have enough, I always want more. If I was to get a big score, I would want another big score. After awhile you start getting bigger ideas. I've thought about doing an armoured vehicle and I've watched them make deliveries.

"It's only a fluke or a set-up that gets you caught. You either get caught cold-cock or you don't get caught at all. If they don't catch us in the first couple of hours then forget it. They don't have a very good chance. This was the first time I got caught, but I think I learned a lot. Next time it will not be so easy. Once you get caught, everyone goes through a process where they don't want to do it anymore. Then after a couple of months, you're willing to do it again. I'm supposed to have a job when I hit the street, but if I have no job and no money I would do a bank for sure. It's your only means of survival. If I have no job and nowhere to stay, of course I'm going to do a bank. It's what I know. I've been trained to do that."

Author's Note: Jules did rob banks again. He was arrested with his older brother five years later at age 22. They were both sentenced to 15 years in prison for several armed robberies. His brother had recently been released from prison and was on parole at the time.

Native Indian

Age 32, this man is a full-blooded Canadian Indian, stands 6'2" tall, and weighs 185 lbs. He is pleasant, smiles easily, and was cooperative in the interview. I was scheduled to interview him a few months earlier but he failed to return from a temporary absence.

"Yeah, I just got back. They sent me to a camp and from the camp they gave me a three-day pass. I got into the city and started drinking and picked up this nice young girl. You know how it is. Being locked up for so long. Bit of booze, some pleasant sexual favours. Because I was on a pass I had to stay at a halfway house. So I phoned the house and told them I got drunk and spent my money. 'What's going to happen now?' They said, 'Well, you're going back to prison to do your time.' Well, I can't handle two more years in prison. It was impulsive because I'd left all my identification, address book, up in the camp. It was just one of those things. It was a quarter to twelve at night and the girl's lying there naked beside me. 'Don't go. Don't go back.' I says, 'Right on' [laughs]. So I called them and told them I couldn't get back in time and they said I was going back to prison.

"I do regret it. Oh, you wanna believe it. The next day when I kind of sobered up and I looked over at that girl laying next to me, I thought, 'Oh my God, what have I got myself into now?' I'm doing two years more than I would have done if I had behaved. But in other ways it proved out okay because when I was out for those two months I happened to bump into my ex-girlfriend and we got back together. We had a son together a few years ago and now I have her and my son back and that would never have happened if I hadn't taken off. I was out for two months and during that time I worked for a lawyer. I'm a carpenter and I built a house for this lawyer and he wrote me a very supporting letter after I was arrested. The fact that I worked proves that I'm not gonna go back to crime. It was terrifying being on the run. Every time a cruiser would pass, I'd jump. Then, at the end, the police came to my mom's house and arrested me. I knew they would show up eventually, but I was tired of running. I couldn't live with that hanging over my head. The police told me that they had the house under surveillance two or three times.

"I told the police that I got the idea to rob a bank from reading the newspapers. I said that to protect the person I was with. The police suspected I had a partner because they said I was seen coming out of the bank and running off with this young man. Plus the M.O.s of other banks being done were the same. Even the wording of the note was the same. So they had the idea that someone was with me and they asked, 'Well, how'd you get into this if you're doing it alone?' I say, 'Well, I read it in the newspapers.' I'm not a rat and I didn't expect him to be.

"I learned how to rob banks from my partner. We used to hang around together. He's only 20 and he always had money. Wasn't working. So I says, 'Where are you getting all this money?' So he told me and he says it's easy. I say, 'How can you get the nerve up, man?' He says it's easy. He says, 'Come with me and you'll see how easy it is.' So I wait outside the bank. He went in, came out, whoosh, take off. He gives me half the cut! So then we went and partied and I said, 'Well, you did one, I guess I gotta do one.' It took me a long time to get the nerve up.

"I went to do three banks and chickened out. I couldn't do it. I walked in, got right to the counter, and I just couldn't do it. But because this guy took his bank down and gave me half, I felt obligated you might say. So then when I hit, we split it again. I'm telling you, after every bank job, for maybe three or four hours, I couldn't eat. Just shaking, man. Just pacing and walking and pacing and pacing.

"The most I got was $3600 and the lowest was $480. Mostly it was in the $2000 range and we split it fifty-fifty. Then he went to jail for a car theft and I operated alone for awhile. When I walked into a bank I walked in with no mask and no disguise. We never cased it. Just walk in and make sure there's no camera. You see where the teller is, you see where the door is. Stand in line with your note and you rob it. I'd look for a bank with an alleyway to make my getaway. When I got up to the teller I'd say, 'How are you today?' They'd say, 'Fine, can I help you sir?' And I'd say, 'Well I hope so, if you can read English.' The note would say, 'This is a hold-up. Don't get excited. Nobody gets hurt. I just want the damn money.' So they'd give me the money and I'd stuff it in my shirt or in my pocket and I'd walk out, run down the laneway, and get rid of my shirt in the garbage can. I'd have a T-shirt on underneath. Run out and get on a bus or hail a taxi. The last bank I did I used the subway.

"The tellers would be shocked. I used a very low key, friendly approach. I always try to take the teller that's young and near the doors because I find that tellers over the age of 35 will give you a rough time. I don't want to scare them. All I want is the money. I had a few that would step back and grab their chest. I'd say, 'Take it easy. Take it easy. Nobody is going to get hurt. Just give me the money. It's not yours so don't worry about it.' I've had some women refuse to give me the money and what can I do? I walked away. It's happened on many occasions. I just told 'em, 'Hey lady, you're crazier than I am.' Because they are 'cause some people are desperate and they certainly will use the gun.

"In the first bank I robbed, I had to wait twenty minutes in line and I started talking to the guy behind me. And when I got to the teller and passed her the note, she starts pitching me the money. She's throwing all this money at me and I'm taking it and sticking it in my pockets. And I figured, well that's enough time. I've been in here too long. I went to turn and go and she was still throwing money on the counter. So I says, 'Oh, my change,' and I went and grabbed all these fives and tens. This guy I was talking to was at the wicket beside me and he says, 'Holy shit! What's going on here?' I grabbed the money and I took off out of the bank. I walked out, then I was gone. I can run like hell. I didn't know that this guy chased me. The police told me after they arrested me that this fellow had chased me. He caught the play, but I guess he was kind of stunned that it was happening right before him. Hard to believe. And I was out the door and I guess she started screaming.

"But my partner was waiting outside for me. I'd be coming down this lane and he'd be standing there having a smoke. If anyone was chasing me, he was to intervene. But nobody chased us except this time, and when I come out of the bank I ran the wrong way. I was supposed to turn left and I ran right. He didn't know what happened. He thinks I'm still in the bank and he hears all these police sirens closing in. He thought I was caught so he took off.

"I tried to make a date with one of the tellers. She was a little paranoid. I just asked her when she was giving me the money, 'Hey, you're kind of cute. What time do you get off work?' I says, 'I'll come by and I'll pick you up. Take you out for supper.' She was a nice little blonde. I would've went and picked her up if she had wanted [laughs]. Sure. I would've gone. Taken the chance.

"Before robbing banks I wasn't making much money. I was pushing hand bills in the city making very little money. Who wants to work for nothing and who likes being broke? When I first did it, it was the money 'cause I didn't have any money. Afterwards, I could see what kind of lifestyle I could lead if I had the money. And I couldn't go back to my former way of living pushing handbills for pennies a day. Just scraping by. Not when I can make $2000 in ten minutes. Like you jump from a poverty level up to where you had women, all kinds of beautiful women around you at all times. Stay in the Holiday Inn at $100 a crack and go to fine restaurants [snaps fingers]. That's it. And you don't have to worry about the money 'cause you know you got it. You get used to the lifestyle. It's very easy to adapt.

"I was foolish. I'd walk down the street and some guy would say, 'Hey buddy, can you spare a quarter?' So I whip out $20 or $40 and say, 'Here. Go into a restaurant and order a nice steak. Have a beer too.' I bought a lot of suits, jewellery, and took some trips. It's easy to spend. One minute it's there and two days later it's gone. I wasn't into drugs, just drinking. I'd go to a party and bring cases of booze. If a girl liked a specific brand of wine, well, make sure I bring that too. It lasted about three months. I pled guilty to eight bank robberies and the judge gave me five and a half years.

"They caught my partner coming out of the bank. The bank manager followed him out and started screaming, 'Stop that man! He robbed the bank.' And a guy started chasing him. He got away, but by then the police were all over the place. He was charged with 13 but plea bargained it down to six and got five years. He was in here for awhile but took off and was arrested for a liquor store robbery. I saw his name in the paper last week.

"They arrested me at my mom's house. The police had a fingerprint on me 'cause I passed a note. I left notes all over the place. I have a previous conviction for marihuana and a shoplifting. They took three months to match the fingerprints to the name. They said to me, 'Believe it, we've got you dead-to-right on eight.' What the hell, why waste the money? I said, 'Let's go. I'll sign the statement.' I like to be free. I go up north hunting and fishing. Do what I want. Go where I want. I was terrified of prison but I've adjusted to it. The first four months, you jump every time somebody slams a cell door. You hear two guys getting into an argument and you tense up. I spend a lot of my time in the carpentry shop and I'm taking a computer course. I'm not scared of some guy shanking me because I don't bother people. I don't owe people. I don't gamble. I don't get into debt. I'm pretty happy-go-lucky.

"What scares me is the change in myself from being around the hatred and the bitterness you find in prison. A lot of people in here have a chip on their shoulder and that chip wears off on other people too. I like watching television — like cop shows. But you can't watch it in here because they'll insult you and turn it off. So now I have my own little T.V. in my own cell [chuckle]. I just hope I don't adopt their attitude.

"I have my girlfriend back and my young lad. She's visiting and I'll work to support my family when I get out. I'm not getting into crime again! This is enough. For me to do any type of crime, I'm looking at ten to fifteen years. It's not worth it. It's a valuable lesson."

Papa was a Rolling Stone

> Age 32 and married with four children, this offender has been free for ten years and owns a courier service that employs 16 people.

"I was 20 at the time I committed these bank robberies and I ended up getting four years and serving two before being paroled. We operated as a gang and were into some very heavy crimes with guns. I was involved in two bank robberies. We got a lot of media coverage for our crimes. It was wild and woolly and heavily dramatized in the newspaper and T.V. Luckily no one was killed. We operated as a gang with 10 to 12 of us ranging in age from 16 to 17 to my father who was 52. Where should I start? I have to go back to my family. I'm adopted. My real father is a career criminal. As long as I can remember he was always in trouble and in and out of prison. I thought that he was my Uncle Leonard until I found out that I was really adopted to his sister. I found this out when I was 13 when I came across my adoption papers. My real father and mother were not my aunt and uncle and vice versa. I have a younger brother Lenny, two younger sisters Ann and Sarah, and an older brother John. Lenny, Ann, and Sarah are real brothers and sisters, but John is a step-brother and really my cousin. But I thought John was my brother and they were my cousins. I was only 13 when I found this out and was I confused. Wow! My Uncle Leonard and Aunt Theresa are my real father and mother and my mom and dad are really my aunt and uncle. I went to Leonard and told him I knew. I guess I wanted a father figure and went to talk to him, 'Hey dad...'

"My father began to manipulate and use me. He got me to do what he wanted because he was my father. My adopted parents had brought me up really straight. We all had to go to school and could never miss a day. We were very strict Catholics and went to church every Sunday. I had a very good family background. My father got me started in crime. We started out shoplifting but doing big shopping carts full. My brother and I would fill the carts and roll them out of the store on signal. My dad would watch for security and keep an eye on our backs. We were into heavy shoplifting when I was 15, and I got chased a few times but never caught. Lenny and I could run. Leonard was always in the background giving us his signal at the door and we would walk out with a cart load of appliances. He would take orders and we would go in and shop for the items: two toaster ovens, a toaster, a blender. I recall being in rooms full of merchandise.

"I was involved in two robberies. The first one was a bank in a large food store. I never went inside to participate in the holdup. I was the driver or 'wheelman' as the papers called me. There were five of us involved. Three went inside, Lenny and two friends that we had recruited. The fifth person was my father who was supposed to run interference by being a blocker in case of pursuit. He was the smart one because if we got busted, he would just drive away. We were all armed and we had portable police scanners with earphones so we could listen to the police. I'm carrying a .38 pistol and two guys have sawed-off shotguns. I'm the driver and I've parked in a no parking zone while they've gone in to rob the bank. I'm watching the entrance when I hear the alarm go off and here come my three partners running out of the bank. They're carrying brown paper bags full of money and bills are flying everywhere. We used my car for the getaway, but we had stolen plates from an identical make and year.

"I can recall listening to the police scanner after the alarm went off. I could hear the dispatcher, 'We have an alarm...' as they were coming out the door. Meanwhile my cohorts are getting into the car and one partner says, 'Now it's your job.' I got out onto the expressway and I could see the lights of a police cruiser coming down the road and turning into the parking lot. They were there fast! We were in the bank three minutes. I hear the police say, 'The suspects left in a Chevy Nova.' I can't believe my luck because this car is not even similar looking. It's like the difference between a mid-size and a compact. Then I hear another police officer say, 'I see that car on the expressway and I'm one mile behind him.' I can see this police car coming behind me with no headlights or flashers. I felt he was trying to catch up to me so I floored it. Then all the lights are flashing and the siren is going. He says, 'I got them. Four suspects heading west. I am now in pursuit of the four suspects. I need a back-up.'

"All four of us have earphones and we're listening to the police scanner. The car is really quiet. Meanwhile, I'm wondering, 'Where is my back-up? Where the hell is Leonard?' I find out later that dad's gone home. He left the bank and drove home. Thanks a lot dad [laughs]. The car is dead quiet. The fear of God is in us all. This is my first robbery and I thought it would be my last [laughs]. We got off at exit number 3 and I cut across three lanes to take the exit. The cop comes right behind me only three car lengths behind on my tail. I could see the police officer in my rear view mirror and I'm thinking, "This guy can drive a car." We hit the exit ramp doing 65 m.p.h. and he dropped back. He was now in another district and the police in this district are on the air. We approached Walker Road and I turned down the ramp. In the meantime, I hear the officer say, 'They've just exited Wellington Road.' But that's the next exit. He was incorrect and we lucked out. I could see his cruiser drive over top the freeway. But as we're coming down the freeway, there's a stop sign that I stopped at. Another cop car comes to a screeching halt inches away from our front bumper. He slid right in front of our car with his sirens and lights going. I could hear one of my partners pull back on the pump shotgun getting ready to open fire. This guy was a jerk, a real crispy critter. I thought, 'Shit, I ain't shooting at no police officer!' I was three seconds away from opening the car door and throwing myself face down on the pavement. I thought that was it. They're getting ready for a shoot-out. I was deathly scared and thinking, 'If I get out of this, I don't want nothing to do with it again!'

"Then the cop roared off across the highway and up the ramp! We drove off towards dad's house, parked the car in the garage, and went into the house. Four guys carrying these brown paper bags looking like we just came from the grocery store. I'm sitting on the couch shaking and my father says, 'What the hell took you so long?' He was at home with the police scanner listening to the whole thing. 'Incidently,' he says, 'great driving.' We split the money — an even share each — and left. My father got his share even though he didn't back us up. Leonard's con was obvious, 'I'll wait here boys, go do it. Don't forget my share. If you get caught, I'll bail you out' [laughs].

"I left on my motorcycle and drove through a roadblock with the police stopping cars but waving me right on past. When I got home I dumped the money on the bed and sat back and looked at it — $10,000. That's the most money I ever had in my life. The next day I started buying things. I bought some furniture and paid some of my mom's doctor bills. I was into nice cars and I'd go out for a drink, but I wasn't into drugs. My partners spent most of their money on drugs and I remember them telling me they didn't know what they did with their money. One time me and my partner went to the airport and went to Florida just to fly there. I was only 20 and that was a lot of money for me.

"Before I did my second robbery I waited a month. I know for a fact that these guys hit a couple in between. I went back for the second because my money was dwindling and I was hanging around with Lenny and Leonard. We would go to these big-time night clubs where a lot of fast movers went. There were limousines and Cadillacs outside and everyone wore nice suits. My father used to go there and he knew a lot of people. There were nice women too. Hell, it was a good time [laughs]. There was good to this whole thing but a lot that was wrong. People could have been killed. Before the second robbery I'm running out of money and I'm used to this being cool thing: new clothes, rental cars, and all that.

"Meanwhile my lifestyle changed dramatically and my step-mother confronted me. She knew something was up because she found out that I had paid her medical bills and I had new clothes, cars — it was obvious. She knew that I was hanging out with Leonard and what I was up to. I admitted it to her and she asked me to stop and I said I'd stop. She thought I did it to pay her bills, but I told her that's not why I did it. I paid the bills because I didn't know what to do with the money, plus it was my mother.

"Then I got talked right back into it. Me and Lennie went and did one on our own with my father running block for us in his car. Lenny goes in and I'm parked on the side. Once again we have police scanners. He comes out and dives in the front seat of the car and I drive away real cool. A cop goes racing by, then another one, then another. Three different ones and they're looking for two guys racing away. Lenny's on the floor and we get a break. Over the scanner I heard them say that the suspect took off on a ten-speed bicycle. 'We got him! We got him! We got him!' We can hear them arrest the wrong guy — some poor guy riding away on his bicycle. I remember there was a guy riding off on his bicycle when we took off.

"On the way home — this will show you how crooks steal from crooks — Lenny is on the floor and he's digging into the bag and putting bundles of money under the seat of my car. Meanwhile Leonard is behind us because I could see him in my rear-view mirror and he follows us home. Lennie says to me, 'We'll get the old man.' We get out of the car and go inside and divide the money. We got about $40,000 out of the robbery and there was $10,000 hidden in the car. So Lenny and I each got an extra $5,000 apiece. My father wasn't very useful, hell no. That's why we clipped him on that one. He used to tell us — I was stupid enough to believe him — 'Somebody has to be there on the outside in case you guys are arrested. Somebody has to bail you out.' He convinced us that he'd be there to help us out if we got caught, but in the meantime he just drives away. He convinced us that he was acting like some kind of lawyer on retainer for us in case we're caught. And we believed him — kind of. My father had so much control over Lenny. If we robbed $40,000, he'd tell Lenny, 'You don't want to carry all that money around. Leave it here with me and whenever you want some, come see me and I'll give it to you.' Lenny would take $1,000 and leave $10,000 behind, and who knows what my father is doing with his money. I would never leave my money behind. I always took it with me. So Leonard was burning Lenny left and right so that's why we clipped him.

"The papers put down that $40,000 was taken and Leonard knows that we only counted $30,000. There is some money missing. He gets us over to the house and I said to him, 'I think that after we leave, the manager probably grabs ten grand and puts it aside and says it was stolen. Who's going to know?' Leonard falls for that and he says, 'Why those sons of bitches!' He believed it and thought the bank clipped him.

"A few weeks later they came to me and said, 'We have one last job. Do you want to be in on it? There is going to be five involved altogether and they expect to get a $350,000 haul. All you have to do is drive.' I said, 'It's a long distance from the bank back to our regular drop off spot.' It's ten miles and we've never done anything more than five miles away. That's a long distance to be driving after a robbery and an extra five miles of being chased. Lenny says that we can park the car at our older sister's place. It's only a few blocks from there. My older brother John was in on this with me. Leonard talked him into it. He works for me now and we never talk about this at all.

"I said, 'Okay, I'll go for it.' In a couple of days, Lenny and another guy came over to discuss the plan. The hardest part they said would be getting into the vault, 'What we'll do is we'll go in the bank and we'll shoot the manager.' I went, 'What!' 'We'll shoot the manager to show them how serious we are.' I said to them, 'I don't want anybody shot.' They say, 'We have to get our point across.' 'Bullshit!' So anyway, they say, 'All right we won't shoot anybody.' I said okay, but after I'm thinking, 'I don't believe that. How can I stop that when I'm not in the bank?' A couple of nights before the bank robbery, I'm thinking about everything — my parents, what I've done, conscience things. I had a close friend who was a police officer. I went to his house and knocked on the door. 'Rick, I'm in trouble.' 'Billie, you look terrible.' 'It's something really heavy and I'm scared.' 'Is it so serious?' 'It's very serious.' 'Bill, you know that I'm a police officer and whatever you tell me, I'll have to do my job. Before you tell me, think of what you want to do.' We talked for a couple of hours and he was in total dismay. He knew my family and he couldn't believe it. He says, 'I want you to come in the office tomorrow morning. I don't know what will happen, but you did the right thing. Someone could get killed.' I go in the next day and the police want me to do a set-up. I was told that if I cooperated, I'd be treated accordingly in my sentence. This was my ace in the hole. If I had to do it over again, I wouldn't cooperate. I was shafted because they sent me to prison for four years.

"I agreed to go along with the robbery in order to set them up. I knew the date, time, the bank. I was to back out at the very last minute and say that I wasn't going to do it. The morning comes and they pick me up. On the way to rob the bank, we got near the house and I said, 'I'm not going to do it.' The crew already knew that I was reluctant. I said that I wanted out and that I don't want to be involved in a killing. They stopped the car and said, 'Hell with it. Let's go.' They left me near my sister's house and drove off to do the bank. Now comes the tricky part. They do the bank and come back to the house. We're all in the house. They got only $1600 because it was a set-up. The staff and manager in the bank are really police officers. They come back to the house and I'm about to leave when all hell breaks loose. I get in my car to drive out when I get hit by another car. I'm right in the middle of it. This lady officer grabs my face and slams it into the car. She says, 'Is this your car? I believe this is your car and you're under arrest.' Now something has screwed up because I'm not supposed to be part of this. The cops jump out of telephone trucks and off roofs and run in the house. Some officers are trying to get me out of this but if they release me on the spot, that would stink and everyone would know. So we're downtown for hours before they finally agreed to let me go.

"As it turned out, both Leonard and Lenny cooperated and started naming names. We all got bail but they surmised that I set them up and I'm cooperating with the cops so they decide to shoot me. I'm walking down the street and they drive by and open fire. I hit the ground and I'm crawling under cars. I knew it was Leonard, my father, and Lenny, my brother. Now, since that didn't work, they come up with another scheme. Leonard and my brother John take Lenny to a street corner and they deliberately shoot him in the leg. Lenny says it's Billie who shot him, 'Billie came up to me on the street and shot me.' Now Lenny is in the hospital. I pull in my driveway and there's lights and guns and cops everywhere, 'Freeze! Police! Don't even move!' I'm padded down and told, 'You're under arrest for attempted murder.' 'What?' Finally the truth comes out and they let me go on that.

"Meanwhile, Lenny and Leonard are still robbing banks on the other side of the city. My brother John was also in on them and they eventually got arrested. When I was going for sentencing, everything screwed up. My name is really Leonard Allen Herbert and my father's name is Leonard Allen Herbert. My brother is called Leonard Allen Herbert. I go by the name Billie, my father goes by Leonard, and my brother is Lenny. I go in front of the judge and he's trying to unscramble all this. The judge calls me to the bench and he has this all goofed up. I have a lawyer who is useless. The judge says, 'Mr. Leonard Allen Herbert, you are one of the most master minded criminals I have ever seen since I sat on this bench.' I'm looking at the police in the courtroom and I'm trying to tell them, 'Hey, this guy's got it wrong.' I say this to my attorney and he tells me to listen, it's going to be all right. I ended up before the wrong judge for sentencing and he goofed up. The judge called me the mastermind. 'Mastermind! Gosh, wait a minute. You got the wrong guy pal. Gosh' [laughs]. Then he says, 'Four years.' I hear this deputy with his handcuffs come up behind me and take my arms. 'Holy shit, this didn't go right!' [laughs]. That's what happened [laughs].

"Afterwards, certain people went to the judge to try to sort it out, but he won't change the sentence. Once they're sentenced, that's it. Next thing you know, I'm on my way to prison just because of that confusion. That's why I said that if I had to do it over again, I'd never do that again. In the media they had, 'Wheelman Sentenced to Four

Years.' They had that in the news with a picture of me being led out of the courtroom in handcuffs. When I was being taken to jail, we turn the corner and there's the prison straight ahead. It's huge and one of these guards turns to me and he says, 'Well son, you've made the big time.' They brought me in and I was put in a cage and they took my clothes. This guard tells me my number and says that I leave my name at the door and I can pick it up in four years when I leave. He says that if I forget my number, he'll beat the shit out of me. My first day there, I cried. When the other guys went to trial and the articles hit the papers it came out that I was the informant and I was moved out and put in protective custody `cause I wouldn't have lasted a day in there. That was hell. In P.C. you're in your cell 23 hours a day and let out only for that one hour to stretch your legs and exercise.

"All this was very hard on my family. My mother died shortly after I was released, but I believe this hastened her death. I feel terrible over what I put my family through. I had an asshole for a so-called father. Am I bitter? Yes. Do I regret what I did? Yes. Do I forgive everybody? Yes. Do I forgive myself? No. I cannot forgive myself for what I put my family through. I wasted a lot of valuable time of my life in prison. I'm educated, I'm no dummy, I can do better than that.

"When I got out I had lost a lot of things. I felt embarassed and ashamed. People looked at me like a criminal and others thought I was a snitch. Nobody has ever said that I did the right thing. Nobody has ever said anything about that bank manager who could have been killed. I couldn't get a job at first. I applied for a job in a delivery service and I told the guy about my past. He hired me anyway and I worked for him for eight years eventually becoming the general manager. Then I opened my own business. Now my older brother John is working for me. We don't talk about what went on before. He knows I took care of my step-mother, which is his real mother. He testified against me and I testified against him. There were a lot of dirty things that happened. So we've just tried to put it behind us and never talk about it. There were very hard feelings with everyone trying to kill one another. My wife saved the articles while I was in prison. I didn't want them in prison because of what I was doing — informing.

My real father took me for a sucker and nobody likes that feeling. There aren't two days in a row that go by where I don't think of it. I have to accept it for the rest of my life — my stupidity.

"My wife and I were going out before I went to prison and she waited for me. That's another thing that helped me to hold it together up here [pointing to his head]. She even moved in with my parents while I was in prison. We've been married eight years and have two little boys and two little girls. We were married right after I got out.

"One of the guys got eight years, went back to prison and got out about two months ago. Another got ten and got paroled and robbed another bank right away and was sent back to prison. Leonard got 25 years and John got off with six months. I think he got the sentence I was supposed to receive. Lenny got 15 years, did nine years, and was released. He's now 30 years old, married with one child and one on the way, and working in the oil industry. I spoke to him last month for the first time in nine years. For awhile, nobody was talking to nobody. He's doing real good and I'm going to see him next week. He called and said he was sorry for everything: 'The old man did me bad. You're my older brother and I'm sorry for what I did. If I come down, would you see me so we could talk?' I said, 'Yeah, sure. Let bygones be bygones.'

"As for Leonard. Papa was a rolling stone [laughs]. He was the kind of guy who would do anything for you. If a kid didn't have some good clothes to go to school, Leonard would take him out and buy them for him. That's the kind of guy he was — of course it was never his money [laughs]. He was good — but as slick as they come. What a hustler. He was a con man, a smooth talker. Leonard had style. He was a good manipulator and could manipulate your mind. After I was out and he was still in prison, his sister — my step-mother — died. He couldn't come to the funeral but he called from prison. We spoke, 'How 'ya doing?' I could tell he was sick by the way he was wheezing. He was in the infirmary section of the prison. His glasses were broken and I went and got him a new pair and mailed them to prison. There were some people who petitioned to have Leonard released near the end because of his failing health, but it got nowhere. Leonard died in prison last year. I have no hard feelings against Leonard, but Lenny is bitter. When he heard that Leonard died, he said, 'Good riddance to the son of a bitch.' He still can't stand him. No acknowledgement. Lenny was used the most by Leonard and he got whacked good in court."

Travelling Bandit

Age 30, this offender is serving a total of 18 years for the commission of 14 bank robberies across Canada. He is university educated (a sociology degree), a self-described former hippie, and a long-time heroin addict. He does not feel sorry for himself, stating throughout the interview that he deserves what he got. His M.O. was always the same: walk in, stand in line, pass a note, show the teller a gun if she or he stalled, walk out, and either take a subway, drive, or walk away. He has been paroled to halfway houses and drug rehabilitation centres several times but has always failed to return. On these occasions he travelled throughout the country robbing banks and is suspected of 50-60 bank holdups.

"I gave them a bag and the note told them to put the money in the bag. 'I've got a gun. Hurry up' [laughs]. I met a guy in here that robbed banks the same way. We talked about it. I guess you can call it comparing notes [hilarious laughter]. I wouldn't try to hurt anybody. If something goes wrong, I walked out. And I'd take a piece, but most of the time I wouldn't even load it or show it. If I can get away with taking the money without nobody seeing the gun, fine. As a matter of fact, it was never mentioned in court that I was armed. They have their doubts, but as far as they're concerned I was not armed.

"The parole board is getting a little pissed off at me. 'We give this guy two passes and he goes out and robs banks.' They gave me passes because I do well in jail. I don't get in trouble and I've finished my university degree in prison. In fact, I was supposed to go to the university campus on my last pass. I went out for a few beers on the last night of my pass and we got into a scrap in a bar, me and a couple of other friends with some other people. When I went back to the halfway house, the broad that runs the house already knew what happened. She says, 'You go back to the pen tomorrow and you're not accepted here.' So I said, 'Fuck this,' and I went through a window and took off.

"I robbed my first bank when I was 24, but I was selling dope for five years prior to that. I was pretty quiet in those days. I did a lot of dope, travelled a lot, and I didn't bother anybody. I was just having a good time meeting people. I went out to Vancouver, San Francisco, San Diego. I was a hippie-type. Before, when I needed money, I played drums in a band. I would maybe work six months, collect unemployment, deal a few hits under the table. I could get by fine. I didn't have an expensive habit then. Then I got busted for some B & Es and got a year in prison. They decided to send me to a hospital for dope rehabilitation and I took off from there. I met a guy I knew from prison in a bar. I was on my own and I had to do something. He explained that they were into banks. Hey, that's pretty fucking heavy man. But the way they were doing it, it didn't sound too bad. I mean nobody was getting hurt, no guns were shown; it sounded easy. So he asked me, 'Do you want to come along?' They explained it to me and I thought about it maybe a couple of days, then I said, 'Yeah, okay. Sure.' I needed some bread and fast.

"We did them simultaneously. One guy would rob one and another would do another. Maybe two in one afternoon. We never went inside to case the bank. I just look around to see how I would get out of there after. That's the main thing, which way to go. It doesn't matter how the bank's set up. I'll find the money [laughter] and the door. That's very important [laughter]. It's their job to hand over the money. The banks don't want nobody to get hurt. Tellers have specific instructions not to argue. Just give him the money and let him go. I'd get a couple grand each. We pooled the money for a bigger job, but one guy ended up fucking everybody around so I took off to the West coast.

"I went out west and I was doing the odd bank to survive. But I knew deep inside that it is not going to work. You're going to end up getting caught one way or the other. I'd try to walk in and not have the same appearance that I usually have. For example, they got a picture of me when I had my hair tied in a ponytail. I let it loose so they would get a good picture of the hair and then I went and cut it. I had glasses plus I had a baseball cap. Then I'd wear a tuque or tinted glasses.

"It's possible to recognize you but not likely. But when they did arrest me, they had a lot man. I mean one broad identified me in a bank. They had a fingerprint from one bank, a thumbprint from another. I talked to my lawyer and he said, 'Plead guilty and maybe get five years.' That's a lot. I was from out of town and they don't like that at all. So I said okay, I'll take the five.

"The police had most of them worked out. They had pictures, drawings, and they looked really good. This cop is saying to me that there are three, possibly four of you and because of the descriptions, it's not always the same guy in the bank. But you work together because it's the same way.

"This one cop, a Scottish fellow, he scared the shit out of me. I got a .357 Magnum stuck up my nose and he says, 'You try anything, I'll blow your fucking head off.' I'll never forget that guy, man. Another cop flashes this picture and he says, 'Do you know this guy?' I said, 'Never seen him before.' Slap across the face. They're fucking rough, man, believe me. But I didn't say nothing. They ended up arresting all the other guys I was with. Some before I got caught and some after. One guy, an American, was arrested in Alabama. I read it in the newspapers. There was a broad with us, but she never got caught.

"I got caught in Winnipeg. I did a couple of valiums and had a few beers. Stupid job to do. This city was not a place to rob banks. I was there just for the day. I hate myself for that, man. Stupid, very stupid. I was wasted, man. Like I had been on the fucking bus for two days. I stopped off for a day. I had a bottle of valium, which I wasn't used to taking, but I didn't have anything else. So I did a few of those and a few beers. I was pretty fucked up. So I saw a bank and I said, 'Here we go.' I just walked in and did it. I got maybe five or six blocks away and there were so many cop cars [laughter]. This city has one main street that splits the city in two, and all they have to do is block both ends and you can't go anywhere. It's a very dumb job. I didn't know the city. Walked right in, walked right out, and said, 'Okay, where do I go from here?' Stupid.

"They caught me with the fucking money in my hand. Ten minutes after the job I'm face down in the mud and all kinds of cops everywhere. They had me fucking cold cock. It was a big thing when they caught me. Escaped from prison. I had an attempted murder charge back East but it was dropped to assault. They always play up the worst. I was on the radio and T.V. as an escaped criminal wanted for attempted murder and bank robbery. The cops were amazed, they had the biggest dicks around to get me out of the cells.

"Once a girl fainted in the bank. I just walked up to her as usual and she just dropped [laughter]. Just like that. So I turned around and walked out. It was in the paper the next day. A guy walks in and tries to rob a bank and a girl faints and he leaves [laughter]. That was it. Just a little thing with a picture of the chick. One broad smiled at me through the whole thing. She handed me the money and she said, 'Will that be all?' I said, 'Yeah, well write your phone number on the bag' [laughter]. 'I didn't really say that,' I said, 'No, that's okay.' Another chick would be really scared. I'd tell her, 'Take it easy. Be cool.' Others would just look down and give you the money and not look at you.

"Some of them are pretty slow. They tend to try to take their time. You have to tell them to hurry up all the time. Except when it's a man. I mean these guys panic man. I mean male tellers. I've never seen anything like it [laughter]. One guy started throwing money over the counter. Actually throwing it over the counter! These guys are office types guys, 5'8" and 140 pounds.

"Some bank tellers think that bank robbers are stupid for some reason. Or the type that never went to school and had to rob for a living are stupid. They act obnoxious. They give you hell, man! For doing what you're doing. One girl was saying, 'What are you doing this for? Why don't you get a job?' I said, 'This is my job.' She says, 'Tch. Jesus' [laughter]. She was pissed off [laughter], 'You shouldn't be doing this. You should be working for a living.'

"Most of them are cool, especially in Montreal. They've been robbed a lot I guess. I try to be friendly. When they're all finished I smile at them. I don't threaten them. Just, 'Hurry up.' I had the gun in case they ask to see it. Most are cooperative.

"In Quebec, some women would not speak English and I had trouble with that. One lady just didn't understand what I wanted. I'm pretty stubborn. I'm French, but I didn't want to talk to her in French because I want the police to be looking for an English guy. So I was understanding what she was saying to the chick next to her, 'What does he want?' [laughter]. The note was in English and she had the bag in her hand but she wasn't doing anything. 'Come on!' Then she takes a pile of twenties and looks at me. I said, 'Come on!' She takes the tens, she puts them in the bag and looks at me again. I said, 'The whole fucking thing.' So the other chick tells her, 'I think he wants it all.' She gave it to me and I left. It was pretty funny after I thought about it [laughs]. She just didn't understand what I was saying.

"I thought about customers interfering, but I don't think people would because they think you're armed. They don't want to get shot. Some guy might try to play superman, it might happen. Not likely. Nobody wants to get involved in anything anymore. When I first got into it, the customers were never discussed because as far as we were concerned, they weren't supposed to know what was going on. It was just discreet. The teller? I figured that if anything went wrong, I'd just turn around and leave. But the guys said to me, 'If she wants to see the gun, show her.' That's it.

"It's not hard to get a gun. If I was released today, I could have one by 3:00 this afternoon. Silencers and machine-guns too. Not that I want them, but I could get them. When they call prison a university of crime, they're not mistaken.

"A large part of my motivation for robbing banks was to buy drugs. It was definitely *the* motivation. That and taking off. Once you've done a few, you get so confident that you figure that you can get away with anything, man. When you start off, you're very careful. After awhile, you just say to yourself, 'Well listen, they don't know me, they haven't caught me yet so why should they? They don't know nothing. They got nothing.' Which is not the case. Like that thumbprint they had and that picture and the pattern, which I didn't think was so obvious at the time but which was. Jesus, they couldn't go wrong. All they had to do was catch me. You make one bad move and then the rest just falls through. Which was what happened in my case.

"Greed has a lot to do with it, and being overconfident, and making mistakes. Because you find out it's easy and you find out there's a lot of money there and you want more. Especially if you're doing dope, and that costs a lot of money. I figured the more money I have, the more chance I have of staying stoned. You're spending money and you don't care. Another thing too is when you have a lot of money, you have a lot of friends.

"Before, I would do one and wait until I needed the money to do another. I'm broke and so I'd wake up in the morning and I'd say, 'Okay, today I have to do a bank.' But the last time it was getting to the point that I would do about four or five a week. I didn't really need the money, just go out and do one.

"I asked for it, man. That's why I don't have a problem doing my time because I know what the fuck I did. Half the guys in here, Jesus, 'When are they going to let me go?' and all that. They hate everybody, they don't realize it's their fault. Don't do the crime if you can't do the time. That's my philosophy anyway. I want to get out too. I'm not happy here. I don't want to come back. I've been in about six years now on and off and I'm getting sick of coming back to these joints. I'm 30 now and I'll be 31 next month. I mean I'm seriously considering not stealing again. The other times I said that it wasn't true. I have to work on my drug problem. I realized that coming back this time. I've got a big problem there, I would never admit it to myself. You always have that attitude, 'I can get out of it.' That you can stop whenever you want. It's not fucking true man. Once you realize that, it's a big step. Because if I could control the drug problem, then I won't have to steal again. And that's a fact. If I can solve the drug problem, I won't have the bank robbery problem.

"Robbery was never a high for me. No, no, no. Definitely not. It's like a job man. I needed the money, I went in and got it. No highs. You feel good afterwards because you got away. But that's relief, not a high. I have a dope problem. That was the main reason for all those banks: junk, speed, morphine. That's the big thing right there, I wasn't doing it for any other reason. I had to get that dope, man! The big thrill was in the dope. The big high was there. Once you had that money, 'Fine, let's go score.' I'd just change my clothes and go get some dope as fast as I could. Come back and get off.

"After you do one or two banks, you start to realize it's not hard. The way I was doing them it's not hard at all. There's risk involved but minimum. And like you do it so nobody notices. You come out of there and you say, 'Man, that was easy.' That's why you tend to do more and you get careless.

"I had a getaway driver for some banks. I met this guy and I knew him in jail and he's a good friend and he was broke and he had payments to make. I knew what he was getting at, 'Are you working?' I knew what he meant. I said, 'Yeah, I guess.' He says, 'Well fill me in, I'm ready to go along with you.' I said, 'Okay. All you gotta do is wait outside.' And for me it was a lot easier because I wouldn't have to worry about getting away. He'd be right there. Except he wasn't right there one time [laughter].

"In one bank, there were two parts. I went up to the security exchange and passed the note. She says, 'Are you looking for the bank?' and I said, 'Oh fuck' [laughter]. She says, 'Next door.' So I went next door and grabbed one till. I shouldn't have taken the risk. She gave the call automatically as soon as I went out that door. I know she called the cops, man. So I was a little longer than usual. I just left the driver in front and when I walked out he's not there! I was really panicking. I said, 'He took off on me.' I'm going, 'Where is he, man?' and I looked down the street three blocks and he is parked on the other side of the street. I said, 'You fucking idiot, don't do that' [laughter]. He said the getaway was really nice. He said that we could just hit the tunnel. He could have said something to me before I went in man. Stupid mother-fucker [laughter]. Usually I'd walk away, but that time I ran. I ran [laughter] because I figured I spent too much time in that place and they'd be getting there any fucking minute, for sure. I just tore up the street.

"And they told me later, 'We were close enough to shoot but didn't because of the people.' The cop told me that and I thought he was bluffing for sure. Then he tells me which way I went and I said, 'Wow! He was close. Fuck!'

"I did one bank four times because it was easy to get out of. I got caught for that one. The second last time I was out the cops did get a couple of photos and one was very good. They put it the paper and I saw it and went, 'Holy fuck' [laughter]. I figured, 'Jesus! If somebody recognizes me I'm fucked.' Because it said, '$500 reward.' Somebody did phone in and tell them who I was."

CHAPTER THREE

From Bonnie and Clyde to Kojak:

The Influence of the Mass Media

- Fun with Dick and Jane
- Bonnie and Clyde vs Kojak
- Counting the Dough
- The Relaxe Bandit
- Lost Love

Daniel Glaser (1956) extends differential association theory by emphasizing the indirect learning impact the media can have on offenders. Glaser maintains that to be influenced by criminal traditions the individual must identify with definitions of deviance conveyed by real or imaginary others who deem nonconforming behaviour acceptable. Criminal values and traditions need not be transmitted through persons in proximity since role models can develop through media images of real or fictional persons. Significantly, differential identification operates in situations in which individuals are not necessarily members of deviant groups or interact with real live persons. The notion of differential identification is thus useful in explaining the media's contribution to criminal conduct.

Research on the media's contribution to crime has largely been limited to laboratory studies of aggression. Studies focusing on direct effects of the media on individuals are uncommon and often rely on anecdotal and fragmentary evidence. Nonetheless, the data that are available suggest that there does exist a criminogenic effect of the media on our society — the nature and magnitude of that effect is undetermined. In an analysis of the studies done on copycat crimes, for instance, Surette (1992:131-2) concludes that the effects of the media are more likely qualitative (affecting the behaviour of persons who are already criminals) rather than quantitative (affecting the number of criminals). In other words, the media tend to influence how people commit crimes to a greater extent than they influence whether or not people actually commit crimes (Comstock, 1980; Pease and Love, 1984; Surette, 1992). Copycat criminals typically have the intent to commit crime before they copy an M.O. learned through media reports.

One theoretical explanation of copycat crimes is the idea that criminal techniques are adopted through a simple process of direct imitation (Bassiouni, 1981; Livingstone, 1982; Schmid and de Graaf, 1982). In this case, the offender incorporates major elements of the publicized behaviour into his or her own criminal conduct. Berkowitz (1984:414) argues that imitation theory fails to explain behaviour that is influenced by the media but not physically similar to the publicized event(s). He suggests that through a process characterized as "priming," the media may stimulate the offender and activate a network of associated ideas and concepts that increase the likelihood that he or she will behave similarly but not necessarily identically. A priming model of crime considers several factors including media content, the offender's interpretations and assumptions, his or her characteristics, and his or her social and economic situation.

A major finding in this study of 80 bank robbers is the extent to which the idea to commit their first holdup originates from the media. Approximately 30 percent of the sample conceived of the idea from reading or viewing reports and/or portrayals of bank robbery in newspapers, television, and movies (Desroches, 1995:84-87). For some, the idea lay dormant for months or years until sudden financial problems developed and the notion presented itself as a means of obtaining needed cash. For others, the process is reversed as they first experience financial problems then conceive of bank robbery as a solution by reflecting upon day-to-day news reports of this crime. The study supports the proposition that the media "prime" offenders and contribute to the "differential identification" process through reports of successful robberies and by portraying the robber as a cunning, daring, anti-establishment individual. Many robbers in this study clearly enjoy their celebrity status and romanticize their crimes through comparisons with famous outlaws. Identifying with the romantic media image of the outlaw may consciously or unconsciously influence their decision to commit this crime. The media also make holdups attractive for people with financial difficulties by depicting robbery as non-violent, impersonal, fast, easy, and a low-risk means of obtaining cash. The present study also found that the majority of men who originate the idea to commit a bank robbery from the media operate unarmed. The most frequent reason given for not being armed was the perception from media reports that tellers and customers do not resist nor do they challenge bank robbers who claim to carry weapons. In addition, the research found that over half the sample used media reports or portrayals of bank robbery, the police, or bank policy to develop their *modus operandi*. Such behaviours as the wording of the note, the choice of getaway, the area of the city, the choice or avoidance of certain banks, and the use of police scanners have all been reported to originate from media reports of bank robbery. Given the fact that the majority of offenders in this study had extensive criminal backgrounds, it is evident that media reports of robbery did not propel them into crime in the first place. Rather, most were "primed" by and "identified" with media characterizations of this crime and "imitated" some of the *modus operandi* publicized but adapted it to their own liking. As Surette (1992:138) suggests, the mechanism behind copycat crime appears most likely to be a process of identification and priming leading to some degree of generalized imitation. The media typically report on successful crime leading the offender to identify with the crime and/or the offender. He or she next makes assumptions about the risk involved, his or her own abilities and financial need. Needing money, viewing the crime as easy, non-violent, and low risk, and having confidence in his or her own abilities, the offender adopts elements of the M.O., changes it somewhat, and goes out and robs a bank. The media also provide bandits with the justifications used to overcome internalized social constraints and to neutralize guilt.

Fun With Dick and Jane tells the story of a married man who moved from employment to unemployment and into crime through his addiction to drugs. He originates the idea to rob a bank and the rationalizations he used to justify it from viewing the movie *Fun With Dick and Jane*. In *Bonnie and Clyde vs Kojak*, the robber is inspired to his crimes by a movie and is later arrested when a teller accomplice informs after watching a television program in which one partner kills another. In the other three stories — *Counting the Dough, The Relaxe Bandit*, and *Lost Love* — offenders report how newspaper articles influenced them to attempt bank robbery as a means of solving immediate financial problems. The impact of the media is also evident in the histories of other offenders: *The Honest Crime* (Chapter 6) is influenced by newspaper reports; *Lifer* (Chapter 10) claims to have been stimulated by a Stephen Leacock story he read as a young child and newspaper reports of bank profits; and the use of a false bomb is described as having been "T.V. inspired" by *The Hunchback of Notre Dame* (Chapter 4).

Fun with Dick and Jane

This interview was arranged through a parole officer and was conducted at the subject's home with his wife present. The couple have been married 15 years and have three children.

"I've been out three years, but I'm on parole for another three years. I was convicted of five armed robberies and I got nine years. I used to work in this factory for 12 years before I was fired. I was missing a lot of time and causing problems. A lot of my problems are due to drugs. I got involved in smoking and dealing at work. A lot of guys do it there because the job is so boring. For a year after I was fired I was on unemployment. My wife was working all this time and taking care of the family bills. I attribute most of my problems to drugs.

"I was out all the time and spent my time hanging around this particular hotel frequented by bikers, strippers, and other bums. I was always stoned. I only usually smoked pot. I was also hustling a little pot on the side for a dealer who fronted it to me. When I got into the robberies, I owed him $1000.

"My wife was ready to leave, but friends and family convinced her that I was worth trying to save. We argued a lot, but I was always stoned and nothing bothered me. I didn't listen. Sometimes I moved out for long periods — in a hotel for awhile and with a friend another time. When I was at home, it was only to sleep. Our marriage was falling apart and prior to that we got along well.

"I was hanging around this fellow Bob, who was 32 years old, and this younger guy, about 21. We were all unemployed and on drugs hanging around the hotels. They didn't have any previous record either.

"I got the idea to commit a robbery from the movie *Fun with Dick and Jane*. I saw it on TV. I saw it about six months before and it stuck in my mind. In the movie, they commit some robberies and nobody gets hurt. Everybody treats it as a joke. It's a big joke and they get all that money.

"When you're stoned like I was all the time you start to lose touch with reality. It was greed. I wanted the money and I didn't want to have to work for it. The movie gave me the idea but also smoking and dealing, you're continually breaking the law. It seemed like a natural progression. There didn't seem to be any right or wrong to me at the time. I started borrowing money from guys, I guess you could say loan sharks. And the guy I was dealing for, I was selling it and not paying him. Smoking a lot of it. I didn't have the inclination to work anymore. It cut into my free time or what I regarded as fun — hanging around the bar and getting stoned. I was looking for a short-cut and I didn't want a job.

"I brought the subject up to my partners. I just said it flat out. The young guy thought it was a joke, but Bob took it seriously. He was like me, out of money. Bob and I did the first one. We hot-wired a van and drove my car to a mall. We got all these ideas from *Dick and Jane*. I thought about it a lot because I didn't want to get nailed and go to jail. We didn't have any bullets in the gun — that was an absolute must because we didn't want to shoot anyone. Of course, the victims didn't know that. We did a gas station and got about $500. Big deal, it was easy. We partied away the money. It lasted a couple of days. My partner told the younger guy what we had done. He also gave him some money. The kid wanted in on the next one. I regret getting him involved. We did four within a three-week period. A beer store, two Kentucky Fried Chickens — and we got chicken feed — and finally a bank. We would tie up the victim before we left.

"After the first one we quit being careful. We stopped using a stolen car. That's why we got caught. Someone took our licence plate number outside the bank. I had already decided that this was going to be our last one because Bob had been drinking a lot and telling others. He hung around with a few strippers and it was coming back to me through them. One guy came up to me and said, 'I heard that you guys have been doing some armed robberies.'

"After we did the bank we went back to the hotel and split the money immediately. We watched TV and saw how the police had set up roadblocks to catch the robbers. People in the hotel knew we had done it and were cheering because we got away with it. Just like in the movie *Fun with Dick and Jane*. Like when they rob the telephone company. I knew then we were done.

"We were sitting there laughing and meanwhile the young guy had gone home and the police were waiting for him. It was his girlfriend's car we drove. He didn't show up for a few days and we got curious and phoned his girlfriend. She told us that he had been picked up on suspicion of armed robbery. We knew we were had. I was so scared. It felt like everything was coming down around my ears. I stopped taking drugs or drinking. I started to get stuff in order around the house. I just stayed home because I knew the police were coming for me. They took five days before they came to arrest me. I was relieved to see them come. I should have given myself up.

"The arresting officers were decent. They put their guns away as soon as they saw what I was like. They were surprised to find that I had a wife, family, and home. They said that in their arrests that was quite uncommon. I initially denied everything and then one cop sat down and told me all the details of the robberies. They knew everything and laid it on me and I admitted to all of it. Both my partners had copped out already, but I didn't get angry over it. I didn't see them as rats.

"My wife suspected me when she heard about the first robbery. She circled the newspaper article and it really freaked me out when I saw that. Prior to that, she caught me cutting the eyes out of a ski mask. I said it was for shovelling snow.

"Behind the wall you never stare at anyone, and on the street when people look at you, you get paranoid. After I got out I felt that people knew that I was just out of prison. I was suspicious of everyone. But things have gone well since my release. I firmly believe that you can find a job if you want one bad enough. You only have to hustle. I'm doing private contracting and I have a guy working for me.

"Back then I thought that as long as I didn't physically abuse anybody it was no big deal. I've changed my mind about a lot of things since this experience. Now I feel bad about the people at the other end. I have nieces working in variety stores and I have a 13-year-old daughter. I know how I'd feel if someone came in and tied them up and robbed them."

Bonnie and Clyde vs "Kojak"

Age 36, this man is serving 12 years on one count of bank robbery. He is a well known among other bandits and regarded as a professional bank robber.

"I robbed my first bank when I was 19. My mother came home one day with a tale. I was 13 years old. She was in a bank and had been held hostage during a bank robbery. That caught my interest, plus television programs. I was a real mischievous kid and grew up in an area of the city where there was heavy gang action. I liked to be chased. I was very fast and I used to get people to chase me. I'd throw a potato at a streetcar and I'd have ten citizens chasing me up the street. I just liked to test my own endurance to see if I could get away.

"When I robbed my first bank, I was going to night school finishing my high school diploma. I remember I went to a movie one night and seen that movie *Bonnie and Clyde* when it came out. I remember I watched that and it was just like a shot of adreneline. I said, 'That's it.' It's obviously something I've been waiting for. I went and did it and that's all there was to it, about a week after seeing the movie. It was just the sort of thing that would interest me because I had that kind of fire in me.

"It was something that had been on my mind since I was 13 years old and one day a particular bank struck my fancy. I just went in and stuck a gun over the counter and demanded the money. The woman was very cooperative and I got away. It became a profession for me. Later I formed a little crew.

"The first police chase I had, a detective shot at me three times as I was going over a fence. It never slowed me down at all. I don't know, bullets didn't seem to be part of the reality of what I was doing. I guess until you get shot you don't realize how realistic it is. That's what it takes. I feel that the media are responsible for getting some people into robbing banks because they have glorified bank robbers over the years.

"Once I have made the decision I am going to do something, there is nothing else in the world that matters after that. Jail is not a deterrent because I have made the decision to go out and do that.

"For me to be here is a very tough experience. I know people think I am mad all the time because I walk around with a scowl on my face. But that's just my way of keeping them away from me. Prison is something you have to deal with. I've gone through some really heavy trips in my head and heart while in prison. One pinch in particular cost me, it cost me so dearly. My wife was eight months pregnant and I was involved in a conspiracy. I didn't really like the whole trip because a bank teller was involved and she knew me personally and the way the thing was going down was kind of shaky. I didn't put enough effort into it as I should have. And time came for it to come down, I was still shaky because I am not the one actually doing the action. I ended up paying for the mistakes of somebody else and if I had gone and done the action myself I wouldn't have had that problem.

"I thought about it for days because even my wife thought I was up to something and she told me she had a gut instinct that there was something happening that was bad. Right. Women have always got those instincts when there is danger around. That's what I chalked that up to and it cost me dearly. The teller ended up telling and I went down on that one. That was a turning point in my life. I was really bitter about that one. I shouldn't have gone to jail, it was my own fault too. It was just something I couldn't forgive myself for. Too stupid of a mistake. It was a costly, stupid, dumb error. That's what it was, you know, because I was working at the time. We just bought a house, my wife's eight months pregnant, I had been on the street a couple of years and I had things going well. I saw it as free money. That's all it was to me, a paycheque coming in that would help with payments and it was something that could have been done if it was done properly. It was just a little... my heart just wasn't in it and that's what happened, that's... [long pause].

"The teller watched 'Kojak' the night before on T.V. and some guy dumped his partner and she got to thinking that was going to happen to her. I am dead serious. That was in her statement to the police. She was charged along with this other guy and myself."

Counting the Dough

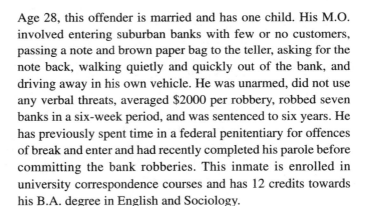

Age 28, this offender is married and has one child. His M.O. involved entering suburban banks with few or no customers, passing a note and brown paper bag to the teller, asking for the note back, walking quietly and quickly out of the bank, and driving away in his own vehicle. He was unarmed, did not use any verbal threats, averaged $2000 per robbery, robbed seven banks in a six-week period, and was sentenced to six years. He has previously spent time in a federal penitentiary for offences of break and enter and had recently completed his parole before committing the bank robberies. This inmate is enrolled in university correspondence courses and has 12 credits towards his B.A. degree in English and Sociology.

"There was no gun involved, just a newspaper that I held under my arm and a note saying that I had a gun under the newspaper. Bank policy says to give the guy the money. Don't be an idiot, it's insured. You read about it in the paper everyday. I'm a newspaper fanatic and everyday there's one in the paper. There was mention of a note but never any evidence of a gun. So you think, 'I don't have to have a gun.' I went in probably a dozen banks before I decided to actually do one. I had a note already written and I'd go into the bank and say, 'No, I can't do it. Just forget it.' Walk out, drive away, and go to another one. Finally I did go through with it. I gave the girl the note and then it's too late, you can't grab the note back. It's incredibly fast. Go in, money, and you're gone. Four or five steps and none of them take a hell of a lot of planning. It's not like you sit there for two or three days with a map of the city.

"I don't want to do B & Es again. It's a serious crime because the home owner can walk in and anything can happen. He can do anything to you because you're in his house. I would classify bank robbery as a low-risk crime and it seemed to me that bank robbery had a lot less of the bullshit. You can do 50 houses in a day and walk out with 50 cents. In a bank, the money is there. You don't have to fence for it and you don't have to carry anything away. You only have to do one, you don't have to go down the street and do four or five. The cash is there.

"I never thought of bank cameras, but after you get caught they've got a fucking 8 by 10 of you. A picture is just good in court, it doesn't give the police your name and address. I didn't have a record in that city, but I could kick myself in the face now. If I had the same intentions today as I did then, I would buy a make-up kit and look like an eighty-three-year-old man when I walked into that bank.

"I used to park my car two or three blocks away from the bank. Whether I got to run or walk two or three blocks away, who cares. Drive away from there up into the suburbs and go into a restaurant for an hour or two. On the last one I drove eight blocks away and pulled over to count the dough. I'm sitting there counting and a white undercover police car pulled up next to me. I looked at him, he looked at me, and I put the car back into gear and started driving away. He turned on the siren and lights and I said, 'Well, catch you later.' I took off. I hit several curbs, bang, turned down the street, turned another corner, hit the median, and the front of the car was shot. And then he hit the side of my car with his car and I wasn't going anywhere. And that was it. When I stepped on it, well it was like pleading guilty without going to trial. Innocent people don't run, supposedly. To this day I'll never understand why I stopped to count the dough. If I wouldn't have stopped there, I would have got away with it. What I didn't know is that I parked next door to a precinct station.

"My wife asked if I gave any thought to being caught. I thought about it a little before I was caught and lots afterwards. Some days you don't feel good and I'm not gonna do it today because I might get caught and go to jail. But then you say, 'Well you got away with the last one and if everything goes like it should, you're not going to get caught.' You think positive and go in there on a positive. You're gonna get away and that's the ultimate. You shouldn't get caught if you do it right. Maybe you get lucky, I mean people parachute all their life and it always opens."

The Relaxe Bandit

Age 24, this man was convicted of 13 bank robberies and is serving a six-year sentence. He is divorced, has one child, a grade 10 education, and a past criminal record that includes break and enter and forgery. This is his first federal penitentiary sentence. He is tall, slim, has long black hair, and is missing several teeth.

"The police called me the 'Relaxe Bandit' or something. I didn't have a gun, but if you indicate that you have a weapon, how do they know you don't? Leaving my notes behind was another mistake. They had a picture from one bank and one an artist had done. It didn't look at all like me. I wouldn't look at the cameras. I'd just keep my head down. The police showed me the notes and they were trying to get me to write so they could get a sample of my handwriting. They played Mutt and Jeff with me, you know, nice guy, 'You want a coffee?' And some other guy comes in and punches you up. Then the two of them come in and the one guy is holding the other guy back. I guess if a person's not knowing what's going on he figures well, 'This guy wants to help me.' But I knew the play. You know, seen it on T.V., right? I knew what they were doing.

"After about ten hours I knew they had me. They knew everything. They knew because of my handwriting. Like, they put it through the computer and the same M.O. came back. They pointed out that the same word is spelled wrong on every note. I gave a statement at the end. I don't know if it did any good or not. I never thought of changing my M.O. because it worked.

"I had one guy who tried to corner me. The bank teller's chasing me up the street and she started screaming. He was in the cab and jumped out and started chasing me down a side street. I never ever carried a piece, but I just put my hand in my jacket and said, 'You get the fuck out of here or I'm blowing your head off.' And he said, 'Daddy,' and he beat it.

"I was considering getting a gun. I had two or three guys offering me pieces. I had it in my hand — thought about it — but said, 'No, if I got it I'll probably use it. Do something I'll be sorry for.' I didn't want to hurt nobody. I have a real attitude problem. Like, I'd sooner give somebody a slap in the mouth than look at them. And go do a bank, it was like an everyday thing. It was just 'I don't give a damn' kind of attitude. I wouldn't hurt an innocent bystander. They're not asking for it, right? But somebody who wants to play hero, I'm not going down for anybody else. It's a natural instinct.

"I quit for three months, but then the money ran out, the drugs ran out. I had some hangers-on. Everybody's your friend when you got lots of money and drugs and stuff. There was a circle of people I hang around with for parties and beers.

"I had a close call in a downtown bank. I walked out and ducked into a bar two blocks away, sat down and had a drink. I had $2200 in my boot. The cops came in, they looked around and left. Ten minutes later, 30 of them came in. Fifteen of them in the SWAT team, guns strapped to their backs. As it happened there was four guys sitting behind me. I turned around and I said, 'Listen, I just had a hit and run there a few minutes ago and I think they're looking for me.' 'Well come on, join us. Party with us.' The cops came walking through and looked around. It was too close of a call, too close for me. I figured It was time to get out of the city and do some in the suburbs.

"On the first four or five I made my getaway on the subway. I'd pick a bank right along the subway line and 15 seconds you're in the subway. I cut off the subway route after I did about five or six of them. I never planned on doing 13 bank robberies. I thought there'd be about one or two just for extra cash. But it got so easy that it becomes addictive almost. It just came natural after awhile. I'd be driving around at night and I'd see a bank that I likes and I'd just say, 'I'll do that tomorrow or the next day.' I never really got into deep thought about it. There's not much to it though. I guess it just takes that nerve to go out and do it the first time.

"I'd wear two coats and throw one away. Go unshaved for a week and as soon as you do it you go and shave it off. And I'm walking around with long hair. I can't just grow long hair. They see you at the bank with short hair because the hair's underneath the baseball cap. After a score I'd go to strip joints and get high. And prostitutes. You go out with $2000 in your pocket, there's nothing you can't do. You want some broads and some dealer to sell you some coke, no problem. Money doesn't mean nothing to you anymore. A hundred dollar bill don't mean nothing. I got $200 today, I'll guess I'll have to do a job tomorrow. It was no big money, $1800 or $2000, but it was a lot better than working a 40-hour week and getting paid $200.

"I'd been thinking about robbing banks for years. I always thought you have to go in there with a gun, you got two or three guys to back you up, and you take the whole joint. Then I started reading the articles in the paper about bank robberies. And they can't refuse to give you the money. And they can't say anything until you're out of the bank. I read that in the papers and I figured, well Jesus, it even makes it easier. I don't understand why they put it in the paper. So I decided to give it a try.

"I didn't give a damn if they catch me? Just a period of my life I didn't care. Other people can go to jail and still survive, why can't I? I don't know why I felt like that? Beats me. But I don't get off on the place though, at all. Being broke on the street is better than being in prison."

Lost Love

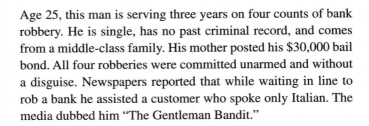

Age 25, this man is serving three years on four counts of bank robbery. He is single, has no past criminal record, and comes from a middle-class family. His mother posted his $30,000 bail bond. All four robberies were committed unarmed and without a disguise. Newspapers reported that while waiting in line to rob a bank he assisted a customer who spoke only Italian. The media dubbed him "The Gentleman Bandit."

"I imagine all of us have the potential for crime. Not necessarily violence but criminal acts. I've always been quite aware of it from a very young age. I did a few things as a juvenile, broke into a couple of places, but I never got caught. Why banks? I went out with this girl for four years and I was shut off the relationship. I was working with my brother who just got his company off the ground so there was a lot of stress and a lot of hours involved. And so, she left! I took it really bad. Started using cocaine in large amounts. I had maybe $10,000 in my own savings. I went through that quickly and I got into debt quite heavily to this guy for the drugs. And I had a falling out with my brother just shortly after that so I wasn't working.

"I owed about $7000 to $8000 dollars for drugs. I was pretty screwed up so it's not like I could think straight. I don't know what initiated the idea to rob a bank. I just remember reading a lot of articles: 'Old man, 65, hands teller note and limps away on his cane.' Everybody seemed to be doing it. I was amused how simple it was. There'd never be any trouble. This is the sense I got from the newspapers. It just seemed too simple. I don't think they mentioned 'limped out' but 'got away on foot.' How fast can a 65-year-old man run? Seemed so funny. I robbed my first bank shortly after. I figured it's gonna be the easiest way. I don't have to rob anybody. There is no thought process needed. There's banks everywhere and it doesn't matter which one you walk into. It was just simplicity. I knew it was there and one day I thought, 'That's it! I'm gonna do it today.' And I went out and did it that day.

"The first one was kind of tough. I was nervous. I was afraid the teller would laugh at me 'cause I didn't have a gun. Didn't want to hurt anybody. That's one of the reasons banks appealed to me. Great, just give her a note and if nothing happens, oh well. When I did see how simple it really was, it came easier. So there was no anxiety after the first one. The more I did it, the easier it got. The fourth one I really got careless. There was a gentleman in line, an older gentleman having problems communicating with the teller. I am standing in line waiting my turn and I overheard this so I just said, 'He'd like large bills. He's asking for large bills.' He couldn't speak English and she couldn't understand him. Afterwards, when it was my turn, I robbed that same teller. They put that in the paper.

"I remember making a concerted effort after the first one to find what they said in the papers about the robbery. Nothing, no mention at all. I felt relief at the time — felt good. That's the way I wanted it. I remember one of them well. The teller fainted afterwards. After she gave me the money she was terrified. I remember as I walked away, I'm seeing people turning their heads, look at her, bend down. Their attention was drawn to her so I just made my escape. There was nothing in the papers about that. She handed me a bundle of large bills [chuckle] which I thought was kind of nice.

"Just prior to the banks, I started using coke heavy. I was... I was shooting it. I spent roughly $2000 a week on coke. This was for a very short period, maybe from May till July. It was quite a turnaround in my life when I started that. I took it hard when my girlfriend left me. I believe that I was quite self-destructive.

"I got caught very close to home. I went down the street, a couple of blocks on my ten-speed. Handed the note, ran out, jumped on my bike and went home. I think somebody followed me. The cops came right to my house three hours later. I wasn't there at the time. My roomate told me, 'Cops were here! What did you do?' I took off that night. I didn't want to turn myself in so I fled. It seemed like the natural thing to do. I was arrested on a train making my way out west.

"They stopped the train maybe a mile before the station. The cops boarded the train. I walked by them the first time, right by them. Went and had a drink, sat down. Then when they came up to me again they asked for I.D. They were talking to each other, conferring, 'Well it looks like him.' These cops were so — I don't want to say dumb — but they were pretty slow. I had to tell them, 'Yes, okay, I'm the guy you're looking for.'

"I was held in a holding cell for three days. That was probably the roughest part of it 'cause after using all the coke I was coming down. An officer picked me up and took me to the airport. I was handcuffed in the vehicle going to the plane. He took them off on the plane. I knew he was going to be prodding. He said, 'We have you for four of them. What do you think of that?' I figured, what the hell. I didn't hold anything back. They're all mine.

"I used coke moderately before I started robbing banks. Buy a gram once a month. Just a few lines of coke here and there. Once I started shooting it, it was wonderful at first. After awhile it didn't get that wonderful so I thought maybe I'm not using enough. Keep using more and more. It was my first experience using needles. When I ran out of drugs, it was pretty bad. I'd be scraping around looking, 'I must have some more elsewhere. Need a fix.' Just die!

"I didn't see my girlfriend again until maybe August, after I came out on bail. It was only brief. We talked about it. It sort of shocked her, shocked her a lot actually. I haven't seen her since."

CHAPTER FOUR

Nothing to Lose —

The Tragic

- • The Reluctant Robbers
- • John Wayne
- • Sad Sack Loser
- • The Hunchback of Notre Dame
- • That Wanderless Feeling
- • Death Wish
- • Outlaws on the Run

Whereas differential association and anomie theory assume conformity and attempt to explain deviance, a social control perspective views conforming behaviour as problematic since humans will violate norms if it is in their advantage to do so. Control theory developed from the same intellectual tradition as Durkheim (1933; 1951) because it asserts that the fundamental cause of crime lies in the weakening of social constraints over the conduct of individuals. People have many temptations to crime — money, fun, power, status, peer pressure, sexual gratification, anger, revenge, and drug-induced motives — and without social controls that keep us in check, we might all succumb to the enjoyment, excitement, and profit that frequently accompanies criminal conduct. Controls that help ensure conformity include both internal and external constraints. Inner controls typically derive from socialization into conventional law-abiding values whereas external controls represent the possibility that other persons may punish or reward our behaviour. Social controls and agents of social control may be informal or formal, such as a compliment delivered by a friend or an arrest made by the police. When both inner and external social controls are strong, people conform. If both are weak, however, people will be tempted to deviate.

Social control theories explain conformity in reference to the strategies that societies use to maintain social order. These include socialization into common values, family supervision, role modelling, reward structures that promote conformity, and a variety of formal and informal mechanisms that discourage, punish, and deter deviant conduct. Control theory often focuses on the effectiveness of the family at socializing children, and the theory has been termed an "undersocialization perspective" since it is premised on the view that proper socialization will yield conforming conduct and improper socialization will result in deviance.

Social control theory has several variations. Travis Hirschi's (1969) social bonding theory emphasizes the positive role that socialization plays in the promotion of conformity by establishing social bonds between the individual and others who are carriers of conformist values. Hirschi argues that people are more likely to become deviant if the bonds to society are weakened or non-existent. The social bond consists of four elements that promote conformity and prevent deviance: attachment, commitment, involvement, and belief. Attachments to primary groups such as the family constrain behaviour because individuals do not wish to hurt, embarass, or disappoint the people they love. Commitment to conventional goals requires people to invest time and energy into conventional pursuits, such as an education, a business, a relationship, or a job. This acts as a deterrence to crime because the decision to commit a deviant act will place at risk a person's investments. Involvement in conventional activity takes time and limits the opportunity to partake in deviant pursuits. And belief in cultural morality arises from proper socialization into values that are internalized and function to constrain behaviour. Thus a person who lacks affective bonds, commitments and involvements in conventional activites, and beliefs in societal values, is relatively free to pursue criminal conduct because internal and external social constraints are weak or non-existent.

One image of offenders that social control theory presents is that of a "loser" (Hirschi, 1986:115) — individuals who have few accomplishments or meaningful relationships that bind them to the conventional order. Having few stakes in conformity (Toby, 1957), they have nothing to lose and are undeterred by the threat of arrest and imprisonment. Research consistently finds that offender populations are made up of men who have few family bonds, low educational attainment, few job prospects or job skills, minimal work experience and motivation, and low self-concepts. One component in their motivation includes a nothing-to-lose or self-destructive attitude. In this view of offenders, social control theory is consistent with rational choice and deterrence theory because it portrays the offender as rational and capable of assessing potential gains and risks inherent in criminal activity. A person who has few social bonds and little to lose is likely to think that the benefits of committing a crime outweigh the potential costs and will be undeterred by potential risks.

Critics of social control theory point to the fact that this explanatory model is incomplete since it does not offer an explanation of deviant motivation. A lack of social control provides a release from persons and values that bind us to the social order and allows us to drift into crime, but it does not explain the attraction that deviant conduct offers. Control theory is also faulted because it tends to focus on the individual and his or her relationships with family, school, peer groups, church, and work yet fails to consider the larger political and economic structure of society. In addition, social control theory says nothing about the interactive setting in which deviant conduct is learned, performed, and reinforced (Linden, 1992: Thornberry, 1987:865). It is clear from the criticisms of social control theory that this perspective offers only a partial explanation of deviant conduct and must be combined with other theories to give a more complete explanation of crime.

As can be seen from the following case synopses, a significant number of the men interviewed in this study describe their social and financial situations in depressing terms. Many have experienced the loss of a relationship or job, prolonged unemployment, and economic dependency and have little hope that their life is about to improve. They subjectively define their situation as one in which they have little to lose and view crime as a means to improve their life. Some even demonstrate a self-destructive component in the motivation to robbery. This is particularly evident with inmates who have escaped from prison, failed to return from a temporary pass into the community, or violated their parole. Over a dozen men in this study were on the run when they robbed banks. Since they already face additional time, many throw caution to the wind and commit their crimes carelessly and in quick succession, spending the money like there is no tomorrow. The emotional state of men on the run varies, but for most it is best summarized as a nothing-to-lose or to hell with tomorrow attitude. The threat of arrest and imprisonment is not an effective deterrent because they fatalistically believe that they can fall no further.

The following cases illustrate the tragedy in the lives of many offenders. Some of the suffering is the result of having been brought up in dysfunctional families, but much of the despair that is their life results from their own actions. The interview in *The Reluctant Robbers* is with a not-too-bright 22-year-old serving time for the robbery of several hotels. After his release from prison he violates parole and takes part in a failed bank robbery in which he is shot and arrested. His life is one with few social bonds and commitments. In addition, his appearance will make difficult his integration into society since he has disfigured himself with amateurish and grisly tatoos on his arms, shoulders, face, and neck. This story describes a group of young, inexperienced, and unintelligent criminals who attempt to rob a bank. Their lack of planning and sophistication sets them on a path to arrest and re-imprisonment.

John Wayne is a 29-year-old career criminal who was interviewed in different prisons two years apart on separate bank robbery charges. He has a lengthy history of criminal involvement going back to adolescence, but states in the first interview a clear desire to go straight. He was recently married in prison, his wife was about to have a baby, he had a job waiting for him upon his release, and his parole application had been approved. His prospects and his commitment to go straight seemed promising. Two years later, I heard a radio report on his arrest on 13 counts of robbery. In our second interview, he explains how his continued association with ex-cons led to his re-arrest, parole revocation, and the loss of his job and family. Having nothing more to lose, he escaped from prison and embarked an a crime spree.

Sad Sack Loser is a sorry case. His life is characterized by family and marital problems, foster homes and training schools, low self-esteem, substance abuse, unemployment, financial problems, and friends who use him, lead him into bank robbery, and eventually inform on him. All of this results in a term of imprisonment that only adds to his problems. *The Hunchback of Notre Dame* is a man injured in a motorcycle accident that resulted in serious and permanent physical disabilities. One side of his face has lost muscle and nerve control, giving his features a grotesque appearance. He has very low self-esteem and characterizes himself as a freak. He describes how this tragedy has influenced his life and resulted in permanent emotional disabilities that led him into self-pity and crime along the road to self-destruction.

In *That Wanderless Feeling* the offender has spent his life behind bars and with little family contact. When his girlfriend ends their relationship he is emotionally devastated, escapes from his halfway house, and commits another robbery. In *I Need Help Not Prison* the offender has previously served time for manslaughter. For the present offence he turned himself into the police in order to receive psychiatric treatment for emotional and substance abuse problems. Unfortunately for him prison has little to offer in the way of psychiatric facilities. He is presently seeking parole so that he can receive treatment in a non-custodial setting. His letter to the parole board is reproduced. In *Death Wish* an 18-year-old man is depressed over his brother's murder and agrees to take part in a bank robbery partly because he no longer cares if he lives or dies. *Outlaws on the Run* describes how one escapee shows another how to rob banks as they begin a series of holdups across the country. They see their arrest as inevitable, wear no disguises, and commit their crimes carelessly. They exhibit little concern for their long-term welfare and have as their only goal a desire to have fun as long as they can. Both express the belief that they have little going for themselves in life and nothing to lose by escaping prison and embarking on a major crime spree across Canada.

As can be seen from these case synopses, the lack of affective bonds or their recent loss creates a self-destructive attitude among offenders who feel they have nothing to lose by committing crime. In retrospect, most see the fallacy of such reasoning and realize that arrest and imprisonment have only made their situation worse than before.

The Reluctant Robbers

This offender was interviewed on two separate occasions four years apart. Several years later I read a newspaper story detailing this man's arrest in the commission of a bank robbery. The article indicated that he and four others had attempted to rob a bank and that he had been shot in the back with a shotgun blast. It also stated that he had filed a lawsuit in excess of $900,000 against the police for damages resulting from his wounds. He readily consented to another interview and the following contains excerpts from both.

First Interview: Age 21

"Both my brother and I are in for armed robbery of hotels and their cash registers. I got six years and he got eight. The way it started is that he escaped from prison and wanted to see me. I made a stupid mistake by coming back from the West coast because I got involved with him in doing burglaries. In one house we happened to find a gun and we figured that was our paycheque for doing robberies. Quick money without the effort. One of us would go into the hotel earlier in the evening and ask for change. Later, when we thought it was safe, we'd put on some nylon stockings and go back and rob the place. We'd have a couple of drinks just to get our courage up. We did five, but I planned to quit because I knew my luck was going to run out sooner or later. I was drinking pretty heavy. We were spending $500 to $600 in the bar every night. We always like to have a couple of hundred just to show off. Pretty silly when you think of it, make that money just to blow it in a bar. What the hell for?

"The gun was loaded, but I never wanted to hurt anybody. I'd never want to shoot anybody and come to jail for it because I'd end up in here for a long time. Not only that, I don't get off on hurting people. Like I never used any violence at all when I was doing these robberies. We would just make people lie on the floor. I did six months dead time awaiting trial. Just thinking of court, I couldn't handlle it. I was surprised I didn't slash or hang myself because I was going through hell. You couldn't even talk to me when I got pinched. I was so screwed up. Other cons felt sorry for me because I was shaking and having it rough. My brother was calm and helped me out because he got along with everybody. I went through too much in these joints just to go out and come back. I went through pure hell and I know if I do it again I'll go through pure hell again. There is no way I'm going through it again. I'm surprised I didn't have a nervous breakdown. Maybe I did and I don't know what a nervous breakdown really is. I guess I did, but maybe I didn't.

"Some guys will sit down and talk to you about this bank robbery they did and when I first started my bit, I'd go, 'Oh boy.' But now, I don't even listen. It doesn't do nothing for me. I don't care anymore. You get sick of hearing all the stories. That's why I think so many guys get out and come back because they listen to all these conversations and you pick up little pieces. They will think they're better, and you've got to admit they probably are better.

"My parents have been split up since I was five. I lived with my dad and I didn't want him to know that me and my brother were pinched for armed robbery. He heard it over the radio. My dad comes up and visits me all the time. My real mom is two-faced. She will write a letter and say she is coming down to see me and she won't come. She plays head games all the time."

Second Interview: Four Years Later

"My brother took off and I was wondering whether I should take off and get in shit again. I was really thinking about it and a week after I decided that I was going to take off from the halfway house and not even bother with it any more. Whatever happens happens. I was there for ten and one-half months and I should have been out of there sooner. I was on the verge of getting out of there, but I was sort of living in two worlds. Like one with the straight life 'cause I was working with people that were straight and then I was living my life with the people in the halfway house. And it was like I was caught in between the middle. I've never been in that position before, I didn't know which way to go. It was like juggle myself back and forth and I decided to take off. It was obviously the wrong reason.

"I got shot in the back. There were five of us living together in this apartment. Me, my brother, and three other guys we knew from prison. Four of us had violated our parole by taking off from a halfway house so there was no sense going straight. The police had us under surveillance for two weeks. They wiretapped the house.

"We stole a car the night before. When we all got ready in the morning we were really scared thinking about it. Like nobody had any experience robbing banks. It was like nobody was in control because we didn't know how to do it. We knew how to do robberies, but we didn't particularly know the procedures of a bank because you got certain minutes and seconds. Anyway, we stole this car and slept in the apartment that night and never drank or nothing, tried to stay straight, keep a clear mind in case anything went wrong. We didn't want someone getting killed — us or anybody.

"That morning I felt really uneasy about it. I could see it in everybody else's face that they didn't either. But we already committed ourselves in a sense. We all jumped in this car, but little did we know we were being followed. But you could almost tell we were because of our feelings, I don't know. We got instincts. You get a weird feeling when you're doing stuff like that.

"We started driving up the street and went to the back of the bank. It didn't look too good so we drove away and we decided to come back. When we went back to the bank, at the last minute, one of the guys said, 'Forget it. Let's not even bother doing this. Just get the hell out of here.' And just as we did that, a car cut us off out of a parking lot right in front of the bank. I thought it was some guy recklessly driving so I jump out of the car 'cause he was just in plain clothes. But when I looked around they were all over the place. There weren't no uniform cops — it was just all of them with guns. I knew they were cops. They were lying over their cars, all over the place.

"Apparently they shot the tire and then this guy cut us off. None of us heard the shot. It all happened at once and the cop was right there and he put the car in reverse and pulled in front of us and we hit him. I thought it was an accident, 'Oh no, an accident in front of a bank at a time like this!' I jumped out of the car and they were all there. I wouldn't dare run when I seen guns because there's always that fear that they'll shoot me if I run. I try to be as participant as I can. Do what they want me to do — everything. This officer told me to put my hands on the car so naturally I did 'cause he had a shotgun in his hand and he was pointing it up in the air. Not pointing it right at me but pointing it up. Another cop said spread out. So I stood there for a minute and the funny thing is I've been arrested so many times I can't count and usually they put the handcuffs on you right away, bang. But this guy was taking a long time to put these handcuffs on me and I knew he was behind me. So he decided to just shoot me in the back with a shotgun. The shotgun was leaning against my back when he shot me. There are pellets in there still all over the place. There's about five or six of them in there still. He said it was an accident — it just discharged. Obviously I'm suing them.

"When he shot me, I sprung straight up. My arm went numb. I didn't know I was shot. I thought maybe he hit me on the back of the head. I felt a tinging in the back of my neck. I didn't feel the pain, no. After a minute I knew I was shot. He didn't say a word, he was in awe that he actually shot me. He couldn't believe it. This other cop told me to lie on the ground and I did. About 15 minutes later the ambulance came and I bled for quite awhile on the ground. I was lucky it missed all my vital organs. I think the reason I did live is the gun was leaning against my back and went off in an up position. If it went straight through, it would have blew part of my guts out.

"But the whole thing was just a crazy idea in our heads. It's too dangerous to rob a bank. We were just praying that it would work. We were very amateur at it. We didn't know what we were doing or how. It was just, 'Let's go do this,' and that's it. I can't really pinpoint whose idea it was originally. From the beginning it didn't sound like a good idea. Once we were sitting there and said we were going to do it, we made ourselves committed. Nobody wanted to say anything because we didn't want to look bad. It was like we were all thinking, 'Well, what are we going to do, sit here and make no money? We got to do something. Nobody is legal and nobody is working.' Yeah. But after awhile we started realizing, 'This ain't going to work.' And you can see it in each other's face, the intensity. Nobody was happy with it. Nobody wanted to go through with it. Oh, we were all thinking that; you could tell it by looking at each other. It wasn't like we did it before and knew what we were doing.

"I got six years in a deal. The judge hated us. When you're going down for a bank robbery they don't usually like you. We thought we'd get 12 or 15 years if we went to trial. You can easily get that if you fight it because the courts get sick of you and they don't want to waste time and money so they do that a lot. The judge didn't like the fact that we had a shotgun, a .32 handgun, and I had a starter's pistol in my coat pocket.

"I'm 26 now and that's old for in here. I was out ten and one-half months and I was doing so well. I wasn't getting in any trouble. I don't know what it is with crime, once you've done it before it's a lot easier. Everybody knows that. I don't know why you do it 'cause you know you're going to have to suffer circumstances again like coming to jail. And you gotta go through all that pain of being in the bucket and sitting in court and going through hell. It's a horrible scene and yet you do it. I don't understand, it's ridiculous. I had a job and I was making money. The halfway house was really happy with me and used me as an example for the other guys in the house. They said, 'Look at Jim, he's doing good here and good there.' I was doing okay and I turned around and went and did this. The halfway house was — they were shaking their heads. They felt betrayed but not only that, they have to put up with the community around them. They're really disappointed when you do something like that.

"I always knew that a person can never say that they will never be back in jail because you don't know. There's so many things out there that you don't know about. You've been in so long that when you get out everything's changed so much so you react to different things. The only thing you know is jail life so you end up back. You just kind of pray you don't come back."

John Wayne

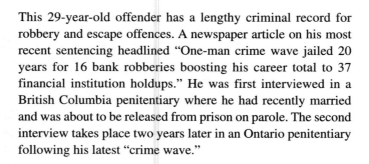

This 29-year-old offender has a lengthy criminal record for robbery and escape offences. A newspaper article on his most recent sentencing headlined "One-man crime wave jailed 20 years for 16 bank robberies boosting his career total to 37 financial institution holdups." He was first interviewed in a British Columbia penitentiary where he had recently married and was about to be released from prison on parole. The second interview takes place two years later in an Ontario penitentiary following his latest "crime wave."

"Drinking has always been my biggest problem. But that's not what caused me to rob banks. I don't know what caused me to rob banks. As a matter of fact I haven't even got the personality for it. I may have been influenced by the glamour in it. I started off in juvenile detention centres at 14 for car thefts and worked my way up. I remember that bank robbers had a lot of class so that might have had something to do with it. From doing time in the penitentiary and associating with guys who had done banks, I was told exactly how to do it. You have a lot of time in jail and you learn a lot about crime.

"I had a kind of bogus John Wayne image. That might have had something to do with it. I know that my act used to parallel his quite a bit. Dressing up, the way I acted, stuff like that, my lifestyle. I used to think I was pretty undercover. I had a vision of myself as a gangster. I used to act it and the guys I hung around with, mostly guys from the pen, they had the same act. Dress nice, go to cocktail lounges and date the cocktail waitresses — fast women, big tipping, and the cars — spending a lot of money.

"We had a favourite bar downtown and my partner and I would go there after the robbery and make the split. Do it in the underground parking lot or in the cocktail lounge itself. I didn't like to wait. Then you can relax, drink, and watch the sunset. We'd sit around the bar all night drinking with friends, mostly partying. I was drinking a hell of a lot, went through a few cars. I had an apartment. I bought a speed boat one time from a guy in a bar and only used it once. I had plans to start up a business and get out of this, but the drinking and partying got in the way.

"I got hooked on a lifestyle. The people I was hanging around with, if not robbing banks, were into something else. A girl I was living with, she never knew what we were up to. Matter of fact she always thought it was drug oriented. She knew there was guns and money, but it was not a topic of conversation. Most of that money went on other people anyways. I seen very little of it actually. When I think back on it, in times past, a couple of thousand dollars meant nothing to me. When I started to get short, I'd start planning to get more because $500 for a night out was nothing. When you worked you only worked for an afternoon. Not even that. Go out, get the money, and be back in the bar an hour later.

"Now I'm married, my wife is pregnant, I've had to acquire knowledge of money and what it's worth. We gotta rent a house and we drive a beat-up Chevy. I think now how even a couple of thousand dollars would make a hell of a difference. That would just take the edge off the next six months or even a year. Just for little things; just that little bit extra. I've never been straight and that's another thing I'm going to have to acquire.

"I met my wife two years ago after I had escaped. I did four bank robberies during that little escapade, got caught, escaped again, and met my wife just two days before I got busted. She didn't even know my right name. Then she started visiting me and we got together a year after that. We got married in prison. I got my parole last week and I get out soon. I've got a job lined up."

Two Years Later in a Different Prison

"I did get parole and was out for four months. Then a friend I was hanging around with went up for murder. He eventually got five years for manslaughter. So anyways I never was charged with anything, but I was in the wrong place at the wrong time. Nobody believed me when I said that I didn't see anything. I was stoned on valium and booze. A fight broke and one guy got stabbed. Technically they took away my parole for using alcohol and for associating with other parolees, but that wasn't the real reason. It doesn't look good for the parole board when a guy who's on parole is mixed up in a murder. It was a drinking party. There was this guy, my friend, me, and our old ladies. We were into the booze and a fight broke out and this guy got killed. We were all on parole and living at the halfway house. It was all in the family.

"Things had been good between my wife and me. I wasn't even thinking of pulling any robberies or anything. I had guys coming up to me wanting to do scores and I didn't touch one. I was working as a labourer and we were poor but doing good. Yeah, I never deviated from my intention. I picked up one speeding ticket, that's it. I didn't want to come back to prison.

"And that killing came down and I went back into prison. My wife had the baby a week later. The police were threatening to charge her with an 'accessory after the fact' and the marriage dissolved. My wife decided that was it. She had waited for me for two years and now I had another four to serve. She came in to tell me. She visited me after she got out of the hospital and brought the kid for me to see her. No hard feelings.

"Since I had almost five years left to serve I just said, 'Fuck it' and escaped. I was pretty shook up. I had other problems too; they wanted me to testify at the murder trial and I didn't want to hang around for that. I could have probably got released if I had put the finger on my friend. That's what the prosecutor wanted. That's why I left. Now that I'm on the run, I'm broke and I've got to get money so I walk into a few banks. Then I came out East and started doing them here. I did 18 banks from July to mid-October. I was living with this girl, drinking a lot, and doing coke. She didn't know — she didn't want to know what I was up to. She still calls me by my alias, Al.

"They charged me for 18 banks and I coughed up to the whole works. Supposed to have a deal. Supposed to get ten years and ended up with 20. Add that on to the 19 I'm already serving and my total sentence comes to 39 years. But it's not as bad as it sounds. I've served ten in total and I'm eligible for parole after a third of my sentence — three years from now. Not that they'll give it to me then, but they're not going to make me wait till I'm 50 either. I used to take university courses while I was in prison out West. I escaped before I finished my B.A. so I'm looking into starting it up again in here."

Sad Sack Loser

Age 37, this man is serving three years on three counts of bank robbery. His three partners received sentences of ten, eight, and six years.

"I spent time in a training school as a kid. I was 11 years old when I started. In the beginning I was running away from school, stealing, B & Es, pulling fire alarms. My mother couldn't handle me so the judge sentenced me to three years. I broke out of there four times in one month. I didn't like it. It was very rough for me. I was always getting into fights. My mother separated from my father and I think I looked too much like him. I reminded her of him so she took it out on me. That hurt. She was on the bottle drinking everyday. It was not a good life, not at all. My mother would hit me with a broomstick or a belt buckle that broke all my teeth. My younger brother got along great with her. I used to call him a 'mummy's boy.' We lived on mother's allowance. We were a very poor family. There were cockroaches and mice and the landlord wouldn't fix up the place.

"I got sent away to training school and I didn't like that at all. I went through a lot of foster homes and the Children's Aid. This was before I was sentenced. No place could handle me. The judge told me I was a very hard case. They had a huge file on me. I stayed in until I was 19. I did six years in training school as a kid — six straight years! In those days it was like prison. I was a loner by the time I got out. I had very few friends. I got into dope then I got into trouble hanging around with the bikers. I got into speed and smack, the hard stuff. I was lucky I was never busted. Then I went into a drug treatment program. I weighed about 90 lbs when I went in and I stayed there for 15 weeks. I got involved in a volunteer group to help street kids; it was something to keep me occupied and out of trouble. That was where I met my first wife. She was a runaway. I was only 21 then and she was about 19. I invited her to have a cup of coffee and she said okay. I asked her where she was staying. She said, 'Nowhere,' so I told her she could stay at my place. We got along well and nine months later we were married. We had to get married because she was pregnant.

"After we had our son we moved to live with her parents on their farm. I didn't like her father and he didn't like me at first. I told him I couldn't do anything on the farm because I knew nothing about it. He put me to work to prove me wrong. We started liking each other after awhile. He said he could tell a lot about a person by watching them work. We had another baby, a daughter, and lived there for three years. My best friend started hanging around us. He started coming up on the weekends. It didn't dawn on me what was going on. My wife took off with my best friend. She took the car and left a note on the table that she had left me. The day I saw the note her father came over to ask if he could help me in the barn. I showed him the note. He and I both cried. He was hurt too. He didn't know it was going on.

"I saw her two years ago walking down the street. I called her name and when she faced me she turned white. She was scared. We started talking and I asked her how the kids were. She was supposed to send me some pictures, but she never did.

"This is the first time I've done time as an adult. My partners were involved in more robberies. They had them on seven and I only did three. I had stopped five months before they were arrested. I had enough of it, I got away from them. My nerves couldn't take it no more and I couldn't take the bullshit no more. I got a job in a hotel and was working there when the cops came to arrest me. They had arrested one partner and he ratted on all of us. The police put the other two under surveillance and nailed them when they did a bank.

"I needed money, it was real hard times. I had been truck driving and I had an operation on my wrist and couldn't go back to work for awhile. Instead of the boss calling me back like he was supposed to, he called his son-in-law instead. So I was laid off permanently. I was losing my apartment because I couldn't keep up the payments. I was on welfare, but welfare wasn't paying enough to keep the place. And I was having trouble with my girlfriend. I needed money badly so I phoned Neil. As it happened the bank robbery had already been planned. They came and picked me up and told me to get in the car. I thought they could loan me some money. Then they mentioned bank robbery, I thought about it and said, 'Might as well, I've got nothing else to lose.' I was losing everything: my relationship was down the drain, I had no job, and I was losing my apartment. I also had a fraud charge coming up and I was on bail. I was frightened about this because I don't like prison. Neil kept saying that I was going to get 15 years for fraud. That added more to my mind. I was confused and thought I'd do some robberies and then get the heck out of the province. I thought I'd move out West. I had 13 charges for bad cheques, they were my own cheques. I told the court that I thought I had enough money in the bank, but the judge didn't believe me. I wanted things: my new place needed dishes, I bought clothes. When the case did come to court I got a year's probation.

"I used to live with Neil, and I knew the other guys from this restaurant where we all hung out. Neil had a record for bank robbery from a few years before, but these other guys didn't have records. So anyway I got in the car and we drove around and started talking about the job, which one we were gonna do. They didn't know where to go or what bank to do so I mentioned this trust company and that's the one we did. They all had money problems too. Neil was a transport truck driver and was making lots of money, but then he was laid off and out of work.

"I was the one who went in to rob the bank. I was pretty scared and I wanted them to stand guard because some guy might jump you. I was very nervous. There was no gun involved, I just handed a note. We got close to $8000. We hit that bank a second time and the teller recognized us as soon as we walked in. We had sunglasses on, but that was all. We should have got disguises, but it wasn't well planned. She pushed the alarm as soon as she saw us, but it took the police quite a long time to get there so we got away. We stood in line and waited for a couple of customers to get out of the way and we both went up and asked for the money. It's scariest just before you go in. Once you hand the note to the teller, you kinda calm down; kind of, not completely. The third time I stayed in the car and drove. They jumped into the car and ducked down and I drove away.

"Then I spent the money on foolishness, having a good time. I met a girl and she spent a couple of weeks with me. We had a good time drinking, partying, and buying dope. It lasted for about two weeks. I was trying to get enough money to go out West, but when I saw that Neil didn't want to go out West with me I decided to break away. He came looking for me and tried to get me to come back, but I said, 'No way. My nerves can't take it.' I seen him a couple of times after, but he never bugged me about it. Never again will I rob a bank. I have a stepsister and she was very angry and disappointed that I did what I did. She said that when I get out she is going to make sure that I get a job and go straight. My boss says I can come back to my old job at the hotel."

The Hunchback of Notre Dame

Age 27, this offender was sentenced to two and one-half years on an earlier conviction for robbery and is now serving a seven-year term for an attempted bank holdup using a fake bomb. His appearance is striking because one-half of his face droops due to nerve damage resulting from a motorcycle accident.

"I had an accident on my motorcycle when I was 18 and I landed on my head. I was comatose for a month before I woke up and I had the shakes really bad. It was just like I had a stroke. My face lost its muscle, my mouth and eye hung down. My whole right side was affected. I used to be right-handed and now I do everything with my left. I used to be a good drinker and a good fighter. I was sort of a rough and tough kid. I was big and tough and I lost all of that. I was reduced to a quiverring little... [tails off]. It wasn't my entity, it wasn't me. I had to slow down, I couldn't fight no more. I could barely move fast. I couldn't play hockey, I was useless. I lost it all. I was shattered — gone. I used to be all right. Suddenly I had turned into a freak. I used to have no problem with girls then after that it was like the Hunchback of Notre Dame. I used to be proud of my appearance and every hair had to be in place. I had to look right on. Tanned, blue eyes, I had no trouble with girls. I didn't have sex for four years with a girl after I fell on my head without paying for it, that's how bad it was. That really scarred me up. I know I looked developmentally handicapped. I looked like a goof. I looked fresh out of an asylum. My face made people look at me strange. I looked like I shouldn't be out in public. I got into self-pity and that motivated me for a couple of years. I couldn't handle none of my family no more because they showed too much sympathy for me. I don't want people feeling sorry for me.

"I tried to find work. I didn't get nothin. I quit school when I was 15 and went to work on the railroad. I did heavy physical labour on a steel tie gang. I liked physical work and I went back after my accident, but I couldn't compete with the other workers. The foreman advised me to quit or get fired. I had no choice so I resigned. I knew I couldn't pull my weight. I didn't care much about myself. I just gave up on everything. The money from robbing a bank was going to provide an escape from the Hunchback of Notre Dame. That's the way I felt. It would allow me to buy so much drugs that I could really get lost. I wouldn't have to worry about how I looked, I could just be high all the time. I was looking for a total escape.

"I was in a restaurant and I started writing out a holdup note on a paper placemat; it was a spur of the moment thing. I was living in a drug-induced fantasy. I did some chemicals the night before and I was pretty high on hash when I did this. I had a meal in the restaurant and I decided that I am going to rob the bank across the street. It took me

18 minutes to do it. I walked in and up to this teller and I handed her my note. It said, 'Please get me my money. Go to the vault. Don't in any way raise the alarm or police because I am crazy and I am terminally ill and I only have a few months to live so I have nothing to lose if I start harming people.' I intimidate people with my looks ever since my accident. I look a little bit off centre, especially when I get high. Then I put my finger in my pocket, which was natural to do since I had no weapon. She went to the till and took out some money, which was about $2000 to $3000. I said, 'No, no. Go to the vault.' She looked at me and said, 'No, no. We can't do that, it's locked.' I says, 'When is it gonna open?' She says, 'It's time locked. It won't open until tomorrow morning.' I says, 'Maybe I'll just wait here.' Then she kinda figures she is dealing with a crazy — the way she reacted, she sort of looked flustered. 'Oh no.' Then she says she can take this key and get me money the tellers use when they get low and that there will be $10,000 at least. That would get me lots of cocaine and a plane ticket somewhere. She was three to four minutes getting my $10,000. I was looking at the clock every ten to 15 seconds. It seemed to go by so slow. That's why I was in there 18 minutes. On the note I put, 'If I hear a siren or see an officer at the door, I am going to start shooting.' I guess that's what instilled the fright in her. I didn't premeditate none of it, it just came out naturally. And this whole time my knees are just rocking and I was pretty frightened. No one knew I was robbing the bank. The tellers just worked as if nothing was happening. Then the lady comes back with a bag and hands it over and says there is more than $10,000 in there. I took the bag and walked out of the bank. I walk down the street and I see a cab and I start waving my arms and flagging him down. He pulls up and I hop in and we drive away. As soon as we lost sight of the bank I started to shake and perspire. I really wet my pants. I suddenly realized what I had done. I went to a friend's home and counted the money — $14,800. I left town the next day because I was so scared.

"I went down to Antigua and it was like T.V. — palm trees, sun, lots of blacks, pina coladas, and Rastas dancing in the street. I was there for three weeks. I always dreamed of going to the Caribbean and here I was with some black little prostitutes, smoking grass, drinking rum punch, playing tennis, and sitting beside the ocean with a ghetto blaster listening to rock and roll. I was arrested a few months later when the teller I robbed saw me in the restaurant and called the police.

"When I got out of prison I couldn't find work and ended up living with a buddy until he went off to university. I couldn't get no positive feedback from people. People viewed me as unemployed, little more than a bum. I was hassled a lot. I was labelled a faggot. I used to go to the pool room and get into arguments with guys who called me a faggot. I was still doing lots of drugs whenever I could. I would go into debt for drugs. I used to trick for drugs with gay men. Then I was on welfare and that was very demeaning to me. I grew up on welfare and I didn't like to admit that I was reduced to a welfare recipient. Then I met this man who had an apartment that was empty 'cause he lived with his wife and his children. He let me stay in the apartment for sex basically. I didn't have to pay rent there. I lived there for eight months and then one day this man's income tax rebate came and I opened it. I took it to the bank and cashed it. It was for $3000 and I blew it. The bank let this man know I had cashed his cheque and he came to the apartment and he was all hot and frustrated and he started slapping me. I had $900 left and my uncle said — now you know it's my uncle — he said, 'Give me the rest of the money or I am phoning the cops.' I was mad and told him to fuck off so he phoned the cops and I got charged.

"I knew after ten months of incarceration that the price for robbing a bank wouldn't be so bad. I knew what prison was. The first time I was scared of prison, but now I knew I could handle it. I knew it was sort of easy. You can adapt yourself to the environment. I don't have trouble doing time. In prison you are not judged by your looks. People don't say a lot about how you look, you just do your time and it's much easier to live in here. This is a much harder jail and a higher security level. The inmates here are more violent criminals, but I have learned how to avoid any contact. I have been through all the ribbing about being a faggot and I have been in three fights already. Sometimes I get so frustrated that I can't control myself and just snap. I got beat up pretty good last month.

"They call me a faggot, but I just tell them I am not. I have been bi-sexual in my time but I am not gay. I want a wife, children, and I love pussy. I am not a bona fide gay person. The only way I could support myself was to trick for queer men. I have become a Christian again since I came back to prison. In here Christianity is a way out for me because it helps me to avoid a lot of problems. I can go to the Bible and when I fall down I can put out my hand and the Lord will help me back up. When I get out of here, I want to take the Lord with me. I want to buy a house in the suburbs, have a two car garage, have children, and make my parents proud of me because I know I really hurt them doing shit like this.

"I robbed the second bank because I was going to pay back my uncle and leave the country. I wanted a big score — $100,000 — so I took a bus to the city. I was just in awe — it is such a big place and people are going so fast. I had to stay at a bath house, which was a gay hotel — very cheap. There was a chance I could make a few bucks so I did. Before I left I had made a fake bomb. I took some batteries and some wire and an insulator and put some hair gel into an empty prescription bottle. It was T.V. inspired. I had a leather shoulder bag with the bomb in it and I walked a dozen blocks and passed quite a few banks, but none sparked my interest. Then I walked into one and it looked like a good score. I didn't want to do the teller again so I walk into the manager's office. He was a big guy, about 6'4", and he says, 'Can I help you?' I unzipped the bag and dumped the fucking bomb on the floor and said, 'That's a bomb.' I said, 'I want $100,000 now! Go to the vault and get it.' He said, 'No, I can't do that,' and gave me the same routine that the vault is closed. I gave him 20 minutes before I would set the bomb off, telling him all I had to do was lift up my foot. I gave him the terminally ill story and told him not to jeopardize all these people. He goes out and I lose sight of him for five minutes and I'm sitting in his chair chain smoking because I am scared. I walk out in the foyer and I see this big guy in a plaid suit with his back to me leaning over the counter. I didn't figure at the time he was a plain-clothes cop and I started walking out behind him. I got three feet away and he turned around and put this gun chest level, 'Freeze!' First time I ever seen a gun — a dull black gun. A few drops came out of my pecker and I just froze. I seen that gun and it was so big and black and ominous, dull black — it looked like a cannon to me. I knew it was all over and I was going to prison. Then he handcuffed me and some people saw this and they didn't back away or stare in awe. Business kept on going. I felt shattered because nobody was giving me any attention. Everything carried on. It's times like that I don't like the big city. It's such a fast pace with people coming and going they don't even give you a second glance. I walk outside and looked up and all these guys are across the street on highrises with yellow helmets and high-power rifles and they were all aiming. There were 20 of them and there was a blue van on the street with bomb squad written on it. They put me in this unmarked car and this television crew comes over and starts pointing the camera at me. I was probably white when they had me on T.V. I thought, 'Here I am on T.V. and I probably look scared,' so I tried to give them a smile, 'If I am going down, I am going down smiling.' Maybe you watched it, it was on T.V.?

"I wouldn't say I was desperate when I robbed that bank because desperate implies it is the only choice I had. It was total abandonment of senses. I was supposed to go to court on the fraud charge and I would be going back to prison. Demeaning, going back to prison for $3000. I thought I had nothing to lose. I thought I would make a good score or try then I could get out of the country and never come back. I abandoned all hope of finding a job and becoming a success. I wanted to leave all the humiliation and degregation behind me.

"I got six on the bank robbery and one year for the fraud. When I first went to prison my mother wrote me letters and I spoke to my dad on the phone. They have washed their hands of me until I can come out and alter their opinion of me — become a success. My life of crime is over, I have grown from it. I've learned and it's provided turns for me to go. Now maybe that I've told my story, it can benefit somebody and it's good to know that I did that."

That Wanderless Feeling

Age 26 and unmarried, this convict was on parole at the time of the present offence. He has violated parole in the past and has a habit of not coming back from passes that allow him visits into the community. He has previous convictions for theft, bank robbery, and a lengthy juvenile record.

"This is my second time in a federal penitentiary. The sentence I'm doing now is seven years, which was added to the eight years I was already doing before I received that. This one is for bank robbery

— one count — and the previous one is for the same thing only four counts. I was going to school [in prison] on the first bit and was doing well. So I approached the parole board for a three-day pass and then a five-day pass and then day parole. I was lucky because I got the help of the staff, but I blew it. I didn't commit any felonies, but I took off out West and was re-arrested for being unlawfully at large.

"I did another year in a pen out there and applied for parole a year after. They said, 'What do you want?' and I said, 'I've had a lot of time to think and I had a problem. I couldn't stay put.' Now they realize that is what was bothering me so much and now I can deal with it. So I changed their decision around 180 degrees and I got out again, paroled to this halfway house. So that worked well for seven or eight months. I exaggerate, seven months. I got into this big heavy relationship and it fell apart for personal reasons. I couldn't handle it. I couldn't deal with it mentally. That was my security. I built myself around that and once that fell apart I kind of lost control. That was my first relationship. I was a real dingbat and when it all fell apart I wondered, 'What is it all for? Why bother anymore?' Plus I was having problems at the house, they wanted a urine sample. The night before I snuck out and had a few beers because I was depressed. I was allowed to drink, but I wasn't allowed out after 11:00 P.M. They discovered my absence and wanted a urine sample.

"I wasn't living with my girlfriend, but I spent more time there than at the halfway house. I spent my weekends there. It was like being married except I couldn't sleep there five nights out of the week, which was a little depressing for both of us and caused bad vibes and hostility with each other.

"I was doing well and I got some roots down for the first time in my life: a job, an old lady, a kid, responsibility, and diapers. It really numbed me, it turned me into a piece of mush. It was a big deal to me, you're out two days and you fall in love. That is a very strong hold that will keep me in check. I had a full-time job and about $500 in the bank, which wasn't a lot but it was my savings and I was secure at the house. Another couple of months and I would have been out.

"I left all that. I just picked up, left the money there, and left. I just couldn't take it anymore and took off just to get away from the parole system. I was violating parole, but I just didn't care anymore. They have three parole officers, they take eight hour shifts. One parole officer runs your life the way he likes it and when he goes home it is a whole different ball game. They play with your personal life too. A weekend pass? One says okay and the other says well maybe and you get stuck in the middle. Then you turn them against each other and they end up taking it out on you. I couldn't cope any more so I took off to the city.

"I felt a lot of heavy anxiety when my relationship ended. You look around and ask whose fault is it, 'Is it my fault? No, I'm doing everything I'm supposed to be doing.' After all, I started from scratch and it's all going down the tubes. So what did I do wrong? Nothing, it is just the system, it is too big and it's not perfect. You are dealing with human beings and not drones.

"It was not so much the house that was bothering me; it was a good setting, a good environment. It's essential that you watch fellows. The agreed limit is supposed to be about four months as you slowly move into society. But it turned into eight months for no other reason than personal bickering between me and the old lady. No assaults or anything. We never did that and that would never happen — but a lot of verbal abuse. I had a lot of problems at home and she had her problems and I can't be around and that is hard for her to deal with. And she is waiting and waiting just like I am. Then we had a big fight and she phoned the house saying, 'Well, I changed my mind. We are not going to be living together when he is out on full parole.' Then a week later, kiss, kiss, and make up. But that phone call changed my whole parole plan. It meant that I had to stay at the house for another four months and make a new one on paper.

"That threw me back. I'm there seven months and 20 guys have come and gone, 20 more have come and are going out and I'm still here. And I've been doing as good as any of them. I just got depressed. That is part of the problem. Most criminals are repeaters and they are hounded by some administrative authority all the time. Whether it be the police, parole officers, or Children's Aid, somebody's always got a grip on you. It kind of keeps them in a childhood state. They can't make a decision for themselves if they wanted to.

"This time I was on parole for about seven months and then it all came apart and I left on a bus for the city. Got a room and I had about $300 on me, just my paycheque. I still had my job and while I'm on the bus I'm pondering whether or not I should turn around. On and on I pondered it, but I decided not to, to hell with it. And at that time when

I made that decision I wasn't planning on robbing a bank. As far as I was concerned that was all over because the next time they grab me it was ten years. But I got there, a beer here and a lady there, and I was broke.

"In the meantime I called my partner back at the halfway house. He says, 'Where are ya?' I tell him and he says, 'Ya didn't?' I said, 'Yeah, I did.' He was just finishing his sentence and he says, 'I'm coming out there too.' I figured he was going to talk some sense into me, who knows, but he came and he stayed with me a few days and we made our rounds, visited a few old friends. The money ran out. I'm broke again. What the fuck am I going to do? I had to get some bread. If the question comes to your mind, 'Why was it a bank?', it is basically because they are insured and the tellers are trained what to do. And it's the bank's money and I don't have that much love for banks anyway. They are no better than your typical Italian loan shark. They have a licence and that is the only difference. They have made people's lives miserable. Look at *The Grapes of Wrath*. I got no use for them, they are just a rip-off station.

"I can't work because I'm on the run. So what are you going to do? Either go to prison or stay free. It was just something I had to do to survive. There must have been other ways, but at that particular time I felt I didn't have much option. I was angry too. We were walking down the street and I said, 'I got to get out of this rut. If I'm going to be on the road, I've got to get something established.'

"Facing heavy time will [snaps fingers] straighten some guys out. Some guys will be deterred, some guys it won't. It depends how much bravado is in them and how much they care about themselves. Once I made the move to go out there I got nothing to lose. If they grab me I'm going back to prison for three or four more years just to finish off my sentence. What difference does it make?

"When I was a kid I was fascinated with movies. My mother would drag me away from the T.V. to protect me so I was all the more interested. I watched guys rob banks and I picked up on it and I always wondered what it felt like, the feeling to actually do one, to get away with it. I'd always been into petty crime but I didn't have enough gumption to walk in and do a bank. It just sat there dormant.

"With me, being young and stupid, itchy feet, wanted to travel. Basically that is because I was locked up most of my juvenile years. So from the time I was 12 years old, I always had that wanderless feeling. Whenever I get freed I like to be free. When I got out the first time and went to a halfway house I stayed there about a month and then I split. I had two full-time jobs and I left all that. I just wanted to be left alone. I'd been locked away a couple of years, reformatories here and there and different places.

"If I hadn't taken off from the halfway house it would never have happened. It would have remained a fantasy that would never have become part of my life. I would have worked like everybody else, but I was in a position where I knew I was now going to have to survive. There is a warrant out for my arrest and it doesn't matter if I'm out there doing stick-ups.

"I had a good family life — very overprotected. My father and mother have been separated for 12 years now. He's my stepfather, legally adopted me, but my mother is my natural mother. Loving mother always around the house, church, doesn't drink, doesn't smoke, or associate with those who do. She thinks this is tragic. I guess I put her through a pretty emotional strain. She doesn't believe it is all my fault. She thinks it's a conspiracy by the government to have me put away. She's a little schizophrenic, my mom, from all the turmoil and beatings she has had from my father. She is not herself these days, but she is a good woman. My dad was a salesman, he did nothing to speak of. No guts, lazy. Couldn't hold down a job and too gutless to steal. Just likes to go around beating up women, a real jerk.

"My partner had about 15 days left when he took off to join me. He received three years. He wasn't in the bank and he wasn't armed, neither was I. The thing was I had robbed that bank before and here I am robbing it the second time four years later. But it was just that I was back in town so let's just see which was the easiest out of them dozen or whatever. I should have never have done it. It is hard to explain. I was out of crime. I was happy. I was just broke and, as I say, a little angry.

"We had this little route planned and down you go into the subway. You try to time it so that you're half way acrosss the city before the cops get there. As far as I'm concerned as soon as I leave that bank there is no catching me. I'm walking, I don't run. You just mingle with the crowd and into the subway. Your stomach is up here and your heart is just pounding and you've made this pick-up. It is just a wonderful feeling. Those subway doors clear and that train starts moving and it is such a wonderful feeling, it is better than an orgasm. But the train never left the station."

Author's Note: His partner's interview, "One Armed Bandit," describes the wait for the subway train.

Death Wish

Age 19, this young man served eight months in jail awaiting trial before being sentenced to ten months in prison for one count of robbery.

"My first partner I grew up with all my life. We went to school together and did some B & Es as juveniles. I knew him well, he was right on. He introduced me to banks because before that I was only working one day a week and selling drugs on the side and stealing clothes and selling them. He talked to me about doing a bank, how to do it, and I thought about it for a day and I figured, 'What the heck.' This guy had lost his partner who got arrested in the subway right after they did a bank.

"At that time my brother got blown away with a shotgun and after that I didn't care what happened to me. I didn't care if I got shot. He was murdered and the guy who was convicted is serving four years for manslaughter. I'm going to talk to him when I get out. My brother had his head blown off by a shotgun and they stuck him in the basement for a month to rot away. People were talking and word got back to my family three days before the cops found out that he was dead. My brother and I were pretty close. He was one year older than me. He was 18 at the time. I felt ...[pause]... I don't know ...[pause]... I felt like killing somebody. I had a lot inside me that I had to get out and this guy asked me if I wanted to rob a bank. I didn't care if I got shot, killed, or whatever so I said, 'Yes.' I didn't care if I died.

"The more money you have, the faster you spend it . The more you have, the more you want. It's such easy money that you get addicted to it and you start doing banks one after another. You don't even have a time gap, such as doing them a week apart. You just do them whenever you run out of money. One time we did three banks in one week!

"I don't like staying with my partner after we've done a bank. Why should the two of us get caught in the same place? Sometimes we'd meet at his place, sometimes at my place, sometimes he'd pick me up in a taxi, but generally I like to stay clear of my partner. He has his friends and I have mine. There's a few things I'd rather not talk about. I was having a lot of problems. That's one of the reasons why I couldn't stick around with my partner all the time — family problems plus I had other things to do. I had people to see. I had a lot on my mind. If you do a bank with someone it doesn't mean that you're going to be with him all the time. It doesn't really change your life that way, just because you did a bank together doesn't mean you have to do everything together and hang together. You still have your own life to lead. It's just that you need some money.

"I met my girlfriend for the first time in a shopping plaza after I had just done a bank. I had the bag of money and showed it to her, 'I just robbed a bank.' She loved it. She was excited by it. She was excited by the fact I was a bank robber. Her family wondered what I did because they knew I wasn't working. I'd be coming up to her house everyday in a taxi. I always had brand new clothes and I was spending money buying her stuff and taking her out to dinner every night. I was always on holiday. Montreal is a beautiful city and I'd go out to dinner every night, bars, strip joints, staying out late, and sleeping in. She loved the money that was being spent on her, but her parents said to her one day, 'What does your boyfriend do, rob banks for a living?' I nearly had a heart attack when I heard that. She loved it, but she was worried for me. She's still my girlfriend despite the fact I'm in jail and I haven't seen her in 14 months. She came down to visit me awhile ago."

Outlaws on the Run

Age 23, this offender escaped from a federal minimum security penitentiary with another inmate and set off across Canada on a bank robbery spree that lasted 49 days. In that time, they robbed a total of 12 banks in Toronto, Edmonton, Calgary, and Vancouver. He is serving a 12-year sentence.

"I was in a prison camp when I decided to escape. There were three of us. My partner and I were good friends in the joint and this third guy, he left us, he went on his way. He knew that if he stuck around us, he'd be facing big time. I wish I would have got that in my head. I heard later that he turned himself in. I only had three months left on my bit, I was only doing two years. I have some big regrets, that's for sure. I'm serving 12 years — I figure in five years I'll be out — that's a pretty heavy toll for the amount of money I've taken from society.

"After we escaped we needed money and we sure as hell weren't going to get a job because we were wanted all over Canada. The guy I took off with, he was into bank robbery, so he knew exactly how to do it. He started explaining banks to me. We could rob a bank and we'd have $2000 for one week. He made it sound pretty straight forward — ready cash and then you're off. It didn't take much courage to do it after I had seen how it was done. He'd go in, hand them a note, tell them to give him the money, don't fool around, and nobody's gonna get hurt, or else, you know? Then out the door.

"I would be there just to make sure no one would jump him or hurt him 'cause he wouldn't hurt anybody. I'd be out by the door watching him when he's in there. He could have did it on his own, but we escaped together and we were partners. After he'd stay outside and I'd go in. We're Federal Express while we're doing a bank.

"It's my first time I ever got involved in bank robberies. I don't think it's worth it. You face too much time for the short amount of money you're getting and the short time you're having a good time. It ain't worth it. I got 12 years for 12 bank robberies and for what? My share was $10,000. You spend a whole lot of years behind prison bars and you can never get back that time. You could make that kind of money in a few months if you had a half decent job.

"I thought about it all before I got caught. I knew I'm going to be facing all that time, but once I robbed one I didn't care anyway because I figured that they had my picture. So I just went on a spree, I guess. I knew I was heading for a fall sooner or later. I just figured I may as well drink myself foolish 'till I get caught. I might as well have a good time while I'm at it. That's how I thought about it. My partner was the same. We were both strung out on heroin. He didn't care anymore and I didn't care no more. I was sort of glad we got caught when we did 'cause we could of ended up with a hundred counts of robbery if we had kept going.

"Since I was 11 years old I've been in prison and pens and every place else. I've got about ten years in jail and I'm only 23. I always seemed to find friends that were criminals, not straight Johns. I guess I'm very easy to convince. I'm not saying someone can force me into doing stuff. I got my own brain, right? But I am easy to convince. I'd rather take a short-cut say where I make $1000 in one day then work two weeks to get it. Now I think differently. You don't gain anything from jail. It's not worth it. I have about ten years in jail and that's the last. Maybe this is what I needed to straighten me out.

"We never used any disguise. We just went in the way we were dressed and took the money and ran. We had an attitude that we didn't care — because of the booze, the drugs, and the fact that we were on the run. Once you got on the run you get low on food, you got no place to stay, you're going to have to do something for money. We chose to rob banks.

"I pleaded guilty. We didn't try to plea bargain. We just pupped out. It took six months to sort it out and they weighed in all the charges from Toronto, Edmonton, Calgary, and Vancouver.

"I don't know how I got caught. All I know is that the police came to my hotel room. I guess the people in the hotel suspected me. I had only been in the hotel two hours.

"I'd just pass a note and the teller would give me the money. No gun. There be nothing happening in the bank. I had a couple of them say no and one passed out on me. Like the lady just.... boom, went down. Fainted! [laughs] I don't mean to laugh, but it was funny. That day when it happened, I was all fucked up on drugs. And if they said no, I'd just leave and go for another one. I never really premeditated my robberies. We'd just get in a cab and go downtown and pick the first bank that we see, didn't matter how crowded it was. Get the cash and run. The note said, 'This is a robbery. Give me the money or else.' Or else I'm not going to wait around and see what happens [laughs]. I watched my partner on the first one and when I seen how quick he came out with $1700 dollars I found it easy.

"You got to look at it from their point of view when they're being robbed. This could be a guy with a gun standing there. Tellers don't want to die. You give the bank robber the money. Then at least you get to go home and see your family. Like I'll scare them. I'll make it sound like I was serious. But if somebody said to me when I was robbing a bank, 'No, I'm not giving you the money,' I'm not going to take their life for $2000. No way, I don't expect somebody to take my life for $2000. I have morals in that way. I wouldn't kill somebody for the money.

"I'd raise my voice a little to get the money. When you give her the note she'll look at you, she'll read it, and she'll try to stall and she'll press her button. You know what she's doing, she's stalling. So you tell her, 'Don't stall. You give me the money and you ain't gonna to get hurt. If you don't give me the money, I'm coming over the counter.' When you tell her that, that's usually when she gives you the money. She doesn't know who you are, you could be the worst convict in the world.

"You get some really crazy trips when you do that, like this lady fainting. When I gave her the note, she fainted with the note in her hand. There was another two tellers in the bank so I went to the next one and I said, 'You're going to give me the money. Don't fuck around.' She looked at me and laughed like it was a fucking joke. I said, 'This ain't no joke lady! I'm here to fucking get the money and I ain't leaving.' She just laughed at me and walked away so I just walked out the door.

"When I got outside and told my partner that I didn't get any money he walked across the street and into another bank. He ran into a male teller who wouldn't give him the money and had to really make some verbal threats to get the money. He didn't get the money until he told the guy he was going to cut his throat and it made him think twice. So he gave him the money.

"When he was standing in line the cops came to the bank I had just robbed. By the time we got out of there they had to go across the street to another one. Like I said, we didn't premeditate anything, we just did it. We just got out of the cab and if there was a bank around the corner it was being robbed. We robbed one right behind a police station in Edmonton. We didn't know. After we'd just whistle down a cab. No problem when you're in a big city. You just walk out and flag one down, real quick. We had cab drivers driving us away from the bank and we seen the cops coming with their sirens on and they'd say to us, 'What's going on?' We'd say, 'There's an accident down the street.' Little did he know that he had two bank robbers in his car.

"We had a good time over those 49 days on the run. We figured we'd move around the country so not to get caught so quick. We were living in hotels. We'd pick up hookers, do some boozing. We'd spend $500 bucks in a night sitting in a bar. When you've got that kind of money you don't care what you buy. You just buy it, don't matter how much it costs. We'd spend maybe a thousand a week on drugs, sometimes two thousand. We'd buy a pound of weed at a time. The money would last a few days. We did two banks a week.

"When a guy does get out of prison, he has that extra tension inside by not being out in society for so long. When you get out there, things are so open and you see so much freedom, it makes you bitter. I don't know if it does that for everybody, I'm just speaking for myself. It makes you bitter for having been locked up and for the things you missed in the past years. Then all of a sudden you see what you've missed. People got cars and families and all those things. I realize now that for people to get that they had to work for it. So I got to realize that I got to work if I want something like that."

The following interview is with this man's partner and took place in in a regional psychiatric centre. This inmate is serving 14 years on 12 counts of bank robbery. He is 29 years old and has spent most of his adult life in prison and psychiatric institutions.

"My partner and I left the institution and had no money. We decided to rob banks because banks are very easy to rob. I mean they're very easy. I have done banks before. I was doing four years for two bank robberies. I learned from guys in the joint that you could get money by just giving the teller a note. You don't need a gun to get the money.

"To me it's a lot smarter to walk into a bank and say, 'Give me the money,' and get a couple of grand then to walk into a Mac's Milk store with a gun and get fifty bucks. I'm on the run and I got no money and I know that I can get money at the bank and if I don't have any money I'm going to get pinched. I have to rob a bank or I have to rob somebody. So I then have to choose what I'm going to rob and it's easier to rob a bank then it is to go punch somebody in the head and take their money. I'm not going to turn myself in so I've got no choice, really.

"We were partying. We kept moving because I figured the pigs are going to move in on us sooner or later. You can only stay in a city so long. You rob a bank and there's heat so rob a few banks in another city. It's awfully hard to catch somebody who's moving all the time. I knew I was going to get pinched, I didn't give a fuck. I wasn't wearing any disguises. I knew I was going to get pinched. I just wanted to make it last as long as I could.

"The money becomes addictive and the robberies themselves become addictive 'cause it's like sex. You get really built up before you go into that bank because you know all the things that could happen. The tension, the psychology of psyching someone out to give you the money, it's a trip. It's a power trip and it's a bluff and that makes it all the more exciting because it makes it all the more dangerous. My partner didn't find it a high. No, he was pretty hyper.

"The one guy we escaped with wouldn't rob banks. I went in and did one and told them to watch me. Both of them waited outside and I went into the bank and did it and came out and they were shocked that it was that easy. But this other guy didn't want any part of it and split. They stood outside and I told them all the different things to watch for: tellers' reactions, cameras, putting your hands on the counter, how to bluff the teller. My partner made a few failed attempts at first. He just wasn't prepared for it. He had to see it done a couple of times before he was ready for it. So I took him to another bank. After that he was fine. He was on his own then, didn't have to tell him nothing.

"Jimmy was more easily led. Then again, he didn't care either. He was out for a good time too. He didn't care. He spent an awful lot of time in jail, you know. He's been in jail almost all his life — since he was 13 years old. These seven weeks we were on the run is as long as he's been out. I'm serious.

"I don't know why we didn't wear a disguise. I just didn't give a fuck. He did sometimes. He said to me lots of times, 'I wish we'd get wigs or glasses or somthing.' I'd say, 'Yeah, yeah,' and then we'd just go out and drink and party and then by the time we wanted to rob another bank we'd just rob it. We wouldn't think about it. That quite definitely was a mistake. Going back to my head space then, if I had to rob a bank, I would still rob it regardless of who was there or how many pigs were around. If I had to rob it I'd rob it.

"We knew we were living on borrowed time so we were spending like crazy. I knew that if I got a chunk I could have taken the whole bank and got $60,000, but I didn't want to take a chance that I might blow somebody's head off and get life.

"We went by bus, train, and plane. Once in Vancouver, we flew back to Edmonton to do another bank.

"It's a mystery to me how we got caught. We were spending a lot of money and we were in a bad area of town. Somebody may have phoned in a tip. We were in a bar drinking and my partner went to buy some smokes and the police pinched him in the hotel lobby. When he didn't come back I was thinking, 'Jesus, he must have gone to China for those smokes.' About an hour later I was in bed making it with this stripper when the police came to the door. I could hear them at the door listening. Dogs. They had been to the room and taken the suitcases, and if I hadn't been so drunk and horny I would have noticed.

"By the time I decide to rob a bank I'm usually pretty fucked up. I'm either pretty down or I'm on the run or I'm pretty pissed off and I just don't give a fuck no more. I just don't give a fuck! The first two that I got pinched for I was totally drunk, totally blacked out. I had no more thought of robbing a bank than shit. I woke up in the cop shop beat up and I figured I must have got in a fight. I didn't know I had robbed two banks. They caught me walking down the street like I was going for a Sunday stroll.

"I think one of the reasons, one of the big reasons, why I robbed all these banks on a spree was because I was so bitter over getting four years for the two banks. I was bitter over getting those four years 'cause I was unbelievably drunk. I was so drunk that in one bank I put my own name on the slip. My own name! I wrote a note and asked for $2100 and put my name on it. That's how drunk I was and that was brought up in court. And they still slapped me with four years. I was polluted. I should have got a year for that. They're going to fuck themselves by handing out this kind of time for crimes where there isn't violence because people are going to say 'Fuck it!' and they're gonna use guns.

"This 14-year sentence really jolted me. It's really turned my whole way of thinking around and it's really made me think, 'I'll be 40 by the time this bit is over.' It's made me take a steep look at my life. I've decided that this is it. Like here and now, I have to decide whether I'm going to spend the rest of my life doing time, because that's what's going to happen if I don't change and get a grip on my problems. I've made my decision, I'm going to buy a new life. I just can't handle this time any more. I just can't, really. It took this bit to make me see that. Before this it's been four years, two years, two years, two-and-a-half years, four years. They're all small bits. You sit back and you do your time and you get out. That's it. It doesn't really do nothing to you. But this one, when the judge hit me with this one, I really sat back because the magnitude of the time is pretty big.

"With me I think I was a victim of circumstances because as a child I was bucking the odds. I came from a fucked-up home and a very large number of foster homes. I was a really messed up kid. I was a bad kid and I was tossed from foster home to foster home. It was very hard for me to settle down because I wanted my family — my family and not all these fucking other families. I wanted my family and I just couldn't accept the fact that I didn't have my family. My parents were both drunks, alcoholics. I was in and out of Children's Aid. Finally the Children's Aid said, 'That's it,' and made us wards. That was it, I was five. I was five years old and my brother was three and we were sent to a foster home.

"When I was 16, well by then I was really messed up. I just didn't give a fuck about a lot of things, bucking the system and full of hate. Bitter and really fucked up. I got into drugs when I was 14 and by the time I was 16 I was shooting speed. There was nothing there for me, it was just the kind of people I knew and the kind of life I had. Just my whole life.

"Now that I'm older this last spree was it. When I look at what I did this last time, it's so stupid, so pathetic. But at the time it was just like so many other things in my life, I just didn't care no more. It's so self-defeating because when you do get pinched you say, 'Holy fuck, what am I doing? How could I be so stupid?'"

CHAPTER FIVE

FEEDING THE NEED —

THE ADDICTS

- COMPULSIVE GAMBLER
- I'M GETTING MARRIED IN THE MORNING
- SPEED FREAKS
- DRUG DEBTS
- HEROIN ADDICT

MANY STUDIES DEMONSTRATE A STRONG RELATIONSHIP BETWEEN FREQUENT expensive drug use and involvement in income-generating crime (Collins et al., 1985; Anglin and Speckart, 1986; 1988; Johnson et al., 1985; Faupel and Klockars, 1987; Chaiken and Chaiken, 1982; 1990). Although the relationship between property crime and illicit drug use is complex, criminologists have developed two theoretical models to explain causal connections at the individual level: (1) the drug use causes crime or compulsion/demand model; and (2) the lifestyle or criminalization model.

The Drug Addiction Causes Crime Hypothesis

The police and the media frequently cite illicit drug usage as a major contributor to property crime suggesting that addicts steal or rob in order to support their drug habit. This theoretical model views income-generating crime as a function of economic need that derives from addictive or compulsive use of expensive drugs. The "drug addiction causes crime" hypothesis (Gandossy et al., 1980) suggests that drug usage comes first, the user becomes addicted, and this creates a dependency and a physiological need. As tolerance to narcotics develops, addicts require increasing doses to achieve the acute effects of the drug and turn to crime to supplement their income. Heavy drug users require money to support their habit and when their cash requirements outstrip their legitimate incomes, they are driven to engage in crime to make up the difference. A simple causal model for this relationship is outlined by Collins et al. (1985:745):

Daily drug use ⟶ addiction/compulsion ⟶
expensive drug habit ⟶ income-generating crime.

Although there is research evidence that supports this theoretical model, critics argue that the economic demand explanation is exaggerated and incomplete. For instance, a number of studies show that involvement in income-generating crime often precedes rather than follows regular use of expensive drugs and that many users of illegal substances who steal and rob did these things before they became involved with drugs. In addition, research often indicates that the majority of addicts have arrest histories before the onset of addiction; many predatory criminals are not drug users; and drug abuse often occurs without predatory criminality (Stanton, 1969; Chambers et al., 1970; Plair and Jackson, 1970; Voss and Stephens, 1973; Greenberg and Adler, 1974; McGlothlin, et al., 1978; Gandossy et al., 1980; Collins et al., 1985; Anglin and Speckart, 1988; Blackwell and Erikson, 1988; Chaiken and Chaiken, 1990). Thus the temporal order of initial involvement in regular expensive drug use and income-generating crime, as well as other evidence, argue against a simple compulsion/demand model of expensive drug use forcing addicts into committing income-generating crime to support their habit.

The Lifestyle or Criminalization Model

The lifestyle model or "criminalization" hypothesis explains the high correlation between illicit drug usage and income-generating crime by suggesting that drug use and crime are common elements of a deviant lifestyle. This interpretation suggests that drug abuse and participation in crime coexist in some social groups and that the onset of drug use and predatory crime can both occur as products of particular social milieus. Thus, for instance, invitations to try drugs in the first place are issued by first-time user's friends (Blackwell and Erickson, 1988). The criminalization hypothesis suggests that involvement in deviant and criminal activities and with criminal associates lead to illicit drug usage. A number of researchers suggest that criminal learning environments and the lack of conventional social controls act as intervening variables contributing to both crime and illicit drug usage. These variables include physical abuse, criminal siblings, the lack of parental attention, and unrewarding school experiences. The more deviant the environment, the more likely an adolescent is to perform poorly in school, to use multiple forms of illicit drugs, and to participate in predatory crime (Williams and Kornblum 1985; Simcha-Fagan and Schwartz 1986; Chaiken and Chaiken, 1990)

The lifestyle perspective suggests that the causal direction in the drug/crime association may be reversed and that economic crime may be viewed as providing the capacity to engage in expensive drug use. In addition, this model also suggests a reciprocal relationship in which expensive drug use and income crime might be seen as reinforcing each other (Collins et al., 1985:747).

Crime ⟷ drug use.   Drug use ⟷ crime.

In this latter instance, substance abuse perputuates predatory crime rather that creates it.

The lifestyle model suggests that predatory criminals may be involved in drug use as a part of their non-traditional lifestyle, which often includes irregular employment and absence of marital ties (Chaiken and Chaiken, 1982). The offender's social network is one which allows him or her to pursue a hedonistic lifestyle of drugs, sex, partying, gambling, and property crime activities. Drug abuse and predatory criminality are behaviour patterns that coexist in certain social groups. Katz suggests that for many robbers drug usage emerges long after they have been involved in crime and addiction is a product rather than a cause of a deviant lifestyle. Heavy drug usage will thus have an amplifying effect on crime with users engaging in increasing crime to support their lifestyle. Drug abuse then becomes a cause of relatively imprudent criminal acts that lead to imprisonment. From this perspective, drug addiction ends rather than promotes a criminal career (Katz: 1991:293).

Peterson and Braiker (1980: 119) suggest that individuals who are heavily involved in criminal careers continue this lifestyle for reasons more general than the economic requirements of an expensive drug habit. They characterize such career criminals as hedonistically oriented with a tendency to view crime as a relatively low risk and an economically and psychically rewarding lifestyle. Goldman (1976) goes even further to argue that illegal income leads to increased drug use as a discretionary expenditure. Goldman's perspective predicts that expenditures on drugs will increase proportionately with illegal income.

Overall, the conclusion of the vast body of research on this topic indicates that no single sequential or causal relationship emerges associating drug use per se with participation in predatory crime. In some cases, the use of illicit drugs may be a primary cause for initial participation in predatory crime; however, for the vast majority of offenders, use of illicit substances appears to be neither a necessary nor a sufficient cause of predatory criminal behaviour. Even narcotic addiction often does not appear to be causally related to property crime. Rather, the onset of heroin addiction is often a key point in accelerating an existing criminal career (Chaiken and Chaiken, 1990:218-219).

The drug addiction and lifestyle models are not mutually exclusive, and neither is viewed as sufficient by itself to explain the causal relationship between drug use and criminal behaviour. The two perspectives emphasize different causal mechanisms each of which appear relevant in understanding the relationship between illicit drug usage and crimes such as robbery. In fact, many studies offer support for both hypotheses. Consistent with the reported research, the present study indicates that in most cases drug consumption precedes bank robbery but excessive drug usage and addiction frequently follow the crime. Most men who rob banks admit to using illicit drugs, in some cases to excess, but few mention the need to support a drug habit as part of their initial motivation for robbing a bank. (The same pattern is observable for gambling addictions). After taking care of their initial needs with the money obtained from their first holdup — debts, food, rent, etc. — most bandits begin to party and this entails spending money on alcohol, drugs, taxis, hotel rooms, gambling, women, and friends. Drug usage (in some cases gambling) is an expensive part of that lifestyle and money dissipates quickly. The offender returns to crime sooner and more frequently because of a drug habit and this often results in his or her quick demise. It appears, however, that the decision to rob again and again is motivated more by the wish to continue this lifestyle than because of drug addiction per se.

Only 13 men in this sample (13/80, 16.25 percent) describe themselves as drug addicts (heroin, speed, cocaine) or admit to using drugs excessively (marijuana) prior to robbing banks. Each of them reports that a major part of their motivation to rob a bank was to maintain their drug habit. In addition to these 13 drug addicts or excessive users, another two-thirds of the sample (54/80, 67.5 percent) admit to using drugs occasionally or moderately prior to becoming involved in bank robbery. None of these men specifically mentions drug usage as part of their initial motivation to bank robbery. Almost half report that their drug usage increased significantly after they robbed banks and they now had discretionary funds to spend. Their increased drug intake typically occurs in the context of drinking and partying and their continued involvement in crime is intended to support this lifestyle (Desroches, 1995:98).

Gambling is the main expenditure in six cases (6/80, 7.5 percent) with each of these men frequenting the race track. All six report gambling before robbing banks, but only one directly attributes his motive to a gambling addiction. In all cases, gambling activity increases dramatically with the money obtained from their holdups and all six report large losses as most bet heavily on longshots with correspondingly poor odds. A police search of one offender's home, for example, uncovered a dozen $100 losing stubs on a 60 to 1 longshot.

A 30-year-old *Compulsive Gambler* recently released from prison began a six-week spree of bank robberies that ended in 14 holdups before being apprehended. He netted close to $40,000 and gambled it away at the track. The police suspected that the person responsible for these crimes had a "monkey on his back" (an addiction) and posted plain-clothes police officers at the entrance to the racetrack. With the assistance of a photograph of the offender taken by a bank camera, they searched the track grounds and almost found their man. The offender spotted the police, however, and slipped away before being seen.

In *I'm Getting Married in the Morning* the 23-year-old offender from a middle-class family talked his brother into driving a getaway car while he and an accomplice robbed a neighbourhood bank. They panicked when a police cruiser drove by and were caught because they took off running. This was his 12th robbery in an 11-month period and the offender spent most of his money at the racetrack. At the sentencing hearing the culprit's lawyer is quoted in a local newspaper as saying: "My client was once a promising professional football player until he became a compulsive gambler and his debts led him into a despicable pattern of behaviour. It was very much a sickness that infected all of his activities." The judge sentenced the offender to eight years. *Speed Freak, Drug Debts*, and *Heroin Addict* are three examples of criminals whose drug usage was a significant variable leading them into bank robbery. Although the drugs involved differed — speed, cocaine, and heroin — it is clear in all three cases that addiction came prior to the crime and was a major motive behind their bank robbery offences.

Compulsive Gambler

> This offender was convicted of ten bank robberies in a six-week period. He was confined to the protective custody section of the prison due to recent problems with other inmates over the non-payment of a gambling debt.

"I'm not that familiar with bank robbery, but I'm familiar with bank robbers insofar as I spent quite a bit of time in prison. I committed 14 robberies and pleaded to ten and got ten years. My lawyer told me the cops wanted 15 to 20 years! So I came across this clipping in the newspaper where this other bank robber had done about the same as me and received ten years. I wanted the same judge and my lawyer said it would take a few months but he'd get him. We went to court in

January — postponement. Went back in February — postponement. Went back in March and I was finally in front of this judge and got my ten years. It took from September to March, but I got my judge. My lawyer said, 'Don't worry, the judge is clued in. He's going to give you ten years.' The prosecutor even brought up the fact that there was no weapon, no intent to commit violence, and that I even apologized to one teller for upsetting her day. I have an extensive record and given what the climate was for bank robbery I thought that ten wasn't bad.

"I've never used a gun in my life and yet the parole board has classified me as a violent offender. I couldn't commit violence if I wanted to. It's just the fact that it's bank robbery and there's a threat. I just passed a note which said, 'I am armed. Give me the money.' It was a conscious undertaking on my part to write it that way. It's an implicit threat. I have to admit there's a threat and that I'm exploiting the bank's policy. They want the guy out of the bank. I don't see it as a violent crime.

"I spent some time in prison out West and was friends with two bank robbers. We did four years in the same pen; smoked dope together and partied together all the time. He was my source of information on bank robbery. I guess I just tucked it away in my mind because I didn't leave prison with the intent to go out and rob a bank. If you want quick cash you have a high chance of getting away if you pull one, two, three, or four. One bank robbery is as independent as the next — like the roll of the dice. One roll is independent of the next. I just ran it too long, pushed my luck too far. Six weeks of madness.

"I had just been released from prison where I'd served four years four months straight. I wasn't ready for the street. You think you are when you're sitting in there and your day comes up. When you get out of prison you're a lost person. Socially you're an outcast whether you accept that or not. You're also living below poverty. There are certain material things that you need just to feel part of society. Also, to compete as a person whether it's for women or anything else, you're shit out of luck when you walk out of prison. I mean you're down there and you're not integrated into a group of persons like everybody else. I didn't get out of prison intending to get into crime.

"I had no plans. I came out East and submitted an application for a job and one to go to school and they were denied. I came here with $300 in my pocket hoping to find a job, but I got distracted and went right into gambling. I don't know what motivates me to gamble. Maybe it's because I'm not socially adjusted into a community. I've been estranged from my family for 15 years. It would be different if upon my release I went into a circle where my family and friends were. Someone to fall back on — some people I know. But going to a big city where I didn't know anybody — what do I have to lose? I don't have anything anyways. I don't have a job; a person takes pride in the fact that they're working. That's their notion of living, to have a job, to be doing things for yourself. I was unloading produce and I said, 'To hell with that.' I wasn't physically in the best shape and I sure wasn't in the best state of mind after sitting in there four years. I had no goals and without that I was lost.

"I chose to rob a bank because it is just a matter of going in there and acting. I've been in a couple of plays in prison and I don't see much difference either psychologically or physiologically. You get the same butterflies and you have to psyche yourself up. Robbing this bank was just like performing. I knew that the tellers are instructed to give you the money so the variables are known. Based on that assumption, it's just a 15- or 20-second act and away you go.

"A lot of people find trouble admitting 'I'm a compulsive gambler,' and that it has been the the ruin or downfall in their life for several years. I've finally come to grips with that; if you're a gambler and you need money and you're not violent, then you go for the money in a non-violent way. My first bank robbery was just that I needed some money and I thought I'd give it a try. I was successful and did a lot of gambling and rang up quite a few bank robberies. But I always felt that being a compulsive gambler somehow doesn't make you a criminal where you want to go out and hurt people. I've been successful at getting money without using violence.

"I was gambling the horses and the money went pretty quick. When money comes that quick, and you're in the head space where you don't value the money, you spend it quick. Especially when you're a gambler — a $100 bet or $1000 bet is just a bet, the value of money is lost. Materially I came away with nothing from these bank robberies. It was all spent at the track. I can't even say I had a good time. I'm not too happy with my lifestyle and what it's done to me over the past ten years. Gamblers don't live a normal lifestyle. I had a girlfriend during this spree. She wasn't aware I was robbing banks, but she was into the horses. She managed to keep a full-time job, but gambling has wrecked her life. She's 28 and back living with her parents because all her charge bills were out of control.

"I started gambling at a fairly young age. I was working for a bookie when I was just a kid and I was making such good money at that age that it impressed me. It did something to my values when it came to money and work. If you take away the gambling, I would say I'm not a criminal. I'm a very normal person in every respect but the gambling and the need for money. Before I did these banks I did two sentences for possession of stolen property. During that period I was more professional in my approach to crime than I was with the bank robberies. I specialized in stealing coin collections. When I was younger I used to collect silver dollars and silver coins. Then the price of silver went up and every dollar I had saved turned into two dollars, just like that. I also traded coins with different people and I was introduced to gambling very young. I worked for a bookie at age 16 and began gambling myself. When my gambling made me broke I thought of this guy who had bought all these coins off me and I went and hit his home. I picked up over $10,000, and since I knew coins I knew their value and how to fence them. For ten years I travelled throughout the country tracking down coin collectors at trade shows, by advertising and answering adds, and talking to dealers. It doesn't take long to find people with healthy collections.

"I was eventually caught when I fenced some camera equipment that linked me to a coin collection. The police spoke to me but they didn't have any evidence so I was just charged with possesion of stolen property. But the camera linked me to the coin collection and that collection linked me to the other coin collections that were missing. One cop said to me, 'You cleaned up pretty good in the coin collections.' They knew it was me, but they had no case. At that time there weren't very many people focusing on coin collections and I was able to penetrate these homes easily. But the police caught on to my method of operation and I was busted again. I got five years for burglarizing a coin dealer.

"This last time out I started doing my research again — looking up coin collectors. Then I said, 'Shit, I might as well rob a bank. Why burglarize a house?' Bank robbery was an instant dollar. Doing coin collections takes a lot of work. I bought a *Coin News* and went through it to see what was happening in the city. It gives you the areas where coin shops are concentrated and you can start attempting to locate the homes of collectors. Then I said, 'The heck with this, too much work.' So I went into banks. After the first one, it's nothing. The first two or three, I had a couple of bottles of beer and a shot of rye to calm my nerves. Then it's not much different than the action of going to the store and buying a jug of milk. Physically it's the same thing although you're doing something that society says is a no-no.

"I walked a lot of blocks before doing the first one. I was hesitant and it took me four hours to go in and do it. I went in there five minutes before closing time and almost got locked in. It was a comedy because I robbed a bank in Chinatown and the tellers were Chinese and were talking back and forth in Chinese and looking at me. 'We don't know what you want.' Finally one of them goes to her drawer and gives me the money. I vowed I would never enter another Chinese bank after that hassle.

"I apologized to a teller who was very pleasant to me. It was a very sunny day and she said, 'Good morning, it's a beautiful day. How are you?' I replied, 'Good morning. Yes, it's a beautiful day. I regret I have to upset your day.' And I handed her the note. She smiled and handed me the money. I apologized and left. Tellers are very efficient. I would hand them the note, give them time to digest what it states, and from that point on try to take control. Once they read the note they hesitate and I'll follow with a verbal demand like, 'Start with the large bills.' In a sense, it puts them in a frame of mind where they're not thinking beyond what's happening in that situation. Some were pleasant, 'Oh, that's all I got, I'm sorry,' and others would stack the money up and, out of spite, knock it across the teller's wicket.

"I think if I remove the gambling from my life I have a good chance of making it without having to commit crimes, because I've done it. I was married and employed for two years, but then I started gambling again. Shot the marriage all to hell. I come from a very good family. My father is a very successful artist and my whole family is very well educated. I'm the black sheep and I've been estranged for years.

"When I'm released I want work. I have a B.A. degree in History and Psychology. I earned it out West in prison through a university program for inmates. I enjoy taking courses. It makes you feel like you've accomplished something. I'm taking a correspondence course in French right now. I figure I'll do six years straight before I get released and I'm going to look for a job. I think that my gambling is out the window. I've had enough of it. If I ever get the need for horses, I'll buy a horse and raise it. But as far as gambling, no way. It cost me too much. I'm 35 and I'll probably be 40 when I get out. To heck with this.

"The reason I'm in here [protective custody] is because of a gambling debt from when I was on the street out West. I owed a bookmaker some money and the debt is carried over into prison. It's quite involved because some people tried to collect and didn't get the better end of their attempt to collect. There's a lot of wheeling and dealing. If I was out West it wouldn't matter because I have enough people that I wouldn't have to worry. Here I don't know anyone. It's something I have to keep to myself. That's why I won't name anyone involved. I'm locked in my cell 23 hours a day and the administration is pressuring me because I won't give them the names of the guys who have threatened me. At least I've been able to get some academic books from the teacher in here."

Author's Note: *This offender was re-arrested four years after this interview and charged with three counts of bank robbery. He returned to the same city, robbed downtown banks by passing a note to a single teller, and was photographed in the act. He pleaded guilty to the charges and received 12 years to be served consecutive to the years remaining on his previous sentence.*

I'm Getting Married in the Morning

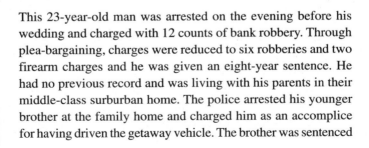

This 23-year-old man was arrested on the evening before his wedding and charged with 12 counts of bank robbery. Through plea-bargaining, charges were reduced to six robberies and two firearm charges and he was given an eight-year sentence. He had no previous record and was living with his parents in their middle-class surburban home. The police arrested his younger brother at the family home and charged him as an accomplice for having driven the getaway vehicle. The brother was sentenced to two years imprisonment on one count of robbery. The arrest interrupted the rehearsal party for the bride and groom. The wedding was cancelled, but the couple were later married in prison.

"The way I got into this in the first place, my fiance got me to go to the bank for her. I went in there and it was very quiet, a pause in the afternoon. I thought to myself, 'This would be pretty easy to rob.' A few months later I needed money. Sure enough I robbed it. I needed money for rent and I was gambling. I'd say the racetrack was my big downfall. I was going to the track and betting with the bookies. I owed a bit of money but maybe just a few hundred dollars. I could have got money elsewhere, like borrow from friends, but I was too proud. I wanted to do it myself. I was tired of having other people support me.

"I guess you could say that I was always a gambler. Even when I was younger I remember jumping off the ferries and swimming to shore on a dare, for five bucks. I started going to the track with my uncle when I was young. I have no criminal record. Gambling was probably the number one reason I robbed banks — maybe laziness a bit, but gambling leads to laziness. I'm not really a lazy person. In here I'm always doing weights and running and looking after myself. But gambling affects your values. I worked for a few years and I liked working, but the gambling did me in. If you lose $300 at the racetrack the night before it's pretty hard to get up in the morning to make $60.

"I had nothing to bargain with when I went to court because I had signed statements against myself. If I would have shut my mouth the police would have only been able to charge me with the one and I would have got three years. You're not too happy knowing you're going to jail, but it's sort of a relief that it's all over.

"It was my fault my brother got involved. He came home for my wedding and I asked him to come along. I know he's young and hopefully it didn't hurt him too much in life. I don't think it did. He was only in jail for three months. Three months isn't really that much time out of your life. He never had a record and never did anything wrong. They gave him two years but he's out on day parole. He's younger than me. He's influenced by me. He would never had done it if it wouldn't have been for me. Hopefully that actually helped him. I know it's going to make me a better person.

"At the time, I counted on my mom too much and I leaned a lot on my fiance. She looked after everything and made sure everything was paid. I wasn't nearly as responsible as I should have been. My family were very shocked, but they support me. My fiance was really upset. We were getting married the next day, but what can you do? If it's happened, it's happened, right? She stuck by me and she still is. We're married now. My life with crime is finished."

Author's Note: The police report that a search of this man's room uncovered dozens of race stubs as evidence that he had spent tens of thousands of dollars at the track. Most of his bets consisted of $100 wagers on longshots. Members of this crew pled guilty to 12 bank robberies over an 11-month period during which they stole over $200,000. None of the money was recovered. This offender was re-arrested three years after this interview and convicted of several armed robberies. He was on parole at the time.

Speed Freak

Age 21, this man robbed several banks with partners, had a falling out, and began a career as a solo gunman committing an estimated 20 robberies over a one-year period. He was convicted on one count of armed robbery and is serving nine years.

"It's an ego trip. Well getting away with it is right on. I got away with it. It all depends where you're living, who you are living with, what's happening, where your life went. If you're a very heavily drug oriented person, there is always somebody around to party any time of the day. My friends were into the same thing, not as regularly though.

"You walk in — you got a shotgun — all these people buzzing their minds out. You just come back with five or six thousand dollars and everybody says, 'This guy's right out of it. Don't mess around with him,' they say.

"Drugs and partying. Speed, speed, speed, and a little coke. I'm from a small town and came to the city and just got caught up in the fast pace. Fast! Whoosh! Like everyone else is standing still. I was living with a hooker. I don't want to be involved with that type of person anymore, it's a different lifestyle. You can't live like that. It's insanity — with a hooker, doing armed robberies everyday, drugs. Fuck, fuck it's wild, too hairy for me. It was a wild time. Yeah, but it was definitely pretty good.

"I was accustomed to drinking, mind you. Drinking alcohol excessively but not doing drugs and drinking. I was used to dope and shit like that. But speed! Jesus, you're awake for 35 days solid. You start to get a little weird after 35 days — not just a little weird, you can't talk to anybody. It's like they're going, 'Um, um, um. Don't know what you're talking about.' Pretty weird stuff. I moved to the city and my brother was doing a lot of heavy stuff I was not accustomed to. Then I moved in with this girl. It was not the trip of a pimp or anything like that. I was supporting myself doing robberies and selling dope. I had money, she had money, we used whoever's money was around. She was into the trip of, 'No, no, no, I'll work and you live off me.' Fuck, I just can't. I don't like the profession but who am I to preach. I'll do my own stuff.

"I never could make money selling dope. You get a big score, then buy the dope and you get home and, 'Let's party.' An ounce of speed would cost $1700 and last two days. You're doing it, my old lady's doing it, so's my brother and other people. They get me high and I get them high. Two days later, it's gone.

"I'd see people going to work everyday and it's like, 'What are these people doing?' I can go out there and in 30 seconds make two or three thousand dollars. If I was smart, I would have done two or three a month and sit tight but when you're not doing anything, you gotta do something right? Get high, party.

"The police, those people are right out of it. Their methods of interrogating people are fucking wild. Oh yes! This is the Hold-Up Squad. These guys are right out of it. First of all, right off the bat, a guy handcuffs me to this chair. He didn't even ask me any questions, just put me in the chair with handcuffs and he says, 'Stay there in the chair.' And he makes me wait for about 15 minutes. Then this giant stomps out of this office and walks right over to me. He doesn't say anything but he grabs the chair and rolls the chair towards the stairs and I'm like [scraping his feet on the floor], 'Are you out of your fucking mind?' And I'm trying to hold on with my feet. Fuck! I'm thinking I've heard that the cops are a little rough but people exaggerate. Well on second thought maybe they are right about this place here. Then it's 'Boop, boop, boop,' down these stairs to the bottom. I don't know what this guy is expecting me to do. Like, 'Yeah.' 'Like that didn't hurt! Holy fuck, don't do that anymore!' I'm looking at him like, 'You are fucking right out of it guy!' Like 'Bang, bang, bang,' fucking head smashing on the floor and the side of the rail. 'Like are you right out of it?' This guy is about 6'10" and he has shoulders about this wide. Oh fuck! I know that they are going to beat me, like start punching me in the head. Seriously, but wow.

"After that, he takes the handcuffs off and then takes me upstairs, and then they have me in a room for about six hours with these guys. Man, they have a whole pile of armed robberies that they knew I did, but they had no evidence — nothing. Nothing to convict me on. I knew I couldn't be pinched on these. Like if I don't get caught then and there you're never going to get me. These guys describe this robbery, 'A friend of yours was doing these robberies and you were keeping six [keeping a lookout].' Yeah, so the copper tells me about this bank robbery right down to the last detail, and nobody's been pinched, and he fucking tells me who did the robbery, who was holding the gun, and who shot the fucking gun! 'Oh Jesus, they know about these armed robberies!' But they can't prove it. I got pinched cold turkey on one. 'Like do you want me to confess to twenty more and get twenty years?' So I'm like, 'I don't know what you're talking about.'

"The copper tells me, 'Your buddy walked in with the gun, in the bank was another guy with him. There were two broads in a taxi and another guy standing outside. That guy was you.' The gun I was caught with was discharged in that robbery, ha, ha. So they ask, 'Where did you get this gun?' Ha, 'Like I got it off an Indian in a bar.' Ha. 'Like, what do you mean, where did you get the gun?' They asked a lot of questions about the gun. The police take that seriously. Some old bag in the bank was saying, 'You guys don't have real guns.' Like you got to be out of your mind lady. Some of those people, I don't believe their logic. Yeah? Well, 'Bang!' Now you know. 'Do you want the next one in the snatch to see if it's real?' The old lady almost had a heart attack. That's nonsense to go in without a loaded gun.

"Fuck, these cops have their methods, you know. Have you ever been surrounded by six people, and here's one guy not giving you a punch in the head but like, slap, bang. And you don't know if he's going to buzz out pretty soon and start — pat, pat, pat — on the side of the head. They only hear what they want to hear. Six hours of that and your nerves are shot, and you're not handcuffed, but there are six people there and I almost lost control, 'You and your little cuffs to the side of my head. Why don't you try one of these to the side of the head?' Oh, he was getting on my nerves. People don't think they do that stuff, people think they just ask you questions and that's that.

"Sometimes I wish I would have stayed totally ignorant of all this stuff. As far as drugs, it would have been a lot easier if I was ignorant of all that stuff. I know what I have done wrong. I cannot say now I would go out and be super straight, but the curves would be a lot more even. Let's keep this a little straighter from now on because you know better. Like if I go back home, like what do you do? There's all sorts of things you can do in the city. In my home town, I was going out of my mind. Like, let's go out to the bar and pick up some women. I don't care, plain women. Well we go to the bar and my friend says, 'You wanted plain women, well....' And that is all there was, very, very plain women.

"All of those people are very, very naive when it comes to city life. Like a drag queen, what is a drag queen? Look at this nice looking broad, and you take a second look and it's, 'Oh my God!' Drag Queen walking around and this guy's saying, 'Nice looking broad.' They just do not know any better. Heavy duty place, the city.

"You know, speed freaks stay at home quite a bit, listen to the stereo, comb your hair for five hours. Sex is heavy machine on that stuff. My girl and I would go to this bar — punk rock to the bone. All these people are weird and there are some people who would consider me strange when I'm high on drugs. But some of these people aren't even high on drugs and what makes them do stuff like that? Dye their hair pink! I seen this one couple. The guy had a dog collar on, a big collar, and this broad that was with him had a collar on her and they were chained together. The guy had his head shaved on this side and the broad had her hair shaved on that side, and they had green, purple, and orange psychedelic hair. Punked out with combat boots, ripped up jeans, ripped up t-shirt, leather jacket, and all kinds of buttons. And this one guy, he's got a bobby pin in his cheek and he's got a

chain going from his pin to his earring. They do slam dancing, crashing, smashing you with an elbow in the side of the head. People were not ready for me on speed, but I was not ready for them period. Wild! You wonder when you look at these people. Like wow! And these people aren't on drugs so you wonder what it is that makes them do these things."

Drug Debts

Age 32, this man was on parole from a previous robbery sentence when he was arrested for another bank holdup. He received five years for four robberies in the first instance and six years for one holdup the second time around. A former drug dealer, he appears unrepentant about his crimes and is critical of family reactions to his lifestyle. A teller who worked in the bank he robbed spotted him donning a mask as he was about to enter the branch. She recognized him as a former high school classmate and later identified him from a police photo line-up.

"I robbed my first bank because of a drug debt. A bank has instant cash so why not go into a bank and get the fuckin cash and get out? Why should I wait till nightime and break into a house and steal a T.V. and stereo? Then I have to find a fence and sell it. Banks are huge institutions and they've got multi-million dollars in assets. They make billions of dollars on outrageous fuckin amounts of interest. They're insured. It's not as though I'm stealing your money or this little old ninety-year-old lady's life savings. I'm stealing money from a fucking bank and it wouldn't matter if I got fifty grand. That's nothing to them.

"The first one was the hardest. My adrenaline was really going that day, but I went in and I did it and I was in there and out and gone and I'm telling you, it was fucking easy, I mean nothing, no sweat. I don't consider myself a bank robber. I sold drugs to an upper-middle-class level, I had a certain clientele and they came and they bought. I wasn't selling nickel and dime bags, I'm selling ounces. These people want it, okay? I'm not going out to sell. They're coming to me and there was a lot of money involved. This was cocaine, nothing else. I was introduced to drugs a long time ago and I've had a coke habit for 12 years.

"So I was selling drugs and I was robbing banks. I had a good income, but I was rather extravagant I guess. I had a nice house. I just rented it, but it had a swimming pool and it was in the country and secluded. I was living with this broad who worked nights at a bar. I had a $2000 a week cocaine habit and I had a partying lifestyle. I'd fly down to Las Vegas sometimes and do some gambling, Atlantic City a few times. Nobody suspected I was robbing banks. It blew my girlfriend away when I got caught.

"She's not around anymore, oh no. She visited me in detention and I said to her, 'Hey look, pack up and move and go and have some fun because it will be awhile.' She's not going to remain a nun while I'm doing five years in jail. People change, you know. Plus it's a headache in here. I don't need Dear John letters and shit like that. So just write it off, pack your bags and leave. Been nice but it's over.

"My folks were shocked, ah fucking shocked. It hurt them really bad. They're still a hundred percent behind me. I've got a great family, but this second time was wild. That really blew their minds that I did it twice. Like I just got out of prison for robbing banks and I was only out six weeks when I was arrested for doing another. That just totally devastated my mom. They're in their late 60s and this was really hard on them. Like they're over it now and they're behind me a hundred percent. My one sister is kinda iffy, but she can go to hell if that's the way she wants to be. She wrote me a letter in here a month ago saying at the present time I can't support you. So I just sent her back a letter with two words, fuck off! It doesn't bother me, I don't care. As long as my mother and father are behind me that's good enough for the parole board. For my sister, if she wants to be a bitch I don't care.

"I went back to robbing banks even though I was on parole because I still owed a drug debt. It was $4500 and these people demanded payment within 48 hours or my parents' house might burn down, that kind of thing. The threats against me, I don't give a shit. But they were threatening my family. So it was sort of a desperation panic thing. I figured I'll do it and give these fucking assholes their money and get them off my back. I had no intentions of going back to dealing drugs or robbing banks. I was just getting re-established. This was a debt I owed them before I went to prison. Just because I got busted and went to jail doesn't cancel a debt. I still owe some of the money but not all of it. It's being taken care of."

Heroin Addict

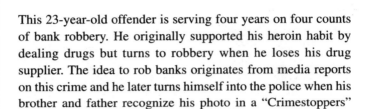

This 23-year-old offender is serving four years on four counts of bank robbery. He originally supported his heroin habit by dealing drugs but turns to robbery when he loses his drug supplier. The idea to rob banks originates from media reports on this crime and he later turns himself into the police when his brother and father recognize his photo in a "Crimestoppers" newspaper column.

"I came to the city and got a job in a bar where my brother worked part-time. I was a waiter and my brother was a doorman. I got involved in heroin and became addicted after about five months — shooting it in the veins. It's not really a high any more after that — it's like a medicine after awhile. It's an expensive drug at $75 a cap and I was up to 3 to 4 caps or $250 a day, that's a pretty heavy habit. Originally a close friend was dealing and I was helping him out and taking my end in drugs. I'd have to say it was curiosity that made me try it 'cause I wasn't destined to use heroin. The people I had been around were using it and you look at them and you say, 'These guys are really enjoying themselves.' Even when you know it's addictive you say to yourself, 'I'm not going to get wired. He's wired but I'm not going to get hooked to it.' A lot of people start out thinking they'll just do it on the weekends, nothing serious. It progresses until you have to use more each time.

"I got sick of working at night. All your friends hang out there and and you want to be the one partying and not the one serving so I just said, 'Forget it.'

"I had a few close calls with the heroin. I was behind the hotel one night talking to a girl who was going to buy some and a police officer in uniform came walking up the alley and told us to hold it right there. I had 12 to 14 caps on me. He was a very big cop and that was his beat. Everybody knew him in the hotel — he'd stop and talk to everybody. He asked me what I had in my hand and I said they were bennies, 'I've been working quite a bit lately and I need them.' He says, 'Ah, you don't need those,' and he put them on the ground and stepped on them. I had a bunch more in my pocket so I could have been caught selling one of the heaviest drugs in the world. With heroin you're dealing in something which the public hates. I've never been involved in a heroin charge but I can just imagine. Anyway, my supplier got out of the business so now I'm not making the end that I was used to making. I have to produce my own money. After a couple of days with the sickness your mind is not thinking of eating or nothing. You're mind is just set on getting that fix. The sickness is in the bones and telling you to get some money. It's an obsession along with an addiction.

"Everyday I looked in the papers and read about bank robberies. It was all with notes. So I just talked myself into it — if these other persons can walk in and do it, it can't be that hard. I did the first one on my birthday, but it didn't even dawn on me that it was my birthday. The drug takes prevalence over everything else. You're cued into one thing and that's it. I didn't single out any banks, I wasn't in the frame of mind to stop and use tactics. It was more that I'd walk until my courage was at a certain height and go into the bank and pass a note. In fact on one I didn't even stop to look that they had a central teller. Surprisingly I went through with it. She said, 'We don't have any money here.' I said, 'Go get some.' I guess she saw the seriousness or determination on my face so she went back, reached over and grabbed a bundle of 20s and brought it back. It was busy at that time so nobody took any notice of it.

"I got away with all of them. I turned myself in. I'm very happy that I turned myself in after four because I don't know where I would have stopped because it was so easy. It wasn't supposed to be that easy. There was no weapon shown in any of them. Even when I stop and think of some of the notes they weren't that threatening. The violence never really surfaces and even the threat itself is a bluff. I'm sure those tellers don't know it at the time.

"In the second bank the teller takes the note and says, 'I'm going to get someone to sign it.' I said, 'No, no, no, you ain't going to get nobody to sign this. This doesn't have to be authorized.' And she ho hummed and then she said, 'Oh you want it,' and she threw it at me. The money was all over the place. I made a big scoop and took off. She was an older teller, about 55 or so. The last thing I wanted was a scene.

"After the fourth one my oldest brother showed me the papers. They had my picture from a side view and there was a $500 reward. My father who lives 500 miles away was watching the evening news and he picked it up too. Both my brothers talked to me and I agreed to turn myself in. I couldn't run forever so I might as well get it over with.

"I think the total of the four banks was $9300. I guess I became a glutton with the drug. I did four banks in six days. I wouldn't say the judge was lenient, but he was understanding of my frame of mind at the time. After the first one I thought, 'All I'm doing is I'm going into the bank and giving her a note. I'm not being violent in any way, I'm just getting the money and leaving without hurting anybody.' I passified myself by saying, 'This isn't serious. I'm not doing anything that drastic. I'm not hurting anybody. I'm taking money without violence.' I convinced myself I wasn't doing anything that serious. It's almost as if the addiction is booting you in the ass saying, 'Go ahead, do it. Go in there and do it. Feed me.' You say to yourself, 'I'm sick, I'm sick. I'm addicted. Nothing is gonna go wrong. Go in there and do everything quietly, be polite and there will be no problem.' You've got to get it because what are you going to do? Walk around all day and sweat it out? It's impossible. The sickness almost justifies it, I can't go through a day like this. I'm sick, I'm sweating. I can't sleep at night and I'm freezing and I'm hot. If you want your medication, it's going to cost you money. I haven't got the money. Well, what are you going to do? I don't want to stay sick like this. I'm tired of this. It's the lowest I've ever felt. You've got to get yourself some money. What are you going to do? Well, you read the papers everyday about all the banks being done, it seems quite easy.

"It's kind of a quick way out because a person can go down the street and do it in two minutes, take a cab, and be back home in 20 minutes like nothing ever happened. He's got $3000 in his pocket and he's not going to be sick for a long time. That in itself makes you happy. You get a certain amount of enjoyment having the money in your pocket and knowing you're not going to be sick tomorrow. That's an addict's security — knowing he has money in his pocket.

"I would say the addiction is 85 to 90 percent of the motive. An addict goes through the day with one thing on his mind and one thing only. People who are hip to junkies will recognize one all the way. He's walking down the street in the middle of winter and he's got a full sweat on. He doesn't look good, he's white. I was down to a drug treatment centre last week and you could spot the junkies a mile away. They go there for their methadone treatment, which is an alternative source for heroin, and it's like they're getting in line for the gift of life. I think I've been able to grab enough from prison therapy classes to fit the lessons into my lifestyle. I was out on a five-day pass and I had no need for it, no craving for it. I didn't want any part of it. I don't think it will be any problem."

CHAPTER SIX

Taking the Short-Cut —

From Respectability to Crime

- The Honest Crime
- Mountie
- The Middle Class Suburban Gang
- Stockbroker

The move from a conforming lifestyle to involvement in serious criminal activity is generally a gradual transition. Albert Cohen (1955; 1965) argues that there is continuity between conformity and deviant behaviour and David Matza (1964; Sykes and Matza, 1957) similarly suggest that young offenders drift between delinquency and conformity — postponing for a time, anyway, their commitment to either. Both theorists contend that the move into serious criminal activity is likely to be gradual and this belief is supported by research. Of the 80 bank robbers in this study, only five had no previous criminal record and two others had only minor records for possession of marijuana. Other research similarly indicates that most men arrested for serious offences such as robbery have lengthy criminal records and do not leap from a law-abiding lifestyle into serious criminal activity. The transition is gradual and is influenced by factors such as delinquent and criminal associates.

From the perspective of social control theory (Hirschi, 1969), most law-abiding people realize that criminal involvement brings with it great risks: position, respect, finances, family, and freedom. What is it then that leads otherwise respectable people to take such drastic steps and risk so much? The seven men with little or no previous criminal involvement all report financial problems prior to their first robbery. Clearly, money is the main motive although no one describes himself as desperate. They emphasize the fact that they needed the money and either could have done without it or perhaps borrowed from friends or family. Once they commit the first robbery and meet their financial need, greed becomes the motive, fear turns to confidence, and like the other men in this study, they return for more until they are caught.

Another factor that appears to contribute to their abrupt move into crime is the loss or threatened loss of their job and/or a significant relationship. Some feel that they have little to lose by committing a robbery or, alternatively, they face losing whatever they have unless they take decisive action soon.

The Honest Crime describes a previously law-abiding 35-year-old man who has been broke for several months, is about to be evicted from his apartment, and is influenced by newspaper reports of successful bank robberies. He has had no previous trouble with the law before embarking on his short criminal career and robbing three banks. His financial need develops because of prolonged unemployment and he chooses bank robbery because he views it as an honest crime.

Mountie chronicles an ex-R.C.M.P. officer's fall from grace. His story depicts a man struggling with financial problems due in part to an extravagant lifestyle. He fails to confide in his wife because of pride, subjectively defines his financial problems as non-shareable, and secretely seeks a solution on his own through robbery. Like the embezzlers in Donald Cressey's study (1971), knowledge obtained from legitimate employment creates the illegitimate opportunity needed to commit his crimes. He uses the knowledge gained from his past criminal investigative experience as a detective in the planning and execution of three bank robberies. Of particular interest in this interview are the reactions of former police colleagues and his family to his arrest and conviction. His description of inmate hostility towards the "cop" placed among them is frightening.

The Middle Class Surburban Gang and *Stockbroker* are interviews with young men from middle-class professional families who take up crime as a short-cut to the lifestyle and riches they have been socialized to expect. *The Middle Class Surburban Gang* included four men in their early 20s who committed a dozen armed robberies in and around the suburb in which they lived. The subject of this interview reports that he was depressed from the break-up of a relationship — suggesting that the traditional bonds of social control had been temporarily weakened. During the time that he is feeling down-and-out he meets a friend who admits to having committed a bank robbery. His depressed mood, a desire for money, and the friend's description of how easy it to do the crime, along with his invitation to participate, is sufficient to tempt him into robbery. Also evident are several techniques of neutralization used to justify his actions. He further admits that he initially hoped that the money could help him win back a girlfriend who had recently ended their relationship. Although his family has supported him throughout this ordeal, several friends have not.

In the case of the young *Stockbroker*, he too has experienced a diminishing of social control and stakes in conformity with the loss of his job. Now that he has financial problems, his knowledge of bank and police procedures is similarly translated into an illegitimate opportunity for profit. Both he and the former subject have had ample work and educational opportunities. Neither have taken advantage of these opportunities, however, in part because they are lazy and unmotivated. Crime becomes a short-cut to the financial goals they have been socialized to desire, achieve, and expect. As might be expected when a former law-abiding respectable person is arrested for a serious and dramatic crime such as bank robbery, family and friends are shocked and angry. While some continue to offer support and assistance, others end the relationship because of their disgust and embarassment over the crime.

The Honest Crime

Age 35, this man had no previous trouble with the law and decided to rob a bank after reading about the increase in bank robberies in his city. The media also led to his downfall when the police published a photo of him robbing a teller.

"I received six years for three bank robberies committed over a three-month period. I think the sentence was a little harsh since I didn't use a weapon and this is my first offence. I knew I was going to get hit heavy because there was a high-profile case in the courts at the same time where this guy had shot a young high school girl in the neck. That was a convenience store robbery and she was paralyzed for life. The judge even said when he sentenced me, 'This city is cursed with persons who rob banks and convenience stores.' I don't think it's fair that I'm being lumped with convenience store robbers. In convenience stores you're robbing from the little guy who's just trying to make ends meet.

"I'm a tool and die maker and there was a very bad recession in my trade and I was laid off from my job. No one was hiring and I was over-qualified for other jobs. I made a lot of money at my trade so this was a big setback for me. I was unemployed for a year, my unemployment payments had run out, and I hadn't eaten for two days when I robbed that first bank. I read it in the newspapers — people getting away with a bank robbery. You can read three, four, five times a day and nothing about anyone getting caught. And I thought, 'Jesus Christ, that must be an easy way to get money. Banks are just giving it away.' It wasn't any specific article but the accumulation of things that finally jelled. I needed money and I had to get it. Everyday I read the paper looking for a job and everyday there were all these bank robberies. And I thought, 'I could go and do that.' Dismiss it because it wasn't my type of thing? You get to a point where you're down and out, need the money, and the foundation has been laid in your mind.

"I was walking up and down the street saying, 'I'm going to do it. No, I'm not. Yes, I am.' It probably took me two hours to get up the nerve before I actually went in. When I went out that day I was trying not to rob a bank if you know what I mean. I was scared shitless standing in line, and when I got up there I was shaking more than the teller. She was perfectly calm, just like it was another transaction. Meanwhile, when I got the money, I could hardly even hold it. She asked me if I had a bag and I said no. I didn't speak, I shook my head. By the time I paid off the rent and bought a few groceries, I needed money for the next month's rent. I was very disappointed at the money I got — she gave me $700. The second teller was very indecisive about giving me the money. She did think about it and changed her mind a few times during that 20 seconds. I didn't speak, I just stood there sweating bullets. I brought a bag that time. I was more experienced in the trade [laughs].

"My note said, 'This is a holdup. Give me all the bills in your drawer and no one will get hurt. Do not raise the alarm until after I have left the bank. I am desperate and do not want to hurt anyone.' I didn't say that I had a gun, but I'm implying that. It's up to the person whether they would think that. The wording was deliberate. I was very surprised I got the money out of them. I half expected the teller had start laughing and say, 'You have got to be kidding.'

"The photo is from the first robbery but wasn't published until after I had done the second bank. When I saw that I thought, 'What the hell, they've got me.' The third time it was down to, 'I need money.' It was no longer whether I could do it because I knew that I could. There was a little less fear because experience tells you what's going to happen. I was broke again. So my picture is in the paper — nothing I can do about that. If they know who I am, they know who I am. A friend showed me the photo when it first came out. We met in a bar on our way to play soccer. He had the newspaper, threw it down and said, 'Who does that look like?' I was stuck for words. It wasn't that clear and he picked up on that. I said, 'It does look a little bit like me doesn't it?' He didn't say anything. Maybe it was his way of giving me a warning.

"An ex-girlfriend called the police and told them where I could be found. I don't know why she informed. Women are strange animals. We lived together for three-and-a-half years and had been broken up six months. I was the one who wanted to end it, but I was trying to be nice. She came to visit me in jail and she didn't know that I knew she had called the cops. I looked at her and said, 'Why?' She was very embarassed and she admitted it. She's sorry she did it. I still keep in touch with her. It's my fault that I got caught, not hers. It was me that went and did the bank robberies. If I didn't do the robberies, I wouldn't have been caught. In prison you talk to a lot of inmates who blame others. Someone has to be blamed and it can't be them.

"Looking back on it there were other alternatives, but at the same time nothing was going right in my life and the future didn't look good at all. The way I look at it, robbing a bank, in my mind, no one is losing off of it. No one is losing out. I'm taking the money, but that bank isn't losing a cent. No one is going to get hurt and the insurance company is going to reimburse them for the money I've taken. It's an honest crime."

Author's Note: This man was arrested four years later while on parole when he robbed one of the same banks wearing no disguise. He was again photographed by the bank's surveillance camera.

Mountie

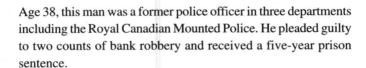

Age 38, this man was a former police officer in three departments including the Royal Canadian Mounted Police. He pleaded guilty to two counts of bank robbery and received a five-year prison sentence.

"I want to let the next phase of my life begin. Get this behind me. There's still the hurt and the pain and the unreality. There's a great deal of fallout for a family man. I have four kids and I tell you [voice cracking] it's just been hell. It's like, oh my God, how did this ever happen? I had to tell my kids that I was going to jail. Sitting in the living room with them and telling them and crying.

"My sentence is five years and I did some time out East before coming here. I was moved because of an almost riotous situation over me.

"I was a police officer for ten years. I was a Mountie, but most of my time was spent in the [names the city] police where I was a uniformed officer for a couple of years then a youth officer for a couple of years and then a detective for a couple of years. I became too big for my britches. I looked at this smaller police force and said to myself, 'I want more.' So I made the move to the Mounties.

"That was a crucial mistake leaving the city police. I was a detective, I was up for promotion, and I would have been an inspector if I had stayed. Anyways, I went to the Mounties and that was a disaster. I was placed in a small community in Alberta and all you do is chase ten or eleven-year-olds for breaking windows. It was very boring. I had done murder investigations, arson investigations, child abuse cases, and worked sex crimes for a whole year. I was impatient. I was about 29 or 30 at the time. Going back a bit, I spent a year in university before joining the city police. I was about 20 at the time and I remember putting on my uniform and thinking, 'This is great. I love it. I love it.' I always kept my uniform neat and tidy. I always washed the police car and made sure it was clean. I would work overtime for nothing. That's how I got promoted. I loved my job and there was great camaraderie. The way I made it into the detective branch influenced my personality. The sargeant came up to me one day and said, 'The chief is getting some political heat and he wants one of you guys to do an investigation.' There were about 30 break and enters in a fairly prestigious area. I went upstairs where the detective division is and you could see all the detectives looking at me and saying, 'Who's this young guy?' You could feel it, 'What in the hell is the chief sending him up here for?' The chief was using me to put pressure on these guys. So I get the file and the list of 24 suspects. The file is in tatters — there's no structure to the investigation. I can say that now, I couldn't say that then. I look at the first name and jumped in the police car, went up to his house, talked to his mother and said, 'I'd like to talk to your young fellow out in the police car.' I gave him the police warning and told him, 'There's a lot of things going on in this city and they gotta stop now.' He said, 'Yeah, you're right. I was involved in all of these and here are all the people who were involved with me.' The case was closed within a half hour. I'm not kidding. I drove back to the police station with this kid in the car, I took him upstairs to my sargeant and said, 'I solved the case I think.' The chief comes out and shakes my hand, 'Young man, I really appreciate the things you've done for us. Let me tell you, there's a place in this police force for you.' That reinforced my personality development — this egotistic, invincible, 'I don't need nobody, I can do it myself' type of attitude. I just kept on rolling. I went into the detective division and worked hard. I would come in in the morning and grab the keys and out the door I go. As a result, I solved a lot of crimes. I had a real good partner. Then they teamed me up with this guy who was too slow for me. He couldn't even walk fast. He was keeping me down. He wanted to go have coffee and I wanted to go solve crimes. As a result of accomplishing so much I wanted to be a member of the best police force in Canada. My ego needed more satisfaction so I transferred to the R.C.M.P.

"The Mounties are the best police force in the world. They were professional, gung-ho. When I was accepted the Mountie who processed my application said, 'Who are you? Are you God or something? I have 17 contacts here and no one said anything bad about you. I even talked to this criminal and he spoke well of you.' That fed my ego: 'I am good.' My wife's father was a 25-year Mountie so she knew the lifestyle. Her and I were high school sweethearts. She was school queen and I played football and was one of the guys.

"When I was going in the Mounties, I started thinking, 'I shouldn't go.' I'm taking the grandchildren away from her parents and she's close to her parents. I remember when I was doing my training in Regina, we drove out to this little prairie town and it was all dirt roads. We get out of the car and I look at this town and it's like the 19th century. It was a horse town. It was a culture shock for a city policeman to go to this small town. I remember looking and thinking, 'Holy cow, this is what the Mounties do! This is boring.' When I was stationed in this small town in Alberta I remember my wife and I having to stay in the local hotel until our house was ready. It was the only hotel in town and it was a dump and I started thinking, 'Oh my God, have I made a mistake. Look where I'm at.' I remember walking through town and looking at the horses in the middle of town. I remember wearing the uniform and the farmers being so polite. They all respect the R.C.M.P. and that was great. There was a lot of respect there, but it didn't fulfil my drive or my needs. It was a place for a retired Mountie. I stayed in the Mounties for a year then left and went back home. Then I joined another police force out West. But my wife got very lonely and I just couldn't put up with the red-necks. Even in the neighbourhood where we lived it wasn't a Canadian feeling — very provincial in focus. My wife wanted to go back home. I enjoyed the force but missed our friends too. I dearly loved the police force. I loved every minute. I remember so many interesting criminals. I remember screaming around the downtown going to bank robberies and the adrenaline going, the heart pumping, getting the shotgun ready, the simplistic cop and robber conflict. You can see that there's a lot of boy in the man.

"We went back home. I bounced around from job to job and still had this feeling in me that I could do anything. I can make it happen. I thought I was invincible too. I always had this drive. Still got it even though I've taken an awful beating. I said to myself, 'Where can I get a job? When you leave police work, you have no place to go. Probation interested me but I didn't have the education. So I went back to university and got my degree and was hired in probation.

"The people I worked for were excellent — the work I wasn't sure about. I spent a year as a probation officer and I was supposed to be promoted to a higher position, but that didn't happen. I did a caseload for a year and I started getting itchy feet. My supervisor told me there was a position coming up as deputy inspector of institutions doing investigations. This would fulfil my drive. I wanted out of probation because it was stifling me. So I studied all the manuals and I was ready when I went in for the interview. The boss told me, 'I want you.' I was expecting the job and when I didn't get it I was really hurt. But I kept it inside. I didn't know how to deal with failure. I felt drained after that. That crumbled me. I kept my feelings buried. When I went back to my office they could tell I was disappointed, but they didn't know how devastated I really was. Then I knew, 'I gotta get out of this job. I'm dying in here.'

"I started looking at businesses. What do I know? I know security. I opened a business installing burglar alarms and continued my job in probation. My wife and I were socializing with people who were financially well off. We decided to buy this house that we couldn't afford. That was the straw that broke the camel's back. A lot of this comes down to bad financial management on my part. We bought the house but that was just the beginning of the expenses because we had to furnish it, get curtains, finish the recreation room for the kids. There was no end to it once you get going. Part of my ego was that I could always provide — I could always make it happen.

"My wife and I were running — whoosh, whoosh, whoosh — ships passing in the night. I remember at Christmas I was working so hard I couldn't partake in celebrations because of the business. I had an alarm installer who was alcoholic and he gave me so much pain. He was a nice guy and very qualified, but he drank. During the night I'd get a call about an alarm going off and he's not available. I've got to go. My mind was never settled, I was always thinking about business. I still had my government job. I was getting desperate for money. Then the crunch came. I'm sitting in my office looking at the figures one night. How in the hell did it ever come to this? Where am I going to get quick money? Rob a bank! The idea just came to me.

"It was no fantasy to me; it was wrong and I knew it was wrong. I was scared to death, but I had this thing in me — the world is not going to stop me. That's how I felt. I was always in good shape, used to box a little, was a policeman, could put up his hand and stop traffic. Never a failure before. Always felt confident in anything I did, any social situation I went into. I would walk up to anyone, I wasn't intimidated. The police training gave me that. I really felt I would escape apprehension; what I feared was failure. So when that came to my mind to rob a bank, it just took off. Once I made the decision I said to myself, 'I'm going to do it. I gotta do it.' I started planning it out. Looking at different banks at the same time thinking, 'This is nuts. Yeah, it's nuts. But what choice do you have? You can't go down!' It was like two people talking inside me. In reality, I had a choice. I was quite conscious and had plenty of time to consider.

"I remember the first bank robbery. Maybe some people get a thrill from it, it was no goddam thrill for me. It was very frightening. I knew I was scaring people. But I remember putting the mask over my face. It was just, 'Ahwhoom, ahwhoom, ahwhoom.' Everything was just going inside me. It was crazy. My emotions were telling me, 'I can't do this. I can't do this.' The key that made me go in the front door was the thought, 'I gotta pay those bills.' The collection company was demanding that I pay my bills. I was in the bank 30 seconds. In and out, over the counter. Boom, ba ba ba boom. People moving fast and I was out of the bank and gone. I remember pointing the gun and saying, 'Everyone down. I'm not going to hurt anybody.' Over the counter I go and I say to the girls, 'Give me all the money. I'm not going to hurt anyone. Hurry up. Give me all the money and I'm not going to hurt anyone.' And pheeeuuw, I was gone. I remember getting a lot of money. I remember getting rid of everything. I said, 'That's it. That's it for me.' I got rid of all the stuff: plastic gun that I used, the balaclava and sneakers for footprints. After I robbed the bank, two hours later I was back at work.

"I started paying bills and then I started getting extravagant: bought some nice clothes, bought a movie camera for my family, bought some frills. Greed was certainly a factor, but I paid a lot of bills too. I felt horrible about it. I think it's immoral to scare people like that. It's just a terrible thing to do no matter what your situation. At the same time, I wanted to survive. Survival came over those feelings. It's like my brother said, 'We weren't brought up that way.'

"The night I was arrested I was dressed up to take my wife out for Valentine's Day dinner. We had dinner reservations and the babysitter was coming over when 12 policemen arrive at my house. I could see some of the policemen I knew. One policeman I didn't know walked up to me, his eyes were just bulging. He was shaking and he said, 'We got a search warrant for your home.' Later, all these policemen I knew said to me, 'What the hell happened to you?' At first, shock, and then it turned to anger, 'You bastard.' I dealt with some emotionally terrifying things.

"I never discussed our financial problems with my wife. It was because of pride. I was a very proud person. I was not capable of sitting down and admitting my failure. I had to keep the show on the road, I couldn't be viewed as a failure. I had to solve my problems on my own.

"Some police officers felt compassion but most were angry. One officer said to me when I was shaving getting ready to go to court, 'Why don't you cut yourself from ear to ear.' Most of them were very very good 'cause I showed true remorse.

"I used to think I was tough, but I folded. I broke. I became a very broken human being. Broken mainly over my kids and family. I considered suicide. I remember being in the police cells. I remember looking at those bars saying, 'Should I do it? Should I hang myself?'

"I was caught because I did something very stupid. I took some of the stolen money, which was American dollars and English pounds, and took it over to my bank. That's how lost I was. Just like a young kid who steals a coat and walks around the store with the price tag on. That's what I did. I put it in my business account. They would never have caught me otherwise. This was money from the second bank I robbed.

"After the police cells I was transferred to the district correctional centre where I had many friends. I worked with these guys as a probation officer. They were in shock, every one of them. The superintendent was a friend of mine — all the guards too. I sat on a board every week with them and here I come in as an inmate. They can't even look at me. And I'm going up to isolation because I'm an ex-policeman. I was in the cells for a week before I got bail. I was beginning to see the criminal justice system from a very different perspective. I started to come around to my senses, 'What in the hell have I done? I'm a man with four kids.' I mean I've always felt like a policeman. I still feel like a policeman inside me. It's something that doesn't leave you — once a cop, always a cop.

"I started falling apart emotionally. I was just about totally broken. It was like an animal injured in the woods crying out. There was no one to cry to so I cried to God. My wife was involved in the church and she used to want me to go to church and I'd say no, 'Me and a few friends are going jogging,' I'd say, 'I belong to the church of jogging.' I'd make jokes about it.

"I finally got bail, but I was going through a real bad emotional time. My wife started to withdraw from me. At first she was just lost and then the anger started to set in, 'How could you do this to me?' She's still angry and rightfully so.

"Then I had a spiritual experience that really turned my life around and kept me alive. If my friends heard me talk this way, they'd say, 'What in the hell is wrong with you John? So you robbed a bank, okay we accept that, but don't give us this crap' [laughs]. I can only say to them that's true.

"Eventually I went to court. They had found some marked money that I had in my house. Stupid eh? Bait money. The rest of it was circumstantial, but they had a pretty good case, enough to convict. I was charged with three bank robberies and I pleaded guilty to two. It was a deal. I was supposed to get six years, but the judge decided on five. He stated that he was influenced by the letters of reference people had written on my behalf.

"My wife and I are still together. She is going through hell. She's deeply wounded — I violated the trust of the marriage. I think it will work out, but right now she is very emotionally isolated from me. I phone my kids every two weeks. I write them every week. I write my wife. Still keeping some contact but as you can appreciate her whole life went out into the harbour. I hope to get paroled and go back to my wife and kids. I'd like to start over and keep a low profile. That's not going to be easy because I can't hide. I'm the cop that became a bank robber. Everybody knows that, but not everyone holds it against me. I have been remorseful. I would like to turn all the negative things that I've done and that have happened to me into something positive."

The Middle Class Suburban Gang

Age 23 years, this young man was part of a gang that received considerable media coverage during their eight-month bank robbery career. Two men would enter the bank with balaclavas pulled over their faces, a handgun, and wearing gloves. They would announce that a robbery was taking place and order people to stand still. One would jump the counter and rifle the tills while the other guarded the entrance with the gun. Their getaway involved running down an alleyway, jumping fences, and driving off in a car driven by a friend in a suit while they crouched down in the back seat. Most of their banks were committed in proximity to a major expressway, which they used as their getaway route. They were caught when a passing police officer spotted them running from a bank and gave chase. The police were surprised to discover that the culprits were all middle-class men who lived at home with their parents in the suburbs.

"I was charged with eight banks and eight firearms and pleaded guilty to three bank robberies and three firearms offences and got one year for each — six years in total. That's a lot! It was 20 months between our arrest and sentencing. That was a hard wait even though I was on bail. I couldn't do anything. I went through three or four jobs. Every week I would take a day off to go to court. It was terrible, a lot of stress. You can't make any plans because you never know when you're going to be sent away. Then you have a date in court in a month and you think that's when they're going to send you to jail. Then it turns out to be another month. It was eight months before we had a preliminary hearing to see if there was enough evidence to take us to trial. Then we waited six months before the trial began. Then after that we were up every month shopping for the right judge. This was supposed to be the most lenient judge.

"I never thought we'd get caught. And if I did think about it, I didn't think of it in terms of what did happen. It was a lot more serious when we got caught then I thought it would be. The cops didn't think it was too funny. When I was first arrested they threw me in the detention centre. They caught us on the Friday night and we spent Saturday, Sunday, and Monday in jail. Then Tuesday we got our bail. Those three days in the detention centre were enough to put me back on my feet. It changed my whole life. This bit is just overkill. It's 20 months after the fact. If you raise children and they take cookies out of the cookie jar, you slap their hands when you catch them, not three days later when you find the cookies are missing. It's a very ludicrous system.

"The day we got caught we split up and ran in different directions. A cop went after my partner and about three or four citizens chased after me. When they chased my partner one cop took a shot at him. I think that put a good scare into him and a few cops jumped on top of him and treated him pretty rough and threw him in the cruiser. I guess that really brought him back to reality. The cops were kind of rough with me when they were getting statements. But at the same time I think there was pity in their eyes. They would slam the typewriter down on the table, threaten to put my head in the radiator, things like that. I signed out of fear. Sometimes it pays to be in trouble, to learn how to get out of trouble. If I was smart then I would have taken a beating and not signed anything. Rather than face the beating, I signed and in the long run ended up screwing myself. If I hadn't signed my own confession to implicate myself I wouldn't be here today.

"The cops came to the house when my parents were having supper, 'Your son has been accused of bank robbery.' They had a warrant and just tore the house apart. It was terrible. My parents were very shocked, very sad. It really tore them apart. But they've been behind me ever since. They went to court with me, they visit and support me. They've been with me 100 percent.

"I got involved in bank robbery because I was depressed over a break-up of a relationship, and I met up with my co-accused while I was depressed. We talked about it over drinks and it just happened. He had already done one and he said it was easy. So I said, 'Well, shit.' You read about it in the papers all the time about these guys going in and passing notes and having a ketchup bottle in their pocket and getting away with a few thousand dollars. And these guys are just fools. They're just asking to get caught. We figured if we do it properly and do it right there would be no problems. I read the papers and it seemed that every time I turned around I would see that banks are making 60 percent profit over the year before. Banks are making money, making money. So there's a target right there. Subliminally it gets in there. For me it was a sort of bitterness towards them. You see farmers getting houses and machinery taken away and the banks making all sorts of money. It formed a bitterness in me and that was as good an outlet as any. Bank robbery is not a personal crime.

"I was living with this woman. We had a daughter and she had a daughter from a previous marriage and her husband came back on the scene and that caused a lot of stress between us. She had to move away to fight him over custody of her daughter. It was just a hassle. I was depressed.I wanted the money to help her with the legal fees. The relationship was over, but I was still hoping that we could regain something. If I did something with myself maybe she would change her mind, but then, after that, I needed the money for self-improvement. I wanted money so I could learn to fly, get my pilot's licence. I thought that's where I wanted to make my career. I was loading trucks and was working 40-60 hours a week even though I was considered part-time. When I started doing this I lost interest in work and would show up only two days a week.

"Coming from a middle-class family and a comfortable living I think my expectations were too high. The bank robbery was a short cut, that's all it was. I had just lost my self-respect. I cared what happened to me but not too much. I wasn't doing it as a cry for attention. It's hard to explain now, but at the time I could sort of make sense of it. It was easier to keep on doing it than it was to stop. The one we got caught on was going to be our last one. We had decided on that. My partner was getting married the next day. I didn't want to even do this one, but he was set and determined. So I figured if I go along I'll make it less likely that he'll get caught.

"Our driver had lost his interest. We would take 90 percent and give the driver 10 percent which might amount to $500. That isn't a lot of money for the risk he's taking. So he wasn't too happy about that. My partner's brother was in town for the wedding and he needed some money so we asked him to drive. He was one person who we could trust for sure. Turns out he got convicted too. I was relieved that it was finally over because we may not have been able to stop.

"To be honest there is excitement to robbing banks, but it's suppressed excitement. You can go around thinking, 'Hey, I'm Jesse James,' but you can't really tell anybody about it. I don't know if excitement is the right word. It was more like a business venture to us. It never got easier on the stomach, like the butterflies and that. Sometimes we'd stand outside in the plaza getting up the nerve to walk into the bank `cause we were afraid. So much tension and stress, then finally one of us would get the nerve up to go do it. It would take a lot to psyche ourselves up. It was always nerve-racking. I know that I'll never be involved with any sort of criminal activity again. It's just not worth it, being locked up like this.

"As soon as I was arrested all my friends and people from the neighbourhood knew about it. Everybody was flabbergasted. My friends have treated me different ever since. One friend in particular, he was getting married a week after we were arrested and I was supposed to be his head usher at his wedding. He called me and says, 'I can't have you at the wedding. I don't want the wife's family to find out.' That was very hard because he was a close friend. That really hurt at the time. I've never seen him since. "

Author's Note: Another member of this crew was also interviewed and appears in Chapter Five entitled I'm Getting Married in the Morning.

Stockbroker

Age 26, this man is serving five and one-half years for a jewellery store holdup and five bank robberies.

"There are two types of robberies: one at gunpoint and one is a poor man's robbery where you use a note. I just handed notes to the teller. I used the same note all the time: I HAVE A GUN. LARGE BILLS. TEN SECONDS. That says it all. I didn't come up with that myself, I got it from the papers. It seemed like a straightforward note. You don't need a weapon. I didn't carry one for the banks, but I had a gun on the jewellery store robbery. That was more scary than all five banks put together because of the gun.

"When I robbed banks I waited until lunchtime when there was a rush hour. I'd go in with a nice business suit and clip-on tie. I had white runners with black rubbers over top, tape on my fingers. I made sure there were no cameras and no big guys working behind the counters. You prey on the ladies. I felt bad about the tellers — some of them were very frightened — but they have all been instructed to hand over the money and not create a scene. I'd walk out of the bank and into these underground shopping concourses. Off comes the clip-on tie, the trench coat, and rubber boots and I'm lost in the crowd. No panic, nice and calm. What gave me the idea originally was that I was in a bank vault counting stocks. I sat down at a lady's desk and by mistake I hit the alarm button. About six or seven minutes later the cops arrive and this was in the morning when there's no traffic. Hitting the button showed me how much time I had.

"I was always into drinking and drugs and I had a low disregard for money. When I was living at home I was making a good income and I couldn't make it from one paycheque to the next. Bouncing cheques like crazy, not paying loans, charging everything I bought. I was riding a fine line but not doing anything that could get me in real trouble. My dad is rich and he would always come through with the funds to pull me out of trouble. But then he got fed up and cut me off: 'I think I'm doing more harm lending you this money. Go out and see what you can do by yourself.'

"I had worked downtown for six years in the financial district for a brokerage firm. I was a stockbroker and my dad and my brothers and my cousins are all in the same business. I grew up in a really nice house, destined to a nice standard of living and all of a sudden this is cut off. I wasn't working hard and got fired from my job and I couldn't find another one. I talked to friends, 'Get me in here,' 'Put a word in for me,' and I got nothing back from it. Fuck you. No one cares about me, why should I care? I just gave up. Getting fired was a great blow to my ego. I think I could have got another job if I had looked hard enough, but it gets to the point where you don't care about nothing.

"My unemployment ran out and now I'm sitting around wondering where my next meal is going to come from. There comes a time when you're on welfare and you've got bills to pay and your rent is due and you are fed up and you don't give a shit anymore. You got to do what you got to do. You still have to eat. I would read in the papers five or six bank robberies went down in one day for undisclosed amounts of cash. You read it on Thursday and then on Friday you read two more go down and you can't see any of these guys getting pinched. A few are caught but it's because of their own stupidity or bad luck.

"The first time I did a bank it took me three days to get up the nerve. Three days with no money, no cigarettes, and I hadn't eaten. I circled the bank so often my feet hurt. I circled the block until the bank closed and then I'd go home. Then I sat outside this bank for a couple of hours and I'm trying to decide and all of a sudden I said, 'Fuck it' and went in. I just calculated the risks. It is like a high afterwards. I don't know if anyone can just do one because you find out that it is pretty easy. Then I did the second, third, fourth, and fifth. I would have definitely kept going until I was caught. It was easy money.

"I paid my rent off and filled the fridge. The rest of it was for partying or going to the racetrack. I was into the races way before that anyway. I'd had fun going to the racetrack with more money than I could count and not caring if I lost it. After the second bank I didn't really care about the money because I can always go back to the bank and make an unauthorized withdrawal. I have an unlimited supply. Why should I start saving it? I was hoping for one night where I could go there and hit a couple of long shots, but it never happened. I think I had 30 or 40 losing nights in a row. I've had a lot of bad luck in my life. I don't have anything to show for the money.

"I have to say that despite all that's happened to me I enjoyed what I did. I never felt better about myself then when I was robbing banks. Finally accomplishing something and looking after myself for a change. I don't have to bum money off my father or brothers. It is a good feeling."

CHAPTER SEVEN

A Dangerous Breed —

Career and Professional Criminals

- •I was a Gunman
- •Street Smart
- •Filou
- •French Canadian
- •The Stopwatch Gang
- •Montreal Pro
- •Brinks
- •Flying Bandit

Sociologists use the concept of a *career criminal* to describe individuals who exhibit a long-term commitment to crime as a way of life; a high frequency of offending; seriousness of offences; an adherence to criminal values; associations with other criminals; and a reliance upon crime as a major if not exclusive source of income. Research with convicted offenders has found that a relatively small group of chronic offenders or violent predators commit a disproportionate amount of crime. Moreover, these offenders are likely to have begun offending as young adolescents and continue in their criminal careers until their early 40s. (Chaiken and Chaiken, 1982; 1989 and 1990; Ball et al., 1983; Ball, 1986; Mande and English, 1988; Petersilia, 1980; Petersilia et al., 1978; Hanson et al., 1985)

One policy implication of this research is to capture and incarcerate career criminals early in their career. If chronic offenders can be identified and dealt with effectively, crime rates should decrease. Selective incapacitation through imprisonment aims to reduce crime by isolating the recidivist from the community and thereby suspending the normal progress of his career. There are serious concerns, however, about the degree to which criminals can be identified early enough in their careers and before they have committed large numbers of crimes. Gottfredson and Hirschi (1986:217) make the argument that since criminality declines more or less uniformly with age, many offenders will be "over the hill" by the time they are old enough to be plausible candidates for preventative incarceration. They point out, in fact, that most of the career criminals identified in criminological research are no longer active and their replacements cannot be identified until they too are on the verge of retirement. Since the commission of crime declines with age, incapacitation must occur during the time that the offender would be committing criminal acts at a high rate to achieve maximum effectiveness. A policy of selective incapacitation is criticized as unjust and costly since the social sciences cannot accurately identify career criminals at an early stage in their careers. Any attempt to do so is likely to result in an undue number of minor offenders receiving extra stringent imprisonment (Gottfredson and Hirschi, 1986; Petersilia, 1980). Regardless of the problems with policy implications, the concept of a career criminal is still theoretically useful to criminology and career criminals are clearly worthy subjects of investigation.

Many of the men in this study can be classified as career criminals because of their continued involvement in crime over a substantial part of their lives. The following selections include eight men who have spent many years in prison and whose commitment to the criminal enterprise is made clear in their interviews. *I Was a Gunman* is perhaps the most dangerous and violent man interviewed. He is an intelligent, confident, and charismatic person whose body language communicates an obsession with power and control. Investigating officers consider him one of the most dangerous persons they have ever come across and they report that he was previously suspected as a hitman for organized crime. *Street Smart* is 32 years of age and has spent most of his adult life behind bars. He is proud, tough, macho, and willing to use violence whenever necessary. His criminal record includes almost everything short of murder — an act he says he has not committed, "only by the grace of God." His value system illustrates a commitment to crime as a way of life and he views arrest and imprisonment as one of the costs of doing business: "I've played and I've paid."

Among the career criminals in this study, it is also possible to single out professionals who exhibit long periods of training, complex occupational skills, and shared sets of occupationally oriented attitudes

— elements usually regarded as central to professional status (Sutherland, 1947; Sutherland and Cressey, 1978). Although the distinction between professional criminals and semiprofessional property offenders is of degree rather than kind, some bandits clearly exhibit greater skill, knowledge, and profit from crime. Among other criminals, men who make their living through armoured vehicle robberies are considered professionals since they view crime as a way of life; they are heavily armed, skilled, and organized and they take on formidable targets. Hold-Up Squad officers similarly use the term professional to describe bandits who are heavily armed, well prepared, rob armoured vehicles, obtain large sums of money, and are prepared to engage in a shoot-out with the police. These men make "the big score," spend accordingly, consider themselves professional, and engage in robbery on a purposeful and sustained basis over various periods of their lives — usually interrupted by incarceration. Individually, each has a reputation among the underworld as solid and competent and is held in high esteem by fellow inmates. These men are not deterred by danger but are respected as much for their intelligence as their courage. They view their activity more as a career or job; they are cautious, patient, and plan their robberies; and they are not deterred by the possibility of violence although they attempt to minimize and control its likelihood.

Filou is a French term used to describe a highly clever criminal — usually a swindler or embezzler. In this interview the subject describes an innovative and dramatic bank robbery that kept him in the bank for 52 minutes — a crime committed to prove a point and win an argument. *French Canadian* was caught for an armoured vehicle robbery in a neighbouring city. He discusses his techniques for disarming guards and the preparation that goes into a big score. His downfall comes from not having sufficient discipline to control his lifestyle. *The Stopwatch Gang* is an interview with Stephen Reid, author of *Jackrabbit Parole*, who describes the activities of his crew "The Stopwatch Gang" on their road trip throughout the United States. *Montreal Pro* is described as an old "bona fide heister" by members of the Hold-Up Squad and has a career that spans 40 years.

Robbery is a dramatic event because of the danger involved and the overt and confrontational nature of the crime. The last two case synopses in this chapter illustrate dramatic incidents. *Brinks* describes the 45-second disarming and robbery of two armoured vehicle guards delivering money to a bank. The holdup does not unfold as planned and the bandits make a split-second decision to go through with it anyway. The respondent's thoughts, fears, and assumptions in this brief and dangerous time frame are revealed. The reader can easily imagine how close this incident came to a tragic outcome. *Flying Bandit* is the story of an escaped convict who hijacks a helicoptor and its pilot in order to assist some friends to escape from prison. When these plans fall through, he uses the helicoptor to rob two banks instead. Later, in court, he pulls out a handgun in an unsuccessful escape attempt.

I was a Gunman

This man, age 38, was sentenced to 25 years in prison for his part in an armoured vehicle robbery when he was 22 years old. He has also been convicted of weapons and kidnapping charges. As part of an organized criminal syndicate, his experiences, values, and M.O. are characteristic of bank robbery in the 1960s. A newspaper article on his most recent sentencing quotes the judge as saying: "[The offender] is completely dedicated to a criminal way of life and is a danger to the public. He should be kept off the streets or he will surely commit other crimes." The article also indicated that the offender has been sentenced to more than 400 years since his criminal career began at the age of 15. In the recent incident the judge sentenced him to a 40-year prison sentence to be served consecutive to 18 years he must still serve for previous crimes. A teller is quoted as saying, "He terrorized the whole branch. He charged me like a bull and pushed me to the ground." The prosecutor is also quoted: "His criminal record is shocking and his release on parole is an indictment of the parole system in this country."

"I started my banking career at the age of 19 and I'm 38 now. I've been out three times since — once on parole and twice I've escaped. It was a short career because I've spent 20 years in prison going back to when I was 15. Prison is my home. I'm doing a 40-year sentence for bank robbery and another 18 left from my previous sentence — 58 years. Yeah, and I have a year in [bangs his forehead on the table and laughs]. Whoaaa, you gotta try to laugh.

"In the criminal element we have different subcultures. You have mobsters, boosters, dope dealers, bank robbers, and other categories. With bank robbers, you have two kinds: the professional and the amateur. I was considered a professional at the age of 19. The difference between the professional and the amateur is how you're doing it and who you're doing it with. I was extremely lucky to be with some of the best, the elite. It was very interesting, exciting, and enjoyable. Robbing Brinks trucks, banks, having lots of money and lots of beautiful women, I loved it. Living it up. It was a trip. It was great.

"I fell in love with the lifestyle of a criminal when I was a teenager. The criminal mind wants to call itself contrary. It's not so much for a need of money because there's other ways of making money if a person has the drive and the abilities and some focus. I remember when I was 12 and watching television with my dad, he would be for the police and I'd be for the bad guys. It goes way back. I'm a criminally minded person. You'll find occasional ones who start at a later age because of financial reasons, but with me it had nothing to do with financial needs — although the financial aspect can be beautiful.

"It's the lifestyle. I remember when I was 17 or 18, I used to wear a pair of jeans, running shoes, and eat pizza and coke. Then I started robbing banks at 19 and hanging around with mobsters. I wore tailor-made Italian suits, big diamond on the pinky, .38 in the belt, and I dined every night. And respect in the places I used to go, when you're a bank robber and you're in with the mob, you're known.

"When I was 20 I was working at this club and I was the *maître d's* assistant manager. My job consisted of packing a .38 and handling things the bouncers couldn't handle. Bouncers run into certain situations where muscle doesn't work so they use somebody like me to do whatever has to be done. You use a name or the .38 or whatever has to be used to give them the message. Once you're in the underworld two or three years people get to know you. I didn't have to use the piece very often. Just the reputation, the vibes I would give off, the body language, that would take care of the problem. Use my fists occasionally. What's going on here? Whishew! Whishew! Boom! Bop!

Kick! Out you go. I was only 20 ,but I wasn't some ordinary 20-year-old punk. I was taking on trucks, I wasn't taking on grocery stores, I wasn't robbing ladies' purses or nothin'. Some people you punch, some people you kill. I'm the kind of guy you have to kill. I've never been punched in my life.

"There's special talent in any field. If you're a physician or a bricklayer, then you have special talents. And in the criminal world there are certain talents; I was a gunman. To attack the trucks, that's definitely a professional's job. The amateur doesn't even think about it. He looks at it and he sees nothing. I look at it and I see a score. What it comes down to is that you're going up against a guy with a gun. If he pulls it out, if he makes a play, you do him in. You have to commit yourself all the way. In a bank the option exists. You can throw the gun away and give yourself up. That's the difference. That's what really separates the men from the boys. You're ready to kill. You've made that decision before you start. On the score, I would take the heaviest responsibility.

"I was approached by the Italian people to work for them when I was only 20 years old. I was flattered. The family ran five or six clubs and they needed a bodyguard. I'd be working at one of the clubs but that was just a front — meet the girls, talk to the customers so that people see you at work. But the real job was delivering packages, breaking legs, shooting off heads, disposing of problems. Heavy stuff, yeah.

"I went to see my friend for advice, an older guy, let's call him George. George says, 'Don't get involved. Keep away from these people because they'll use you and flush you down the drain.' So I went to Tony and said, 'Tony, thank you very much but no thanks.' I was lucky at the time to have someone to explain things to me. The Italians, they take care of themselves. Anybody else, they use. If a guy becomes too ambitious, knows too much, that's it. They shoot him. Life continues.

"George was my *protégé*. He set me up for my first bank robbery — me and another guy about 20 years old. Both of us were cherries. George wanted to test us before we got to go on the big scores. He was testing us to see if we could do it. We did the score and George introduced us to some other guys all about eight to ten years older than myself. I was just a youngster and some of them I looked up to as my idol. Idolism is just a high form of respect. If you have potential and they happen to like you, then they'll give you a chance. And if they like you and you do a good job, other trips come up and you just become one of them.

"Everything depends on your reputation — on the respect you have. Whether you're in the hash business or the gun business — the underworld — we don't sign on the dotted line. 'Here, I gave you fifty pounds. Sign here.' There's no such thing. It's your word, your honour. Either you're solid or you're not. A guy has values or he doesn't have values. A guy has courage or he doesn't have courage.

"It's also who you know. I know so-and-so. Yeah? Nice guy. Boom, boom, boom, we're doing business together. Or so-and-so says he's a jerk, 'Okay, hit the road.' There's a hell of a difference between criminals. You don't compare someone who's selling nickels and dimes on the street to someone importing a ton of hash. A guy who takes on a truck and a guy who takes on a grocery store are not in the same league. Not in here. Not on the street.

"I remember sitting around a table at this club, two tables together, eight, ten men. All these guys must have been ten years my senior. And I got to know their stories and these guys were bad people. I mean there'd be mobsters, killers, robbers. A rogues gallery. And I'm part of it. When you're young, you're impressed. You get respect just being part of this group. I remember going into a club with George and another guy. The *maître d'* comes over with a bottle, 'Gentlemen, champagne on the house.' The manager comes over, 'George, how are you?' We get introduced. I walk in with my girlfriend two days later and they remember, 'How are you Joe?' I wouldn't get the bottle of champagne, I was just a kid, but I was known and that mattered. Just the little things. It counts.

"When I was working at the club we had maybe twenty dancers. Any dancer I wanted, I could dance with. You know what I mean? You see a dancer, 'Hey baby, watcha doing? Let's go for half an hour.' That was it. Go out back and throw a fuck into her. Come back out, 'What'll we eat today? Oh, lobster looks good. Ahh, maybe a little escargots, champagne perhaps.' That was the lifestyle. I loved it.

"One time me and my partner had just done a bank about 10:30 A.M. and we had about seven thousand in our pockets. This is winter time and I see this advertisement for Miami Beach. So we go in and ask this travel agent for some brochures, pleasure scenes. I said, 'Lady, what do you advise for a couple of weeks?' 'Oh,' she says, 'Miami Beach.' So I said to my partner, 'Let's go. What's stopping us?' In the plane. Bing, bang, we're gone. Going to Miami Beach [snaps fingers]. We stayed a month. That's what I mean by the lifestyle; it's a trip.

"I also became a junky on banks and trucks. It was a rush. I'm a bit of a fanatic when it comes to guns. God didn't make man equal but Colt did. To some people, a gun is just a gun. It's just steel. To me, it's power. In one of my escapes, I had two .38's and some other things smuggled into prison. Me and three other guys took 12 guards captive, tied them up, put on their uniforms, and drove out of the prison with two guards as hostages. I was only out ten days when the cops caught up to us. We were about to do a bank when they drove a car into us. I had a machine-gun beside me, but I didn't get a chance to use it before they opened fire. The car hit us, bang! I grabbed the gun and was coming up with it when they opened up. They wouldn't have known that we had this weapon in the car. They just opened up. There was just me and my partner and neither of us got wounded. It was a miracle. The windows were blown out and I had glass chips in my face. I was coming up with the machine gun and, poom, poom, poom, poom! Holes, bloody big holes in the car the size of quarters! I got down on the floor. I had said that I'd never come back to jail alive, but I did because it's hard to die.

"On that same trip, just before that run-in with the police, this guy had given us a car, guns, a few other things. He asked us for a favour, 'There's this guy I want you to talk to. He's trying to muscle me.' My partner says, 'Let's pay this muscle guy a visit.' He wasn't too far away so we stopped in. A big guy, six-foot-two, big arms on the fucker, two hundred and fifty pounds and black. We walk in his office and my partner starts talking to him. I'm off to the side and I don't say anything. I've got the gun out and every time my partner gets the message across as to what we're going to do to him I go, 'Bam!' with the gun. I just look at him. I don't say a word. I hit this filing cabinet 'Bam!' At first the guy smiles. 'Bam!' His size didn't make any difference to me, I had the gun. 'Bam!' Here it is. If the guy was to do anything, then 'Boom, boom, boom, boom, boom, boom' [pretending to grab him by the hair and shoot him in the head]. So it was an act and it wasn't. And just as we leave, I said to the guy, 'If I have to come back here again, You're dead.' I never fucking sweat when I have a piece in my hand. My partner and I had a good laugh over that.

"In the old days when I did them, the 60s, we worked in a crew. Three or four guys, machine guns, hand guns, stolen cars, vests, 'Everybody hit the floor!' I did 28 banks and maybe once or twice I struck somebody or had to shove them along. It's not necessary, only rarely. It would take months of work to do the big score. I would want to know where every cop car was, what every detective looked like, what their cars looked like, what their routines were. We had three or four guys do that; sit around in restaurants, following cars; study the cop station, check out their shifts, a car pulls in, got the number, walk around, see their faces. They only got so many. So maybe when you're doing a score a car's there, whoops-a-daisy. It's happened where some guys will do a score and the cops are there and they get their ass shot off, 'Boom, bam, boom.' For banks and for trucks you need professionalism. You gotta have discipline, get up early, go to work and do it day after day just to set up the score. I never got caught on the score. The pros that get caught, usually it's something out in left field, something you can't forsee.

"From the moment I pull down my hood and I commit myself, in those sixty seconds, I become another person. The adrenalin rush. You become aware of everyone around you. It's a hell of a rush and your whole life is on the line. You could get shot, you could get caught. It's your head. When I'm doing a bank, I'm aware of that.

"I never got caught for the banks. I got caught on this Brinks score when we tried to take the whole truck — more than four hundred thousand dollars. I always wanted to be successful in taking a whole truck instead of just a few bags. I never was. A shootout occured and a guard got shot. I was pinched and got a twenty-fiver for that. It was too bad because that was gonna be our last. You see, this was in the late 60s and drugs were just coming in. We were getting into the dope scene. Hash was coming, speed was coming, acid. The late 60s, early 70s — Janis Joplin, long hair, all that stuff. I was aware of that and I was robbing that Brinks Truck to put the money into dope. I was getting nervous about banks. Not just banks, I was doing other things. That would have been our last venture.

"On my last trip out I was on parole and working on a delivery truck taking home $140 a week! Today! Clear! What's that, half an ounce of sensimilia? You know what I'm saying? I was wearing other people's clothes, leftover scraps. This was eating at me like a cancer. I met a lady with a child, she was a beautiful dark brunette and I married her. She was a hooker. She used to be a hooker. I remember her saying we were made for each other. I guess the bank robber and the hooker is something that goes back many years. Jesse James was probably married to a hooker too. But ah, I fell in love with a hooker. I can't believe it too this day — how can this happen? I guess I felt at ease beside her. I could pull my gun out, I could smoke my dope. I could do whatever I felt like doing.

"I was out only seven days and I robbed a bank because I was broke. It was that simple. The banks were just going to be stepping stones to bigger and better things. I have a certain drive, a sense of manhood. I couldn't work on that delivery truck for the rest of my life. Forget that. I had to do it for awhile because I was building other parts of my world.

"I knew all the main dealers in town. The biggest dealer in the area was the best man at my wedding. I called a guy for some toys and he sent over a .38. I hadn't had a gun in my hands in 15 years. It was a rush. I remember standing there, the sun was shining, I had it in my hand. The thrill it gave me. Ah, I'm in business, ah. I looked at that gun and I said, 'Ah, it's either gonna bring me a lot of the good things in life, or it's gonna bring me a lot of pain.' And it brought a lot of pain.

"I was going to unite these guys and organize the territory. Anybody comes with 20 pounds of hash he goes through us. The bank jobs were only to give me the cash to buy the dope I needed to get into business. I drove down to the city and did them, but in one score things went bad, we got shot at, shot back, someone got shot, and we got caught. It was a heavy trip. I didn't want my wife charged so I took the rap. That's how I got 40 years. My wife visited me about a month-and-a-half ago. She said, 'I love you honey, but life goes on.' Well, she's a beautiful young lady and what should I do? I understand that, especially a hooker.

"You go back a hundred years and look at Jesse James on his horse, a bank, or a stagecoach. Today, the horse becomes a car, the man is still a man, the gun is still a gun, and the bank is still a bank. Nothing much has changed. You gotta have the courage, you gotta catch them by surprise, and you gotta get away. The lifestyle's still the same."

Street Smart

Age 32, this offender is serving seven years for one count of bank robbery. A bank employee followed him from the bank and alerted a female police officer who followed the getaway van until her back-up arrived. A brief chase followed and the culprit rolled the van and was caught after a foot chase across a field.

"I don't want this interview recorded and I'll tell you why. If I'm going to talk to you, then I want to be truthful and I won't be with the tape recorder going. I don't know how you're going to use this because I don't know you from Adam. I'm not concerned about the police because they know me and what I've done, but how do I know this won't end up in my file and be seen by the parole board? It could prevent me from getting out sooner.

"I was acquitted for an earlier bank robbery. They had the licence plate number of the getaway car and it was registered to a lady and she was picked up by the police and shown mug shots. She knew me. We had met a week before. She lent the car to this guy, call him Bill, and was shown my mug shot and she fingered me. In the meantime a friend of mine got busted for something else and gave information on me. I was arrested one and a half weeks after the crime and I went to trial before a lady judge. The woman witness took the stand and said that she couldn't see me in court. The police didn't have a strong case and there were some inconsistencies in the testimony. During this time I was held in custody for 80 days and had my parole revoked, but then I got bail and had the parole reinstated. I'm surprised I got parole back. They had my record and they could see I was a pretty violent criminal. My lawyer argued that bank robbery was a sophisticated crime and that this guy is the violent type. My lawyer implied that I was too stupid to be guilty of bank robbery. I didn't care what he had to say about me, he had my consent. I wanted back on the street.

"I had been sentenced to four years for robbery — not a bank but a dope rip-off. I had come into contact with the Hold-Up Squad before, but they've never given me problems. It was always a Mexican stand-off. There was no give on my part. I give no statements and they kind of respect that. I was never subjected to any beatings. They know I'm a stand-up guy. They get no cooperation from me. I give them no quarter. I'm black, I dress nice, I travel with white women. The social part is one reason. I'm black and hey, I'm a man. They know that and what I'm capable of doing. We have a professional relationship. Nothing personal.

"I'm a street person. I live by my wits and my balls and I don't give a fuck what people think. You should see my sheet. I have a horrendous sheet — drugs, violence, robberies, assaults, burglary. It's only by the grace of God that I've never killed anybody. And I come from a good family — poor but good parents. They were very religious and all my brothers and sisters turned out just fine. I'm the black sheep in the family.

"When I was a kid all the other kids always seemed to do a little better than me — money, cars, clothes. I looked at my rags and I started stealing. I was eight years old. Even then I wanted the better things in life. I liked the respect I saw criminals get. I learned about crime from the kids in the ghetto. I saw myself as the sharpest kid on the block. I'm a lone wolf. I always work alone. I had a couple of cars when I was 15 and because I couldn't drive I had local toughs drive them for me. I spent time in juvenile detention. After that, there was no turning back. I had a taste for the good life. Soon I had a street gang of 20 and I was the boss.

"I've been arrested a few times and I have lots of convictions. They just accumulated. I've been into crime all my life. If you're caught, you're caught no matter how ingenious the plan. I've played and I've paid. I live life in the fast lane. I used drugs and was into burglary, robbery, pimping, you name it. I was always a downtown man. The downtown is wide open. The whole city is wide open. I defy somebody to tell me I couldn't do what I wanted. I can't fathom someone telling me I can't do what I want. I've always supported myself through crime and I got good money. I had drugs, two or three hookers on the street. I was making a minimum $1000 a week and I spent it. When I was young and things were going good I didn't think of tomorrow. I was the star of the show. If I'd lose a hooker then I'd get another. I did a lot of speed. I'd go into a bar and gamble away $2000 and leave broke. I didn't look after my girls the way I should have.

"I got into the revolving door of the justice system. I went to jail a few times and while I'm in there I'd lose everything. I'd get out and have to start over again. Each time I'm a little older and more impatient. I'm a step lower each time. I'm falling out of the groove. I'm thinking that I'm a has-been. It's a gradual progression. I thought I knew it all. I had a gangster's complex. I slipped and fell a few times. I was caught up in the Hollywood gangster stereotype — the big time roller.

"Now when I'm out, I can't take the chances anymore to make the money I did then. I have to start over each time. I'd get out on a Monday — my wife was a wild young girl — I'd be back in jail on Friday for assaulting my wife. Stupid stuff. I had a hot temper. People tell me now, 'You were a terrible young guy,' but I tried to be dignified in my moral standards. I can live with what I did. I'm not ashamed, but I'm not proud.

"Robbery is defined in so many ways. I had already done robberies by doing dope rip-offs. I'd get a whore to bring a sucker to me and I'd rip him off. She'd call and tell me he had a big bank roll so I'd rip him off. I was a tough kid. I'd hit him, spin him, and put my hand in his back pocket. Often I'd be on drugs and I thought I was Superman. I had been in lots of street fights and I always came out on top. I'm a boxer.

"This last time out me and this friend got high and go out to an after hours joint and end up in the crap room. Gambling has always been a big problem. Guys got to know it and they'd entice me. I was a sucker for it. I had an 11:00 curfew and I'm late. I've got a beautiful wife and two kids and I'm supposed to be at home. Instead of taking it easy I'm in the back room gambling. The night goes on and at 8:00 A.M. I'm broke. I lost $1400 in cash, $3000 in jewellry, and on top of all this I owe $4000.

"I'm not in a good mood. I get a ride home and the guy giving me the ride tells me that they had been playing with bogus dice all night. To my way of thinking, somebody is going to die. I've been insulted by guys who know me, who know what I'm capable of and they still take a shot at me. I had told my wife that I had a big stash put away. I did, but I blew $140,000 in the summer and I lied to her to keep her. So I'm sitting there in the morning and I feel like a country bumpkin having been slicked by these guys. My wife gets up and sees that the money I had stashed in the cupboard is gone. My friend had been calling all night, but I didn't know that. I lied and told her I took the money to his house. She knows I lied, but she doesn't say it in those words. She just tells me he called all night. Now I'm behind the eight ball. I had a couple of dope things on the side that would have paid for everything. I should have waited it out. That was my big mistake not waiting. I was feeling closed in when there was no reason to feel closed in. I was not using common sense.

"I lost $4000 that night and I don't have the money. I have to pay this debt and I'm under pressure to come up with the money. I won't let anybody strong-arm me, but I have to keep my gun on me and fully loaded all the time. It gets to the point where I don't know who I'm shooting at. I was talked to twice in two weeks. They send somebody capable of doing it. They say, 'Hey, you owe some money. We'll be reasonable to a limit.' I wasn't forced to do what I did. There's a deadline and you had better be prepared to go to the lengths I did to get out of debt. There were better ways of getting the money but none easier.

"When you're living life in the fast lane you're only as good as your money. The environment I hung around, the company was hookers, pimps, drug traffickers, and strong-arm men. To keep that company your money has to be right. I had to make a score. I needed that $4000 plus money for me. I knew what I had to do to get the money. I had talked to a few guys on the street about banks and I knew what to do. I call my buddy and he picks me up. I was looking for a bank out of town. My M.O. was to go into a bank, give them a big bag, and they take the money out of the tills and fill the bag. It's 30 seconds of yelling, swearing, and psychological abuse. I knew if I was arrested I'd get a considerable amount of time. That made me only more determined. I'd show the gun, ask for the fucking big ones, and, 'Let me out of here quick before someone gets hurt.' I knew that my life was on the line. It was a shot. I was taking a risk.

"My friend is giving his girl a ride to the airport and I tagged along. On the way I see a plaza and I told them to pull in and park around the side. I told them I'm picking up some cocaine. I knew my buddy was scared and didn't buy the cocaine story. I get into the van with a big bag of money and we drive away. One mistake is that we didn't know the area and we're stuck in traffic. Two minutes later there's a couple of police cars behind us. I feel like a caged animal. There's a female cop behind us and she's radioing ahead. I tell the driver to keep going and he says, 'They're all over. I can't.' He's slowing down and we stop. The cops have their guns drawn and tell him to get out. I'm in the back of the van. I have a gun and the money. I'm on parole and bail. I don't give a shit if I live or die. I jump into the driver's seat and smash the gearbox into drive. They open fire and the female cop hits me in the ass. Meanwhile the girl is still in the van. She is terrified and she hits the floor. I got six miles on the freeway before they catch me. I lost them a few times, but the police radioed ahead and some transport trucks straddled the highway and blocked me in. I see this exit and I think I've got a shot. I've played it this far, I'm going all the way. I guess I'm fortunate I'm not dead because I hit something. I'm doing 90 mph and the van flipped and I got out and ran into this field. The police converged on the area and I was arrested, but I went down like a man. I didn't just give myself to them.

"My wife and I broke up a long time ago and were separated three years. I had moved to another city then moved back and went to see my wife and we got together again. We've been married 11 years and never spent a Christmas together because I've been doing time. I have a daughter who doesn't even know me. I never spent much time with my family — I'm not a family man. I've always looked after myself. My wife is an independent lady. I didn't steal for my family. It was all for me. I was not ready to be a family man then, I am now. My wife visits me and we're still together. She's even more solid. I love and respect her.

"I was given seven years with a promise of a life sentence if I ever show up in court again. I'm retired. No more robberies. I'm not telling you I won't go back to crime at all. Who can say how things will fall into place, but I want to try a square endeavour. I don't want to spend any more time in the slammer. I don't have another bit in me. This last judge gave me a scare. The next time they'll put me away for good. I know I could go down as a dangerous offender."

Filou

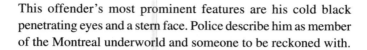

This offender's most prominent features are his cold black penetrating eyes and a stern face. Police describe him as member of the Montreal underworld and someone to be reckoned with.

"My age is 30. I was sentenced to seven years and I have close to five years in. My lawyer tried to get four but the prosecutor — a female bitch — wanted 17. I pled guilty and the 17 came down to seven. I was transferred to this institution for attempting to smuggle two guns into another prison. I'm in here because I was convicted of an armed robbery of a bank. I have a past record for armed robbery for which I did a four-year bit. I was young. It was a gang bang, over the counter, through the tills, cowboy stuff. Somebody wasn't satisfied and ratted. The police charged me with 14 banks and managed to get me for two. When I was younger I had bad experiences and always got caught. I learned the hard way.

"People see my expression and they know not to fuck with me. Guards don't say anything to me, inmates don't say anything to me. It's not cultivated. That's the way I am. People know. I am always serious. I am deadly serious. If someone is bothering me, I just say, 'If you're willing to die keep on.' I go into a trance. People back off. I never back down. I consider the people in here lowlife.

"I'm not saying I'm proud of what I did, but there's only been one job done that way — mine. I had a .357 Combat Magnum and went into the bank and asked for money. I didn't touch the till but got the money from the safe. If you have to risk your life you might as well go for a big one — it's the same risk. I picked up a lousy $50,000. I could have got more but my briefcase was too small. I got four packs of $20s and two packs of $10s. There was more money to take but no room. I put one bullet in the gun. It was for me. If I got into a tight situation, I decided to do that rather than get caught.

"Suicidal is not depressed. I was at work. It was a job. It's not depressed. It's a state of mind or mood I put myself into. We have a saying, 'If you want to kill time, work it to death.' By that I mean you do something to keep busy and kill time. By suicidal I mean that I put myself into a mood whereby I'll get this money or I'll die trying. It's a self-induced state. It's not down-and-out or depressed. It's determination.

"I prepared for this the night before. I picked up the weapon from a friend and returned it. I work alone so I can't be double-crossed. I don't have to shoot a partner if I'm double-crossed. That's *omertà* — the law of silence. The informer is someone who can't take the pressure or the time. I would rather die than talk.

"My philosophy in doing a bank is different than most people. For most people, $2 + 2 = 4$, but $.5 + 3.5 = 4$ as well. People are used to working with units and when someone introduces fractions they're confused. That confusion works to your advantage. I use fractions. Bank robbers worry about time. The time lapse was not a concern, it did not exist. I was 52 minutes in the bank. It's very easy if you're suicidal — either I get out or I don't. I will not use hostages. I am not there to harm innocent people, I'm there for the money. You can go a lot further without using violence. I use atmosphere to control people. There were 30 people working in this bank and only three people knew what I was doing — the manager, credit lady, and the accountant.

"I was dressed in a three-piece suit like a businessman. I am there to do business. It's a fact. It's not a comedy. I'm not playing a game. It's my fucking life. It's a reality for me. I walked in with my attache case, which was empty, I had to act like it was full — give that appearance. I had a gun in a shoulder holster. I went into the manager's office and shook his hand. I told him I was doing a $50,000 transaction.

"He brought me to the credit woman and told her I had $50,000 to deposit. I sat down to talk to her and she's getting the rates on the phone. I said to her that there was a mistake and I took out an envelope with a message made of newspaper letters that said, 'We are doing a holdup. Want $50,000 cash. Small bills — four packs of $20s and two packs of $10s. Unmarked money.' She said, 'You're kidding?' As she said that I opened my jacket and showed her the gun. I told her not to touch the alarm and to call the manager because there was a problem that needed his help. She called him and the same thing happened with him except that he said he didn't want to play cowboy. In the bank nobody wants to play cowboy. In the movies the bad guys lose and the good guys come out on top, but that's not reality.

"He said he'd get the money from the till and I said, 'No. Nobody knows about this and there's no panic. Let's keep it that way.' You have to be cool and cold-blooded — a suicider.

"He had no choice. I'm calling the shots. You're king and master of the situation if you can control yourself first. You have to stay cold and on one track and you lose if you get sidetracked. I go in straight, no drugs or booze and no empty stomach — I ate beforehand. I eat a good meal and then I go for it.

"I told him to get the money from the safe, 'Please don't touch the alarm. Don't get me angry because you wouldn't like to see me angry.' I told the manager to call the accountant and explained the situation to the guy. I then took the envelope and put it in my pocket. He looked at me and smiled. I don't smile, I took out the gun. It's 18 inches long. I put it down and cocked the mother-fucker. The one bullet is in the second hole and not ready for the chamber. He doesn't know if it's loaded or if it's a bluff. Am I bluffing? What do they know? One thing they know is I have a big mother-fucking gun. Never underestimate someone who's in that position. I kept the gun down and he looked at it and I said, 'I have six bullets and five are for you people.' He knew I was a suicider and he came back with the exact amount. As he counted, I also counted and put the gun away. I had the gun out for three minutes and he took the briefcase and got the money in three minutes. The job took exactly 52 minutes and most of the time was taken counting the money. The cops didn't understand why I did that. The cops expect the 30 second job — in, out, and gone. Those guys get what 30 seconds will buy.

"I wanted to see if it was marked or not. I was also looking for bandit packs. There are spots on the money because it's greased. After I counted the money, I got up and shook hands with the manager and walked out. I never touched a thing except the ashtray and I put it in my pocket before I left. I used the word 'we' in my note to give the impression that I am not alone; they have to believe I'm not alone.

"I was arrested three months after. The police didn't have a clue who I was. The girl I was living with gave me to the cops for the reward money. She didn't know I did it, but she put two and two together and figured it out. She caught me counting the money but didn't ask questions. The papers had three pages of publicity on that robbery because it had never been done before. It was on T.V. and the radio.

They called me '*Filou,*' someone who passes through the gate. Nobody knew it was me. My uncle was reading the newspapers saying, 'This is how you work. This is a professional.' When he found out it was me he was impressed. I was only 25 and before that the people in the underworld treat me like I'm a punk. Now I get respect. More that that, they look up to you. The job offers I got!

"They had a picture of me from the bank. I changed my appearance for the robbery and the picture didn't look at all like me. My uncle didn't recognize me. She turned me in because I was getting tired of her and she knew it. I didn't know at first who put it on me. I got some people to look into it for me. When you've got money and contacts you can find these things out. That's the kind of broad she is. She was arrested for prostitution and she turned me in to get herself off and to claim the reward money. I had just taken a shower. She had just hung up the phone. I was getting dressed and my gun was underneath my clothes. The cops flew in from everywhere. I reached for the gun and the gun's not there. It had been moved.

"The police talked to me in the car. I smiled and didn't say a word. The Hold-Up Squad tried talking to me. I said, 'Fuck off' and smiled at them. They started getting rough — the usual. They kicked my balls in. I still have marks on my wrists from the handcuffs. That was over five years ago. My feet aren't the same. They're gentleman. I love them. You know what I'm saying? They're doing a job. I have nothing against them. I'm not really bitter. I'm philosophical. I'm not in love with them, but reverse the situation... [tails off].

"They wrote up statements and put my initials on them. But they didn't try to introduce them in court. They had a witness say she recognized my bottom lip. How can you regognize somebody from their bottom lip?

"I don't understand why I got hooked up with a hooker. It's their job to know how to attract men — they're professionals. She makes nice eyes, shows her ass and the next thing you know you're in bed with her. The broad sees something in me. I know I'm not beautiful, but the broads still flood in. This broad is not dead and I would not kill her. In fact I stopped others from doing so. But she's paranoid and hospitalized in a psychiatric ward.

"I was married before and fine until my wife left. At the lowest point in my life, when I was in jail, she quits on me. I'm going to have problems with women when I get out because I've been betrayed by broads. I've been turned into the cops by a broad and betrayed by my wife.

"I didn't do this robbery for the money. I did it to prove a theory to someone; to show that it could be done and to win an argument. For me $50,000 is fuck-all. To me that's pocket change. I didn't need the money. Money is not a problem for me. I was doing well. My problem is going to be in adapting myself. I will have problems getting along with people — their reactions, yellow hair, pink hair. I haven't seen that. They didn't have those things when I went in. Have you heard the song by Queen called 'Criminal Mind?' Do you remember the line, 'Ask anybody who knows me if I'm really bad. I am'? When I get out it'll be, 'Surprise! Surprise!' Nobody will look at me crooked, believe me. Somebody tries to talk to me, 'Take a hike. Take a fucking walk. Are you so important to think you can talk to me?'

"It's going to take control for me to succeed — control the rage. Your self-control is the most important thing in doing a job. If you lose that you've lost yourself. I feel that I might lose control outside. I don't drink or take drugs. I've had lots of time to think in prison. I've got a lot of hate, anger, bitterness — it increases day to day. I'm dangerous to society. Guys who I did good, they spit on me. In past days I would walk away; today I would kill. If I'm going to be treated as a low life, then let it be. Pray you don't meet someone like me on the street. Don't even look at me funny. It will take a couple of years of routine for me to get used to being back in society. I last saw the street four and a half years ago. I've had no passes, no breaks, nothing for four years and six months. I will have been in five years when my release date comes up. I'm trying to develop faith that I'm going to see better days.

"Banks are out of the question. They're peanuts. I'm not going to face big time. I've had enough. As you get older you ask yourself, 'Do I want to spend my life in jail?' When you're younger you don't calculate the risks.

"I have no shame for what I did. I didn't harm anyone. I never shot anybody or intended to shoot anybody. I had one bullet in the gun for myself. I am not out to hurt anyone. That's a big difference. People think that all of us in prison are the same. It's the punks who kill for $150 who give us a bad name. The rapists and the child molesters are treated better in the courts than the armed robber — it's sick. People are more attached to their money than to their soul. I don't do grocery stores and steal from the poor people who are just trying to make a living. Banks have insurance and they rob people. If you think the robber is bad, take a look at what the banks steal from ordinary people."

French Canadian

This 34-year-old man is well known among the underworld as a highly professional armoured vehicle robber. He was cooperative in the interview but would not allow the use of a tape recorder. He had recently been convicted of three armoured vehicle robberies totalling over $250,000, of which only $32,000 was recovered. A newspaper article reported that he acted as a lookout while two other men disarmed and robbed two Brink's guards of $100,000. Two months before, he and two other unknown men robbed two Brink's guards of $153,344. "[The offender] was sentenced to 15 years after pleading guilty to three counts of robbery, the use of a handgun during one heist, and trying to escape custody. He also faces 17 robbery charges in Montreal."

"I left Montreal to rob an armoured vehicle because guards in the rest of Canada have their guns in their hands. In Quebec they have their guns in their hands. I wouldn't do one if I had to hurt someone or if I thought there would be violence. I don't want to shoot anybody. There is no need to hurt people if you know what you're doing. You have the advantage because you can surprise them. You're the boss. They're not expecting it. It's only kids who don't know what they're doing who'll kill.

"There have been a few where guards have been shot dead from behind. They were killed cold-blooded. That's unnecessary. I never did a Brinks in Quebec because they have guns in their hands. I wouldn't trust a partner not to kill. Guards shouldn't carry their guns in their hands. They get killed because of that. I don't want to be up for murder. I don't want to hurt people. I have trouble trusting a partner not to kill. If you're going to do one, why not do one with their guns in their holsters? You pay the same price in jail for doing a Brinks and getting $100,000 as you do for a bank and picking up $5000. So you might as well do a Brinks, it's just as easy.

"It's psychological. It's communication. In doing a Brinks I get very close to the guard. I move right up beside him and put my gun in his face and tell him to freeze. At the same time I put my hand on his gun to prevent him from grabbing it and then I disarm him. There's nothing he can do about it. Don't give him any space. If you give him a few feet he may make a move or he may start thinking, but not if you take his gun. I don't make him get on the floor, that's only in the movies. You just lose time. I just walk away. I don't like to yell. I don't say a word. You don't have to.

"It's fast, only ten seconds to do a Brinks and it only takes two guys because there are only two guards. Three or four guys give you that extra confidence, but you don't need it. You can even do it alone, but it's harder. With three you have to split it three ways and there's no need.

"Banks are stupid. I did a lot of banks. I've been convicted for about ten. When I was 17 I had just got out of the orphanage. I had spent 16 years there, but that's not the reason I robbed banks. I did it for the money. I saw an article in a newspaper where a guy in a suit went into a bank and went to the teller and took the cash. I was only 17, but I figured that if this guy could do it, then I could do it. I can't do frauds because I don't have the nerve. Brinks and banks are not dangerous if you know what you're doing — banks are boring. I began doing banks with security guards because there is much more money in the tills if there's security in the bank. I'd disarm the guard and ask for the money or jump the counter and take the money. I wouldn't use a partner. A partner is needed to give yourself confidence. I don't need it. If you can't do it alone, you shouldn't do it. I've done over 200 banks and I've never had a problem. If there's even a small chance of trouble, I won't go. There has never been any violence in my robberies. It's not true that bank robbers are violent. It's more dangerous to do a corner store because you're robbing people of their money and they do things you're not expecting.

"It goes fast, very fast. I may stay 30 to 45 seconds. I don't yell or scream in the bank, I don't like that. I'm very sneaky. I'll approach the guard and hide my gun. I'll get very close and then disarm him. I'll sometimes jump the counter if people see what's happening or if the guard makes a noise or commotion. Otherwise I'll sneak around the counter.

"I start counting from the time the tellers know what's happening. Often they don't know anything is going on until I'm right beside them and I reach into the till and they see the gun. Then they'll be surprised and jump back and I'll go through the tills and throw the money in the bag and hop the counter and leave. I don't talk, I just take the money. They know what I'm doing so why talk? I don't look at them either because they'll cry and panic. Many of the women are at their desks and they don't even know it's a robbery. Customers don't even know, just the one being served. I have the gun in my hand and the customer will look at the gun and the money. They'd like to rob the bank, but they don't have the nerve. Sometimes I go through the tills and only the tellers know it's a robbery. Then I walk out calmly. I just walk, I don't run.

"I used to drop the guard on the floor — the first two times. I don't do that now. The first time I did that I jumped the counter and he didn't even stay on the floor. I looked over and he was hiding behind a desk. I made him come out and lie on the floor again. Now I don't even bother. He can do what he wants to do. It's a piece of cake. I take his gun and then I don't even care what he's doing. Someday I'll hit a guard who'll have a gun hidden and he'll shoot me, but that's the chance I take.

"Guards will sometimes reach down and grab your hand instinctively. It's a normal reaction, you have to expect that. You have to prepare yourself mentally. They're there to protect. It's their job. If they make a move you just push the gun into their ribs and say, 'Hey!' It's robbers who aren't mentally prepared who act savagely. You have to think about what they might do. You're human and so are they. Put yourself in their place. If you think about it then you'll know how to handle it if it happens.

"Some robbers just go in and they don't think and then they panic and they shoot. There's a young guy in here for killing a teller. He didn't know what he was doing when he went into that bank.

"I did a Brinks one time and the guard had a pellet gun! He's crazy! A fucking dummy! That's stupid! People don't know he doesn't have a real gun. He could get shot for carrying a pellet gun. Maybe he doesn't like violence, but that's stupid. I hope he quits his job before somebody kills him.

"I've never had any problems with guards, but some guards are very proud. They want to be a hero. There was one guard that I know was wild and special. This guard, I knew he would be a problem, I wanted him not for the money but for the challenge. I meant to do him many times, but I always backed out. I backed out 10 times. I was sure he'd react. He was special this guard. I was right because I read in the papers that he was killed. That was two years ago. He was a big guard and I wanted to do him just to see if I could, but I said to myself, 'Why try to prove something to myself? Why look for a problem?' That's why I didn't do it. After I read that he was killed I said to myself, 'I was right.' They had his picture in the paper.

"I learned how to rob banks from reading the newspapers and got some ideas, but mainly I just thought it out. I've done 13 years in prison and in a place like this you'll find three or four guys, that's all, who have done Brinks. We talk. It's a job. I'd get up at 7:00 A.M. and go out each day and check and check and check. I'd do this for three months or more. I don't do them if they have guns in their hands. I watch their approach. The getaway is the important thing. I check the amount of money they're carrying and the places they go. In some cities you can use underground shopping malls to get away. If you go to a place where people wear suits, then you wear a suit. If you're in an area where people are dressed like bums, then you dress like a bum too. For a disguise, you can get a phoney mustache or fake tattoos. You can get a make-up kit from a drama store.

"My problem is that I don't have enough discipline. You need discipline to do this. You can't go out to clubs every night because that's stupid. There might be a police raid and you're arrested and then they know you're in town. Or somebody who knows you sees you in town and then when something goes down they're looking for you. You should be straight for the whole time. I always go straight on the job. I don't drink or take drugs. On the weekend I'll go and party, but I shouldn't even do that. I don't have enough discipline. I wish I had more discipline and I wouldn't be in here now. I would have done it better and I'd be rich.

"I didn't want to take the cab. It was stupid! Stupid! My partner wanted to go to Montreal right away and celebrate and we took a taxi and were caught on the highway. I knew we shouldn't do it and I could have said no, but instead I said, 'Okay, let's go.' No discipline. If we had stuck to our original plan to hold up for a few days or go in the opposite direction, we wouldn't have been caught. They knew it was Montreal guys so we should have gone in the opposite direction.

"I don't have discipline with money either. I was stupid, stupid, stupid. A businessman cannot be a holdup artist and a holdup artist cannot do business. Once I spent over $400,000 in eight months. I thought I was Robin Hood, I was giving it away to everybody — to anybody. You've got a lot of friends when you've got a lot of money. Maybe I was trying to buy friends, I don't know. Maybe it has something to do with my coming from an orphanage. It's a problem I have to work out for myself. I've spent a lot since I've started crime. I'd buy cocaine and give it away. I'd get $400-a-night hotel rooms. I'd send some coke and hash to my friends in jail. I have no money left. I spent it all."

The Stopwatch Gang

Age 33, this man was a member of the notorious five-man crew from Ottawa known as the "Stopwatch Gang." The crew was highly professional and robbed banks and armoured vehicles in Canada and the United States.

"I'm convicted for Brinks, that and the airport robbery, which was supposed to be a Brinks pick-up, and some bank robberies. I go whereever the money is and where the danger isn't, if possible. Strangely enough, when we were in the United States, the F.B.I. thought we were Vietnam veterans robbing banks and all we were doing was robbing banks like any 18-year-old kid in Montreal. They called us 'The Stopwatch Gang' because on some scores I had a stopwatch hanging upside down from around my neck and set to buzz at 60 seconds or 90 seconds. The F.B.I. thought we were veterans of Vietnam and were militarily trained. It's just that 99 percent of the bank robberies in the U.S. are kids with heroin habits, a note in his hand, and a finger in his pocket. And here we were three, four, five people with automatic weapons jumping over counters.

"Then one day a funny thing happened. The American newspapers did a big thing about the this Stopwatch Gang robbing banks in Southern California in full hoods and automatic weapons. So in comes another gang and they decide to immitate us. The police cornered them and a sheriff's deputy was killed and they killed two bank robbers. The F.B.I.'s having big interviews on television saying, 'We got the Stopwatch Gang,' and then the next morning they said, 'Oops, we have another group, also very dangerous bank robbers, but we didn't get the Stopwatch Gang.' These guys play rough. We left California that week.

"I've been on the run four times. You are an outlaw in the pure sense of the word. Being a fugitive means that you cut all ties and you leave everything behind. The three of us were on the run, outlaws. We were non-drug-using outlaws. We drifed to the U.S. to escape from the heat of our prison escapes and rented a house in Arizona. I had a house up the canyon, an airplane, a car, a wife, and a dog. This was our sanctuary and our base for doing things. We were doing a lot of robberies and spending a lot of money. That's the main reason why I love to steal — I love to spend money. One of my partners wouldn't spend a dime to see an earthquake. I like to spend $200 on a shirt, but not Roger Dangerfield. We did a lot of spur of the moment things like take a boat trip down the Colorado River, go to L.A. to a party, travel to a Caribbean island.

"Here's what happens when you hit the bank. You use your opening line, 'This is a holdup. Don't anybody move,' or whatever. Everything that is happening in the bank immediately shuts off. It's like crashing a big vase in a room. Automatically you stop all sound, all conversation, machinery, clanging drawers. Everything stops, dead quiet. You're standing there and full of adrenalin. I'll go a little Freudian now. A gun does something to you. I think there is something to his theory of it being an extension of your manhood. You put the sucker in your hand and slam a clip home, holy fuck you're invincible! That and the adrenalin in your body — it's a shot!

"What we do generally is go into a town, rent a car, pick up a map, and go through the Yellow Pages. We find the banks and go out and look at them. Some are obviously impossible and some look so good you'd think the architect had us in mind. Some have great back alleys and corner ways and little cubby holes where you can dress and undress. Some have nearby an underground parking lot where you can switch cars. It's all things you learn only by doing. Next you look up all the police stations to check where they are in relation to the good possibilities. Then you watch for Brinks pick-ups and get to know when the cash is coming in and coming out. Some things you have to practice. You time yourself dressing and undressing in a car and try to figure who can get dressed, who can't, and who's kit is this. You get four grown men in a car changing clothes, 'Where's my fucking shoes?' You only do that once or twice and you learn that everybody has kits and everybody practices.

"Bank robberies aren't too complicated. There are only so many variables you are dealing with. You get an apartment A and you set up. You get your kit down, your gear, what you're going to wear, where you're changing, where you're taking it off, where you are splitting the money, and all that. From A you get in the car and go rob and come back to B and that is basically it. It is not a complicated sort of thing. Usually, before I'll rob a bank, I'll open an account and a safety deposit box. I'll go in and know I'm going to take this bank. I'll love it. It's got a lot of the right things. I'll talk to the staff. I love the management trainees, they're the ones that give you your safety deposit box and you can pump them for a lot of information. A Brinks arrives and you say, 'Geez, is that all real money?' 'That's nothing, you should see what gets taken out of here on Thursday.' 'Is that right?' We went back and, sure enough, we did take a lot of money out of there on Thursday [chuckle]. It's a lot of fun sometimes.

"One thing you have to watch for is a police car in the vicinity. A quick alarm and a car shows up. Although usually, with no back-up, he'll wait before he comes in alone. One time I was leaving a bank, coming across the parking lot, and this cop is driving in and there are those speed bumps. There's four of us in the car and I'm in the back seat behind the driver and the cop pulls into the parking lot. We've just done a Wells Fargo and you can see them in the window, they're screaming as we're leaving. I'm like this, cradling my gun in the back seat. These people in the window are pointing to us in the car. Now remember this cop is coming to investigate a bank robbery and here's four guys in a car leaving the scene and we're about to pass within a foot of one another. Our car is moving very slow, the window in the back seat only rolls down half way. The cop car is moving slow. I'm thinking I'm going to have to go over the top with this .357 close to my chest. I'm thinking, 'I'm going to have to shoot a cop!' We pass by slow, real slow, and his face is two feet from mine. This cop drives by us and he keeps both hands on the wheel and he is staring straight ahead. He knew who was in that car. He pretended not to see us just like we pretended not to see him. Everyone in our car was just as terrified as he was, of course, and we passed each other not more than a couple of feet apart. We pulled away just like we were customers leaving the bank. He went roaring up to the bank and it was like, 'What's going on? Where are these guys?' It was weird, that's what it was. That was a trip. I don't care who you are, you don't want to shoot people. Same with the policeman, they're not the policemen you see on T.V. They're people and they have a wife at home with curlers, kids, and snowmobiles. That's their life. Being a police officer is a job, and the idea of a shoot-out probably terrifies them as much as it does me. We always try to hold violence down to a minimum and apply everything we can not to have to take somebody out. We'll pass on a lot of scores because of the possibility of violence.

"I've been in a couple of shoot-outs and I was shot once, but I can't tell you that everything went into slow motion and I answered fire over here and did three of these rolls and came out like Charles Bronson over here. Fuck that. They're shooting and I'm shooting back and screaming to my partner, 'Get the fuck out! Where's the car, the guns? Let's go. Get the fuck out of here!' Bullets are slamming into the car at 3200 feet a second. Fear is what the fuck happens. Charles Bronson my ass. Guys who tell you they enjoy it, they're telling you an out-and-out lie. What they enjoy is cutting up the money afterwards, which is what I enjoyed too. And I went through a few stages of doing them. I went through the terrified, then the cockiness and the arrogance, until a couple got whistled by me. A couple of fracas inside of a bank took the wind out of my sails. I've been through it all and back, and when I'm on my way to a bank robbery I'm scared. When I say fear, I don't go in wearing it. It's a very important thing to show that you're in control. But for the actual moment of being in the bank with the gun in my hand I'm prepared 100 times better than just about anybody that you've probably spoken to. I've been there and I'm fucking terrified, and I hate being there.

"Doing a Brinks is like landing an airplane, you're okay until you're a foot from the ground. Anything that happens with a Brinks is going to happen in an instant. It's a matter of being good enough, your partners are covered, and having the guard well enough covered to prevent that. You've got to get close enough to disarm them. You can't be desperate and do a Brinks — a hand to mouth thing — because you'll cut corners. You'll try to take them on days when it is not quite right because you're in a hurry. If you're patient you'll see they are fairly regular, and as much as they'd like to change their routes and habits, they can't. They only have so much time in a working day and they have to come to the source of the money — the bank. They can come at 10:00 A.M. or at 2:00 P.M., but they have to come.

"There are a lot of places where they become inattentive or security breaks down. Armoured vehicle companies are always looking to cut manpower — one less set of wages. I might look at the same truck in five different spots. I might look at them on different days in different spots. I might work backwards and say, 'Beautiful, the guy is alone here and we can get out here.' Or here we go, another spot, 'The truck is blind, we can get dressed here, park the car here, okay, we got him.' 'Oh fuck, the money isn't right. The guy is only taking out $35,000. We'll pass.' 'Here's another one. Oh no, we can't do it. The truck can see you from here.' An on and on and on it goes. A process of elimination. I will look at 40 or 50 scores usually before I find one that's right. You do your homework and you stay at it and develop it and pretty soon you will find a way. Find some small city with a lot of blue-collar workers and you'll probably find a quarter of a million dollars being moved around somewhere by Brinks. These people in San Diego had never had a Brinks robbery before we walked off with $283,000.

"Once I looked at taking six guards, four on one side of the truck with shotguns and two inside. They were guarding $25 million dollars, but you are talking an 'A Team' or 'Mission Impossible.' You are talking a military operation, spending tens of thousands of dollars, but I still think it could have been done without anyone being killed. It could be done real easy if you want to open fire, ambush them, but that's never been our style. By the time you're really seriously looking at a Brinks you have usually been at least moderately successful at robbing banks. You have to have a crew, you have to be able to get up 6:00 or 7:00 or 8:00 A.M. every morning, Monday to Friday. You have to be able to go to work and you have to have the money to do it and to live comfortably in the meantime — and be patient and not partying until you've got that money. It's a lot of work and persistence and discipline. The imagination comes in later. Usually, if you follow someone and you are diligent enough, you'll spot a security breakdown. They fall into a routine and they overlook something and that is when you make your move. They roll up, park their truck, two guys come out with shotguns, bring the money into the bank, stroll out, slam the truck door, and drive away. In the meantime, 62-year-old Mrs. Willobee who has just signed for it is finishing off her egg salad sandwich before she puts it into the vault. So there is $280,000 sitting on the counter just inside the bank. It happens.

"The old fashioned bank robber seems to be disappearing because there is no money in it. Willie Sutton robbed banks because that's where the money was — no longer true. Cash is disappearing in our society. Drugs are a more lucrative enterprise. I can name 25 bank robbers who are now selling hash."

Author's Note: Stephen Reid has published a book about his adventures, was married in prison, received his parole, and now lives on Vancouver Island with his wife and two children. For additional information on the Stopwatch Gang, see Reid's book, Jack Rabbit Parole. *Greg Weston's* The Stopwatch Gang *is an accurate and detailed portrayal of the crew's early days and final arrest. See also Desroches'* Force and Fear: Robbery in Canada *for an interview with one of the five members of the gang (pp. 157-159). For a description of Stephen's wedding and honeymoon, see "Maximum Security" by Susan Musgrave,* Vancouver Magazine, *December 1986:142-145.*

Montreal Pro

This offender was convicted in a million-dollar armoured vehicle robbery. Since he is appealing this conviction he spoke cautiously about the crime. The police file describes the incident as follows: "The suspect with his co-accused and a third person [unidentified] went into the [department] store and robbed two armoured vehicle guards during a large cash pickup. Suspects used wigs, moustaches, hats, and other clothing. Armed with

> revolvers, they made the guards kneel and handcuffed both. Handguns were then taken from the guards."

"I'm 55-years-old and the judge gave me 30 years — 25 for the truck and five for the weapon. If I don't get parole, the earliest I can get out is 20 years from now with good behaviour. I'll be 75 years old. He also prohibited me from carrying a gun for the next ten years. How the fuck am I going to carry a gun in here? Can you imagine the stupidity of the thing? The prosecutor was asking for life, but since I didn't shoot nobody the judge says I'll give you 25 and five. Thanks judge. The court was full of reporters and the judge made a big speech.

"I have a long criminal record. I was a thief when I was a kid and as far back as I can remember. When I was 17 I got a penitentiary term for breaking into a house. In prison I met some people who took me along to do some banks. Then I got my own clique and we did banks, then cigarette and booze vans. We had a warehouse and we had people who would buy the whole load. I've done a lot of time. After my first bit I was out three years, went back in, I was out another three years, back in, out about four years, in, out five years. On the last one before this we robbed a big payroll and met up with the cops. There was a chase with a shootout and I got 14 years for my part in that. I was on parole when they picked me up for this one. I had been out five years.

"I'm appealing this conviction so technically I didn't do it, but I can tell you what the guard testified in court. This guard is 6'2" and 200 lbs and someone my size is supposed to have taken this guy's gun, thrown a gun in his face, turned him around, thrown him on the floor, handcuffed his hands behind his back, and all in 30 seconds. This took place in the department store after the guards have made the pickup. They walk back through the store down these aisles filled with clothing. One is pushing a pushcart and the other is guarding the money. But his gun is holstered. My co-accused is standing at a pay phone. The guards walk down the aisle when I'm supposed to have come up behind them and yelled, 'Freeze.' So they turn around and the guy at the phone blocks their path, grabs the guard's gun, and they're sandwiched. The guards are put on the floor and a third guy is supposed to have taken the bags. I was convicted, my co-accused was convicted, and the third guy got away.

"Let me explain it. If the guards carry the guns in their hands, you've got to be ready for a shootout. Here the guy's got his piece holstered and he's got someone aiming right at him. He hasn't got a fucking chance. It's real easy. You've got two men to take care of two men. In a bank there are more variables because you don't know who might walk in.

"The guards have guns, but it's no big thing. They haven't got it in their fucking hand. If they've got it in their hand that's a different thing, you must be ready to shoot. If you figure there's enough money there to go for it, that's it. Another thing, when you case the place, it's always the same two guards who go to the same place and you look at them. You see the way they go and you get a certain feeling. You know whether he is going to shit or go for his piece. I feel that I can read a guy pretty fair. It's instinct. You get a feeling that if you point a gun at him, you know what he is going to do. The element of surprise is the biggest thing. It doesn't matter what you say to him as long as you make it loud so they can hear.

"It's only human nature. It's not their fucking money. If they got a chance they're gonna shoot you. I know that. But you don't give them the chance. You're not there to look for trouble, you're there to make a buck. Only a guy who has no brains is going to shoot a guard because it's putting heat on you. If you do a job, the police will come look at you for awhile and then another score will come up and they'll go away. If they happen to catch you, they catch you and that's all. Murder is different. Not only are they going to look ten times harder, they're going to work it forever. It is a different thing. If you go this far you have to be sure of your partner that he's not going to shoot someone foolishly.

"That's why a job like this takes time and a lot of work and it's got to be checked and re-checked. It takes from three to six months to set up a score like this one. From what I heard of this job it was found by luck. Somebody was going to look at another job and on the way they saw the truck stop so somebody got off the car and they checked it. They came back the next week and they checked it. That's how it went. You see the Brinks truck and you see the department store and you add it up.

"This took place in broad daylight in the store and they had no witnesses that could identify me. They didn't find no money, they didn't find no gun, they didn't find the third guy. The one guy who was at the phone left a fingerprint and he was arrested. First they put us under surveillance and this guy gave me $17,000 to go into the arcade business. So I'm on parole and I get picked up and I've got this money and I'm not going to say who gave it to me. The coppers say to me, 'You don't want to cooperate, you're on parole, you've got a record that fucking long, you're it. We are going to frame you.' They had me for 36 hours and said I never asked for a lawyer. I've been around all my life and I'm supposed to be involved in a million-dollar robbery and I won't ask for a lawyer?

"They said that an employee counted a pile of 10s and they put them in piles of 50. In one pile there is only 42 so she writes on the bill 42. I'm not denying that part because the money was given to me. The thing is that the guy gave me the goddamn money to go into the arcade business. They brought in other evidence. I don't live in that city, but I had an apartment there for awhile prior to the robbery. My brother-in-law jumped bail from Montreal and went there to hold up in my apartment. The police went to the apartment and they said they found a coat and a bullet in the coat. Now this armed guard said I was supposed to have a .38, same caliber gun as the bullet they found in the coat. The police said that they followed my co-accused for a week and that he met with me, but he never took the stand to testify against me. He gave me the money to go invest in the arcade business. He's got the money and I was going to manage it and we'll be 50-50 partners. Just the $17,000 was recovered.

"In my day we used to rob the bank and clean out every teller's cage. One guy used to check the vault to see if it was open and sometimes you'd get lucky. There'd be four or five of us and we'd get $50-$60,000, $75,000 if we got lucky. Tellers had $10-$12,000 in each cage, but now they have $1000-$1200. Now they've got exploding bandit packs and cameras; before, it was big gangs. We had a mob. We were five or six guys, but normally we'd rob a bank and we'd go two or three at the most. One guy would call me and I'd ask where it was and who was going. If a certain person was going I wouldn't go. One guy called my name during a bank robbery so I wouldn't work with him anymore. I was standing at the door and there were about 90 people on the floor of the bank. There was 11 teller's cages and I was giving signals, watching for cops, and watching these people on the floor. This fucking dummy is supposed to be in the vault and I felt somebody coming up beside me and I turned around and it's this guy and he said, 'Can I stay beside you?' and he says my fucking name! Well I wouldn't work with the bastard no more. It was an Italian district and nobody understood French so nothing happened.

"Another time it was a one-way street so we park the car right in the middle of the road. I get out with the machine-gun and stop all the traffic and the guys are in robbing the bank. We just blocked the street and I stand there so nobody moves. They hoot, hoot, hoot — all that shit. Then one guy lets out a big German shepherd and he comes and jumps at me and I gave him just two shots, and with his height and the bullets he flew over our car. The men they go in the car and I'm the last guy to get in so I should get the side seat. But this guy was so stunned because I shot the fucking dog that instead of moving to the middle so I can get in, I have to jump over him to get in the middle of the car. I had a brand new leather coat and I cut my coat because he was too dumb to move in the middle. That happened and after he called my name in the fucking bank I wouldn't work with him no more.

"I had another partner and he used to be perfect in the bank — real peppy. I didn't know he used to drink before the job and that was where he was getting his courage. One time we had this huge job to do — it would have been the biggest in the country. We had a big apartment and I was in charge. It wasn't my job, but I was the foreman because I had experience and I was kinda cool so this guy puts me in charge. I had five other guys with me and we stayed in this apartment all day 'cause the job was the next night. Nobody drank, nobody took dope, nobody took nothing. You had to be cold sober on that job because it was a big job. I didn't know that this guy used to drink and we were in a post office truck waiting for the Brinks truck and he was sweating. One guy in a forklift truck passed by in front so this guy said, 'He saw us! He saw us!' The driver was nervous too so he slammed the gas and the truck took off and the back door opened and the employees saw us. We were burned and missed that job on account of this guy.

"This job was perfect, but we missed it. We were in this post office truck in an underground tunnel in the building where the Brinks came in. The tunnel was a U-shape and there was no way for them to get out. We had them with their pants down. We just had to open the back of our truck with our machine-guns and they were there in front of us. In big jobs like that you always have somebody inside. We missed fourteen million dollars in old money that was on its' way to be burned — not even traceable. It would have been the job of the century.

"Things are a lot different now. When I was younger, it was easy to rob a bank in a small town because you could go through the goddam bush and you'd get away from them. The coppers didn't have helicopters and shit like that and they didn't go into the bush. They just circled around the goddam bush and that was it. Like today they go into the bush with dogs and you can't lose them in the bush.

"You know, I've never been convicted of robbing a bank. Payrolls, Brinks, and other things but no banks. I've been a thief all my life. Some guys steal to buy big cars, but it's not my trip. I never drove a car in my life, never had a driver's licence. I like to eat and go out. I'm a tripper. I like to be around people, party and have a good time. In my head, it's Christmas seven days a week and when I was out I always could afford it. I lived well — too well maybe. I'd go to a club every night, dress well, eat well. At one time I had an apartment in New York and I'd fly in for a few weeks, come back for a job, and fly back to New York. I knew people and every night I used to smoke up and go out to a jazz club.

"The last time I was out I tried selling drugs. I had a good contact and I was getting good stuff very cheap and I was making a good living out of it. There is a lot of money in drugs, and people in the past who would have done a bank are going into drugs. Less time if you get caught, less strain on the person, more money. But there's no excitement. Some people just keep in it for the challenge."

Author's Note: This offender was unsuccessful in appealing his conviction and sentence. Police recovered only $17,000 of the cash taken in the robbery. An interview with the arresting officer describes the trial.

Pierre put on a good show in court. It was a jury trial and the defence didn't call a single witness and didn't present a case. The Crown's case included overwhelming evidence. Pierre fired his lawyer on the last day of trial and was allowed to make his own presentation to the jury. It was the best acting job I've ever seen in my life — a one-and-a-half hour presentation. He was constantly instructed by the Judge that he couldn't say something, but he would already have said it and the jury heard.

Pierre didn't take the witness box — he simply addressed the jury and got away with a lot. He made a passionate plea and said that he had never done anything in his life — that he would die in jail. 'I'm a sick man.' The jury was out for a long time and came back with some ridiculous questions. We figured there was a hold-out because all the jury members looked down at one female member. They came back later and she was crying. They delivered a guilty verdict and the judge invited the jury to sit in court for the submission for sentence and three women took him up on it. I was glad to see it because I knew they felt sorry for him.

The Crown asked for a life sentence and explained that Pierre had a lengthy record including convictions for numerous robberies and one in which a citizen on the street was shot. Two of the jury members were crying. I was watching them. I was upset that after so much time, cost, and effort that we almost lost it on an 11th-hour passionate plea to the jury. Everyone realizes that you occasionally get victimized by juries. It happens.

Brinks

Age 28, this man was partners with "French Canadian" whom he refers to as "M" throughout the interview. Three out-of-town bandits planned and executed an armoured vehicle robbery and escaped with $100,000. Two of the culprits were arrested in a taxi travelling along a busy highway to another city six hours away. A suspicious police officer pulled them over and discovered some of the stolen money and two handguns used in the holdup. A newspaper article reports the officer as stating: "The first thing that struck me was that it was unusual to see a cab on this highway so far from the city it came from. I wondered if it had been stolen. I began to follow it, but the thing that made me really suspicious was the amount of interest the two passengers were paying to me. They kept turning around looking at me. A description of two men wanted in connection with the robbery had been broadcast a number of times on the police radio. It seemed to fit the two guys in the cab so I called for back-up and pulled them over."

"M was giving me money and I was spending it. He asked me if I wanted in on a big score and I says, 'Yes.' I was at the halfway house and I had a job, but it paid nothing. And he was giving me money so I could pay the telephone bill, be a little bit more at ease, and sometimes buy myself a little bit of drugs because I use them. I had done banks before so I knew this thing was — I don't want to say easy but ...[pause]... let me put it this way, anybody that's going to have a gun in his face, he's going to agree with you. Put a gun in my face and I'm going to agree with everything you want from me. That's the kind of easy it is — if you call that easy. So when the time came my heart was beating hard and I was scared shitless, but it went pretty easy I guess. Fast too, faster than buying a pack of cigarettes.

"I wasn't expecting any problem, but because it's such a busy street and the cops drive past every two or three minutes, then something could happen just by chance. The thing about a Brinks is that it's a cracker-jack box. You don't know how much you're going to get. I was figuring $50,000 to half a million. Turned out to be $100,000. I gave 15 percent to M because he planned it and I owed him some money so I ended up with $31,000 as my cut. I never even met my partner before. I knew his face from prison. We did time in the same joint years before, but I never knew his name. I don't think he was ever caught. I haven't heard from him since.

"The Brinks guards were coming from the street into the bank. My accomplice and I were in the hotel waiting for a call from M telling me that they're coming. My partner was sitting on the toilet because he had to shit. He said he couldn't go through with it — he was scared. When M saw the Brinks on the street he gave me the call saying they're coming! So we run, and we got to the bank at the same time the guards came in. I walk in front of them and then I figure that I couldn't do it because it's all mixed up in the middle. So I've got to let the mix-up release. That's what I figure at the time because I was going to get the gun out and grab them. I just walked away and come back and that's when I grabbed them, when they split. Because together it was making a mess and I figured that I couldn't do anything at that time.

"It was too crowded in the middle. Customers and guards at the same time. It was too crowded and I had to let them split. One stays at the door and the other carries the money to the vault. That's the one I grabbed, the one with the money, and told him to freeze. I grabbed his gun and put it in my belt and grabbed the bags.

"When I came in the bank I came in another door and my partner came in behind the guards. That's when it was too crowded and my partner wasn't ready and he wasn't even looking at me. He was — I don't know — he was trying to get in and trying to get out at the same time. He was too slow I guess. I don't know. He went past the guards, maybe about five feet, and began playing that he was filling out a cheque. So when I turned around to look at him and he says, 'What's going on?' I says, 'Just go at it, right.' Because the other one had his back to him, so that's when I started to walk fast to get mine so we can get both at the same time. We just looked at one another and we agreed with our eyes on the move first. When he saw me start to walk towards the guard that's when he started towards his man.

"I had to turn my back on his guard. Then I got the idea to drop the Adidas bag I was carrying for the money. It had four metal pins on the bottom. When I dropped it, it made some noise and I expected the guard to look because of the noise. See, I heard about this robbery in prison — maybe it was a movie or maybe it was real, I don't know — somebody told me about it in prison and I remembered it. Two Brinks guards are in an elevator and the door opens and a box of ping-pong balls falls on the floor and catches their attention. Somebody had told me the story.

"It incidently came to me that if I drop my bag, the guard will look and in the meantime my partner will have time to put his gun on him. That's exactly what happened. I was worried about my partner because if he doesn't get his guard, I get shot. That morning M tells me that this guy never did a robbery in his life. So when I passed by the guard that's why I wasn't sure to grab them right away because this guy wasn't there. He was there, but he was not there — he wasn't ready. He was five feet away from the guard and I said to myself, 'How is he going to grab his gun?' If he takes his gun out and he's five feet away, the guard will see him and will take his gun out too. So I couldn't figure out how he's going to do it — how I would do it. When I see him over there I says to myself, 'He's not going to make it. I'm going to get shot.' That's why M was there, in case anything went wrong.

"The Brinks guard is near the door and my partner is beside him at five feet. The other guard is walking and I'm about 20 feet back. So I started to walk fast and I dropped the bag. The other guard will wonder why the fuck I'm leaving the bag there. By that time my partner can grab his gun. I just left it there. I had to walk fast and faster to catch the guy with the money because it was kind of far and I didn't want to run. I just wanted to keep it peaceful. When I grabbed his gun I grabbed mine at the same time, and by the time he found out what was going on and he turned I put the gun in his face. I wanted him to see the bullets and the barrel. I didn't touch him with it, I just put it in his face so he could see the gun. It was a Brinks gun from a previous robbery and he would know that this gun was real. I just wanted to scare the guy, I didn't want to hurt him. I wanted him to cooperate and that's why I wanted him to see the bullets, that they were true, and that he can't mess up. It was a Brinks gun and they use all the same guns — .357 depending how cowboy they are.

"He wanted to give me a shot, but he didn't want to give me a shot. It was a nervous reaction. He was just trying to protect himself and he was scared. And that's when I got mean and told him to freeze. Then he realized that nobody will hurt him. He was nervous. I was not there — I mean I was like a robot, I was on automatic. I was going for one thing. As soon as I step into the bank I stop thinking. Then, when I saw it was not possible, I started to think again. Then, when I saw it was possible to do it, I stopped thinking — I just went for it. I was feeling scared before, but during the robbery I'm not scared while I do something. But when I get out of the car to go into the bank, I'm shaking like hell. My legs shake, I can't stand up. I can hardly stand up when I get out of the car — then I can hardly walk — make the first step. But when the first step is done and I got the first four or five steps done, then I'm going. I'm going like a routine on a machine. I'm just going. I've got the handle on the bank door and I'm going in like on automatic. I jump the counter and I grab the money. I go out on automatic too. I get in the car and I start to shake. Only afterwards do I think, 'Hey, what's just happened is dangerous! I could get caught for this or hurt or anything.' That's what I'm thinking after, but on the moment when I'm doing it I don't think I could get killed. It doesn't come to me to think. I don't know because it is decided I guess. I am going to do it so I just wave everything away. I just keep up my end.

"But to do this I need to tell myself for the whole week ahead, 'I'm going to do a Brinks.' For a whole week I had to put it in my head and M had to drill me to do it. It's as simple as — it's harder to buy a pack of cigarettes than doing this. It takes more time: 'What kind do you want? Filter or plain?' This is just mechanical.

"He had his hands on the cart so I grabbed his gun and I had mine to his side so if he turned I just push it into his face. I don't know, maybe I'm really like this, into crime. I don't think I am, but it seems to be easy when I do that and everything else I do seems to be so hard. I find that easy. They keep their guns in their holster so they can't be faster than you. You make the move.

"After I had his gun, I bent down to pick up the money and there was a box. I didn't know at the time what was in the box, it was kind of heavy. I was stupid. I was thinking it could be gold or something valuable. So I just picked it up as an extra. I left other boxes there, but I wanted to grab this one to see what was inside. There was just one bag of money and the rest was boxes of change. Then my partner started to talk, telling the people in the bank to stay still, nobody is going to be hurt. If he hadn't said that I would be free today because nobody would have seen anything. Because when he started talking, everyone turned and everyone knows. He's telling everyone that we're committing a robbery, 'Nobody make a move and everything is going to be fine.' And he's telling me, 'Come on, just make it fast,' and I'm trying to pick up that box of change and it keeps slipping from my hand because it's big and my hand cannot get a good grip on it. And I'm trying to grip it and this guy is telling me to go faster and he's pulling open the door. And every time he tells me to go faster I drop the box because I'm trying to go faster. And I just grab the fucking box and I just went with it. I said, 'Let's go,' because I had the bag and I knew how much time we had. I'm doing this and he's got the door open and he's screaming at me to make it fast and he is about to leave me on the job! I still had to put the money in my Adidas bag.

"The bag is for the money, the gun is in my belt, my pants are a size bigger because I couldn't find a belt and so I had to grab the gun and the box and the bag and my gun and the Adidas bag. I tell this guy to hold the fucking bag. I don't want to leave the bag there because I got my prints on this bag. I almost left it there and I said, 'I can't do that. It's like leaving my name and address.' So I screamed at him, 'I'm not done yet.' And this guy is about to run. If this guy was cool and stayed there and waited for me the time I needed there wouldn't have be no problem. He could even have thrown the bag over and I could have used two hands to grab that box. In court nobody would have been able to identify me if he hadn't spoken.

"I had dyed my hair black and wore a bulletproof vest. My partner didn't wait for me, he took off and I had to walk by the guard. He just stood there. They have no guns so they cannot run after us. This partner, as soon as he seen me start to walk with the money, he starts to run. He didn't wait for me. We went into the subway and we looked back and seen the cop go into the bank. Then we were gone. We split the money back at the apartment and he went his way and me and M got arrested with the money and the vests. I got 15 years, but one was for an escape attempt with a hostage after we were arrested. So I got 14 years for the job.

"The robbery only took about 45 seconds. It was 15 seconds just to pick up the box of nickels [laughs]."

Flying Bandit

This inmate was interviewed in a penitentiary known as the Special Handling Unit (SHU), which houses prisoners whose behaviour within prison is considered to be dangerous to staff or other inmates. He is handcuffed and escorted by two guards who unlock the door and allow him into an adjacent cell. A small flap in the door opens, he shoves his wrist through, and the guards remove the cuffs. We are separated by a metal screen. The grate is too small to shake hands so we cross fingers instead. This man is well known among other inmates for dramatic prison escapes, a bank robbery in which he used a helicopter, an attempted escape from court, and his conviction for attempted murder of a judge.

"The helicoptor thing was a lot of fun. I didn't have to do that. I was going into the joint with the helicopter to get some guys out, but there was a strike going on in the place at the time. The prison was divided because guys on the inmate committee were interested in getting their transfers. Another group wanted to make a riot, my friends wanted to escape. Because of what was happening they couldn't be in the yard when they were supposed to be.

"I was on the run at the time, but I wasn't on a hobo trip like when you go over the fence and you ain't got a nickel in your pocket. Then you've got to cross somebody's back yard and look for a pair of pants your size [laughs]. I was established. You get out of prison and you want a gun, you can get a gun. I had a friend, he's not a partner, you could say he was a friend. He's an old bank robber only he don't do that no more. He's lost his nerve you might say. He has a wife and kids. He lives in the suburbs. He was going legitimate on the surface. He couldn't afford to go back to jail — not with his kids and wife and everything. But he was an expert driver and he had a good car, modern car, and he would drive me around the city. He was dressed like a businessman. He knew all the underworld figures. Anything you want he can get. You want a Cobra with silencers? I bought two of them, brand new and right out of the box. Identification? I had seven or eight complete sets when I was arrested. One guy would come up with birth certificates and somebody would have drivers' licences and social security cards. Everybody down the line gets paid. All this allows you to rent a car or apartment and pass if you get stopped by the police. I had three apartments. That's where the police picked me up, in an apartment I hadn't been to in three months.

"This was the first time I had ever been involved in organized crime. I found these guys who were big in the underworld, who had known me from inside. I had no trouble with contacts, with getting weapons or anything. I had a *carte blanche*. I was not familiar with the city, but I had a girlfriend who took me all over and showed me the subway system, underground concourses, how the buses run. I studied the city, watched it wake up in the morning, timed trains, how long it took to walk from here to there. I hired a young guy to do odd and end jobs for me — nothing dangerous. Chain a set of doors to block pedestrian traffic and create chaos after a robbery. Then he'd just disappear into the crowd.

"The helicopter escape plan fell through twice and I got fed up and robbed the bank. I had been casing banks all over the city and I was getting into some technological things. I had five police radios and they cost me $500 apiece and I got them wholesale. I had a friend who put the police crystals in them so I could pick up police messages. I had one of those little beepers so that I could get my messages and nobody knew where I was.

"I had picked out two banks to rob in shopping malls with the helicoptor. I stopped at one mall and I walked all the damn way. These damn malls all look the same from one side to the other. They're huge. I had to walk all the way through this mall to the other end and I get to the bank and there's one girl and one customer. I'm standing there with the handgun and my machine-gun sticking out of my bag. There was nothing to rob. For one teller? I went back to the helicopter and we took off again. Then I hit the other one and all the tellers were there.

"I had rented the helicoptor. I checked different companies in the Yellow Pages and drove around to see what they were like. They're on little properties outside the main airport and they don't have airport security — no metal detectors. The one I chose was side by side another company that had a forestry service. It was a little shack with two trailers set end to end with an office in between. There was a waiting room, and while you had your coffee you could look out the window at three big helicopters sitting there. And they had little models of them on the desk. I went there with cash, but they like to send you a bill and have you pay it afterwards. I told them I was Detective da da da. We had two police uniforms. 'This is my colleague, Sargeant so and so.' We were going someplace to pick up three juvenile girls and we're taking them back to the airport. My girlfriend is the female correctional officer who's going to accompany them. This is the story we gave. An ex-partner of mine found himself a telephone booth and pretended to be a Detective Sargeant. They asked for a phone number. This is how silly they are. I gave them the phone number and they ended up talking to my partner for 15 minutes. The guy believed him, agreed to the helicopter, and we were to leave at 7:15 in the morning.

"When I rented it I told them we were going to this place and I figured it would take three hours. I had three hours before he had to report back. I showed up the next morning and I had the girl with me. We took off and I waited a respectable time before I pulled the gun on him...like about five minutes [laughs]. I gave the guy a note. I didn't want to scare the pants off him by sticking a gun in his ear. I can't shoot him anyway or we'd all be goners. My girl took his earphones off and I handed him a note that said to land at a quarry we had picked out. Then I'd explain to him what we were going to do.

"He was cool as far as flying the helicopter, but he was pretty nervous, especially when I moved to the front seat and I started putting the machine-gun together. I'm going on his testimony at the trial where he said, 'When I was in Vietnam, I hoped that I'd never see a machine-gun again.' He was sure we were going to kill him. He was convinced without a doubt that he was going to die after this robbery because he was the only witness. I didn't have a disguise because there was no point. I'm on the run. I'm planning to leave the country. We never had it in mind to kill him. We landed in the quarry and I went out to put some police decals on the helicopter. The plan was that when we land in the prison yard the guards are going to think it's a police helicopter and they won't open fire.

"But the pilot made a break for it! He made a run for it across this field. Well, I shot over his head three times with the .45 and went after him. I had to run him down. Then I handcuffed him. I hated to do it, but I brought some just in case. I've been in prison so long and I hate handcuffs so I didn't want to put handcuffs on the guy. There were a bunch of big gravel trucks and the drivers were watching us but I wasn't worried. We had machine guns so what could they do? I even had a little rocket launcher originally intended for a Brinks truck, but I brought it along just in case I get trapped somewhere. Who knows?

"The second bank was a strange trip because there was a police cruiser sitting right in the parking lot when I went in to rob that bank. Two cops were at the far end of the parking lot. Because my helicopter was the exact model of the police helicopters they probably thought it was some V.I.P. coming in. The police mind their own business. They're used to stuff like that. The trouble with that place is that there were so many people there. We were swooping down like a big hawk in the parking lot and all these people were looking up. 'Hey, get out of the way! I'm trying to land there, you know' [laughs]. So I told the guy to land slowly and this pilot knew how to handle this machine. The people scattered and he landed it with the blades about six feet from the wall of the bank. I hopped out and my girl stayed in the chopper. She put the gun to the pilot. I had an ammunition belt with a .45 in it and I was carrying the machine-gun. All these people were standing there looking and they're blocking the entrance to the bank. I walked in through the double set of doors and into the bank. Jesus! They were ready for me! It's like landing a flying saucer. You can't get people more stunned than that. I had a leather bag and I cradled the machine gun and scooped the money into the bag. Afterwards, we landed at a major intersection in the downtown. We can't go back to the gravel pit or the office and then have to drive back into the city — that's ridiculous. So we landed downtown and sent cars scattering all over the place, up on the sidewalk. We landed in the middle of the intersection and got out. The pilot was still handcuffed to the joystick and we had taken away his earphones. He took off and we went into the subway. I had a car waiting seven stops away. I got under $20,000 for all that work [laughs]. It was more dramatic than anything.

"The courtroom incident was an escape attempt. They ended up charging me with attempted murder of the judge and gave me a life sentence. I never tried to kill the judge. I fired a shot over his head to try to stop him from leaving the courtroom. He stood up when I produced the gun and started towards the exit. I yelled, 'Stop' and put one over his head. How I got the gun is one of those secrets that remains a secret. I can never tell."

Author's Note: The Flying Bandit label has been attached to other bank robbers. A U.S. man who pleaded guilty to over 50 bank robberies in Canada was named The Flying Bandit by the media after it was learned that he travelled across Canada and the United States by plane to commit his robberies. The exploits of a Canadian bank robber (Ken Leishman) in the 1950s is the subject of a book by Heather Robertson, entitled The Flying Bandit.

Violators of the Code —

The Informants

- The Swamp Gang
- Informant
- Jimmy the Rat

For partners engaged in high-risk activities such as crime, trust is of particular concern. Criminals who work together seek assurances that each will perform their assigned tasks and refrain from disclosing their illicit activities to others. For people involved in crime, prohibitions against informing have special significance because of the serious consequences of being apprehended and imprisoned. Criminal enterprises require secrecy in order to avoid detection, arrest, and conviction. The most prominent feature of the criminal/inmate code is the prohibition against informing. So serious is this norm that the penalty for violation is often the murder of informants. The criminal/inmate code against informing is evidenced by the existence of protective custody in prison and government witness protection plans. Frequent death threats, beatings, stabbings, and the occasional murder behind bars testify to the brutal reality of this prohibition (Desroches, 1974; 1981; Caron, 1985). Partners in criminal enterprises thus work with a shared world-view — thou shalt not inform! The present study indicates that this agreement is one that is typically assumed without being spoken. Few men discuss the issue beforehand since the code is known and understood: "It goes without saying that you don't inform." Three aggravating factors that make informing an unforgiveable act include: (a) the betrayal is by a close friend and partner; (b) one partner sells out the other in exchange for lenient treatment by the criminal justice system; and (c) the offender would not have been caught or would be serving a shorter sentence had it not been for this betrayal. The violation of a profound trust combined with a selfish motive that results in a lengthy prison term adds insult to injury and is the ultimate betrayal.

The normative system of offenders is generally restricted to other criminals and persons who are in trusted relationships. Ordinary citizens are not considered informants if they should pass information onto the police — criminals expect this. In addition, there appears to exist a number of mitigating factors that diminish the seriousness of informing by partners/friends in the victim's eyes. These factors represent a recognition of conventional values that compete with and often override the criminal/inmate code. The acceptance of the conventional normative and value system allows informants to explain their actions and gives the victims reasons to forgive the person who informed.

The present study finds that surprisingly few men victimized by informants express any lasting anger against their former partner, friend, and/or lover. Despite the existence of the prohibition against informing and the lengthy jail terms most bank robbers are serving, few men express intense bitterness or anger against those whom they say have betrayed them. Given the fact that (a) many of these men are in prison due in part to the fact that they have been informed upon, and (b) the act of informing is a violation of friendship, trust, and the inmate/criminal code, why is so little animosity expressed towards those who inform? What accounts for the lack of animosity and the willingness to forgive these indiscretions or betrayals. It is clear from discussions with offenders that there exist countervailing factors and competing values that excuse the crime of informing or diminish the injury and consequently lessen the desire for revenge. Not all offenders, for instance, subscribe to the inmate code. A 23-year-old man from a middle-class background *(The Middle Class Suburban Gang — Chapter 6)* escaped from a police chase but was arrested after his partner was captured and named his accomplices. This man is no longer angry, however, and explains his reasons as follows:

In a place like this [federal penitentiary], that's murder material. I don't hold any grudges like a lot of people would. I'm not from the same element as most people in here. I don't consider myself any better or above them, but I'm not of the same element. They've been in crime all their lives. For us, this was a one-time thing and it didn't work. I'm intelligent enough to realize that anything could have happened. I could have got caught and I don't know how I would have reacted. I was relieved that it was over. At the time, I was mad at him — upset — but that's past.

As the above example illustrates, some men have not been socialized into the criminal/inmate code that prohibits informing and stipulates that such offences are to be severely punished. However, because norms against informing are not exclusive to the criminal world but reflect widespread societal values, this offender is nonetheless upset. The main difference perhaps between criminal and societal norms is the degree of retribution prescribed and pursued. It is also significant that this subject lists several reasons for his willingness to overlook his partner's betrayal.

Some offenders are willing to overlook indiscretions because their friendship is an overriding concern. A career criminal whose partners named him as an accomplice in more than 50 bank robberies explains:

The police said to me, "We got enough information from your partners to convict you. Here read this." I went offside! I was gonna kill both of them. I could have been walking the streets if it weren't for them.... But then I got into jail and started thinking. Pete's been a friend of mine for 25 years and I'm not going to let one mistake ruin everything we've built up together. I felt a weight come off me because I've been so tied into this code.

Other men similarly express a willingness to forgive friends who have informed, particularly if their indiscretions result from extenuating circumstances such as police brutality. Bandits are most willing to overlook a person's betrayal if they believe that the informant was pressured into the confession by police tactics. Many suggest that they may have acted similarly under the same circumstances. It is commonly believed and asserted that the police use a variety of techniques to extract information. A typical comment follows:

> You're supposed to be angry, but show me anybody who's going to go down to the police station and not talk. The Hold-Up Squad is not stupid. They're capable of hurting you physically and mentally. There are different types of pressures you have to withstand. Who knows what your limit is to pain.

It is also common to find offenders who blame themselves for their imprisonment. Several men express anger not at their partners who informed but at themselves for having become involved in bank robbery in the first place. Others similarly blame their own judgement in having trusted the person who later informed. An offender who had escaped custody and committed several spectacular holdups *(Flying Bandit —Chapter 8)* was arrested at an apartment whose location was learned from an informant.

> If I allow somebody to know something about me like that, then it's my own fault. I blame myself for lack of judgement. I hold myself personally responsible unless the guy was close, really close, and he double-crossed me. Then I would take it personally.

A few men are willing to overlook their partner's indiscretion because of his inexperience and/or youth. This explanation is common in situations in which they are both under arrest and the police convince one to confess. One bandit explains:

> The guy I did it with, he was inexperienced, okay, or else I could have gotten off. It was his car so he's pinched. But that doesn't mean that I have to get pinched. Now the police lay a trip on him and he put the finger on me. When I saw the confession play by play I knew the police didn't write it out 'cause they wouldn't have known all the little details. I knew I was pinched through him so I just pleaded to it.

Other reasons for not being angry with informers include: (a) the person responsible is remorseful; (b) he or she gained nothing from it; (c) the offender is not unhappy with his sentence; (d) there was no intent to inform and the indiscretion resulted from careless talk; (e) he is relieved that his crime spree is over; and, (f) he has a religious belief in forgiveness.

In the first case synopsis, *The Swamp Gang*, a bank robbery crew was observed casing a bank by a mail courier who wrote down their licence plate number and passed it on to the bank manager. When the bank was robbed a week later, police used the lead to place several men under surveillance and later arrested them as they emerged from having just robbed a bank. This individual expresses no animosity toward the citizen who provided the information, but he is quite upset with one of his own crew who gave statements to the police and agreed to testify against him at trial. He finds it difficult to understand his former partner's motive, however, since the latter received no special consideration from the criminal justice system. He also expresses a sense of hurt since he considered the man a trusted friend.

Informant explains his reasons for having cooperated with the police in religious terms. He also expresses the view that his partners should take responsibility for their actions and be convicted for all robberies committed. His interview reveals anger against former partners and suggests that his reason for informing may be motivated in part by revenge for having been talked into the offence in the first place. His cooperation with the police was entirely voluntarily and he was not coerced nor offered any incentives for his assistance in the prosecution of gang members. In fact, he gains nothing by way of a reduced sentence for his cooperation.

Jimmy the Rat is a career criminal who is pressured by the police to inform on his co-accused in an attempted murder case. He faces a lengthy prison sentence and the loss of his wife and children if he is convicted. Jimmy has accepted immunity from prosecution in exchange for his cooperation in the investigation and his testimony in court. He clearly does not enjoy this role and uses a number of techniques of neutralization to justify having become an informant. His main reason for granting an interview, he insists, is to "put the record straight" and explain why he has betrayed his criminal associates and will testify against them in the upcoming trial. He argues that his cooperation with the police is justifiable because he is betraying only those people who have betrayed him.

The Swamp Gang

Age 39, this offender is serving a 16-year sentence for 12 counts of armed bank robbery. He and two partners robbed banks in a commando-style attack over a one-year period. The subject has a lengthy criminal record including a previous conviction for bank robbery. He is a burly and muscular man with an intimidating appearance but was friendly and candid in the interview.

"My partner turned cooperative. In the preliminary hearing things were going good for me. Their identification wasn't any good so I figured the worst they could do was connect me maybe to two robberies or just the one. But once he took the stand, he put me in the bank with him and so now I am automatically committed to go to trial on all the robberies. My lawyer says, 'If you go to trial, with all they got on you, they might ask for life.' So I figured there was no way I could grab less than ten years and I didn't want to gamble for life. I expected maybe 12 years at the most. I didn't expect 16. I didn't expect to plead guilty to 12 bank robberies either and I didn't expect my partner to turn rat on me. I was a repeat offender so they gave me twice as much time as they usually do. He pleaded guilty a week before I did and got eight years. I imagine he's in a protective custody institution. News like that travels fast in the prison system.

"And we were good friends, oh yes. I had known him throughout our teenage years. I trusted him, definitely. We done a lot of bank robberies together, risked our lives together. Kind of like a war, we were in the trench together, watching each other's back. I didn't expect him to break on me. The thing is that he took the stand after he got the eight years. That's what is really baffling. It's not like they were twisting his arm. He had his time. I don't know why he did it. I never had a chance to talk to him. I'm not too happy with him, but he's going to have to walk with his head down.

"I had known him through our teenage years and I seen him a lot at the racetrack and one day we were talking. I was on parole and he had known I was in jail and I was into something like that. It's hard to find anybody you can trust. He was interested. He had the balls for it though he was probably high on drugs when he did it, but he seemed to be able to operate. The two of us would go in the bank. We used a couple of different getaway drivers. With a driver you have someone behind the wheel to watch the car so that you can't get boxed in. There were four of us pinched and the other two guys were just drivers. They're all gung ho for sitting in the car, but you couldn't get them inside a bank. They wouldn't go into a bank if you sent them in with a tank. It's hard to find guys with balls.

"I prefer robbing banks because it's my kind of thing and the odds are at least 90 percent for getting away. That's the only way of getting cash. I'm not interested in jewellery. I don't want to go around and ask who wants to buy this. Then it's a double risk. Or if somebody told me how to make a lot of money by fraud, I couldn't do it. I'm not a talker, I'm not a con man. I can't dress up in a suit and try to con somebody out of their home, selling something that ain't worth shit. I can't do it. All I can do is by force. I can't sweet talk people. Others, that's their thing, I'm not a talker.

"I gambled a fair bit. I never got too lucky at the racetrack. Some people live on a couple of hundred bucks a week. I would blow that at the racetrack in one evening and I might be driving home and I may see some good looking hooker and I would spend another $50 or more and not worry about it. Then repeat it the next day and not worry about the money and what I lost. I drove an old T-Bird and lived in a little batchelor apartment. I'm not a spender, like walking around like a big shot. I guess most of the money went to gambling, for sure. You can only handle one broad a day, or eat so much and all that. I spent about a thousand a week from the bank robberies.

"I did have a job when I was released on parole. I was working for a year and a half, but then the company decided to scrap the night shift and I was on the bottom of the seniority list so I was the first to go. I guess if I hadn't lost my job I probably wouldn't have really got into it. I was doing just as good, living just as comfortably as I was robbing banks. Except I wouldn't attend the racetrack as often with the same amount of money. But all my other needs were met. I even had a credit card. Then when I got laid off, I used that credit card to the hilt till they took it off me. When I was robbing banks, I would sleep till noon and then get something to eat. If there was afternoon racing I would probably go to the racetrack. If there wasn't then I'd probably go to the poolroom and kill a few hours. Even if I didn't play a game of pool, I spent a lot of time at pool halls. I'm not the travelling type. I'm not big on buying expensive clothes or dining out, but I get bored if I'm broke. My partner and I didn't have much in common except we both enjoyed going to the racetrack. That's about it. And we would get together for a robbery. He's not that outgoing. He won't go out to a hotel for a drink. He doesn't like to play pool. The man's 40 and he's still living with his mother and father. He has a hard time getting along with people. He didn't really have many friends.

"The media gave called us the 'East End Bandits' because we were operating in the east end of the city. Then, maybe six months later, they changed our name to the 'Swamp Gang.' The reason they did that I guess is my partner said, 'Move it. I can shoot the eye out of whatever. I've been in the swamp for two or three years.' The press just picked up on it. It got blown up. They got nothing to do anyways. I'd read about it, but then I could just as easily be reading about somebody else too. It doesn't really seem like me. Even after a bank robbery, like if I didn't have the money in my pocket, I could just say it never happened. It didn't seem like a big thing. I don't do it for the publicity, just for the money.

"Once you know you've made a clean getaway there's no reason to be looking behind your back. You get rid of all your stuff, you get cleaned up, and if for some reason they question you, they've got a hell of a time getting a conviction because they've got nothing on you. If you're going to worry, you're better to have another trade rather than scaring yourself half to death. You wouldn't be enjoying your money.

"This one particular day, we were parked by a side street having a cigarette. So here comes this nosy mailman that sees us parked there. Any other mailman would have just walked by like no big deal. So there's a couple of men, maybe they need a shave. What's the big deal? They are parked on the side street. Apparently this guy took the licence number and I guess he had some mail to deliver to the bank so he gave it to the bank manager. A couple of weeks later his bank was robbed. Then he gave the licence plate number to the cops. Then they started surveillance on my partner, then the other guy, then I came into the picture. They knew which bank we were going to do because we made repeat trips to check it out. They watched us do the bank. Maybe in a different area they might have shot us. There was a woman standing there and she wanted to know what was going on. I don't think we wanted to do any shooting. It would probably have been suicidal when you have four machine-guns looking at you. Three machine-guns and one guy with a shotgun, plus the shock and the surprise. You read about these things and you see them in the movies, but you don't really expect them to happen to you. You think about getting pinched, like maybe them busting your door in one day.

"At the rate we were going, a monthly pace, you're bound to get caught. The police, they've got the time. They can make all kinds of mistakes, but we only gotta make one and that's it. There's always the unexpected no matter how long you plan. It's pushing your luck. You're a fool to believe you can go indefinitely. In the back of my mind I was ready for it too, 'cause it's not like I've never been in jail. I wasn't terrified of getting caught. I know I can do the time so in that way I had an edge over my partners. I knew what was ahead of me if I took a pinch. I don't mind talking about what I've done. It's no big deal. You should go interview my partner. Maybe a book with a rat in it would make it more interesting."

Informant

Age 40, this offender was a member of the Swamp Gang and is serving eight years in prison for having taken part in 12 bank robberies with three other men. He informed on his partners after his arrest and is serving his sentence in a protective custody institution.

"I have no previous record. I'm not a criminal. I wouldn't take nothing off the backs of other people, no way. I never ever stole a dime from anybody. When I did the bank robberies, I looked at a brick building and said to myself, 'A bank's a bank.' I was taking from a brick building. That's what I put in my head and I know that's bull. Twelve robberies were committed by three imbeciles and one person high on drugs. And I really want to say 'imbeciles' because that's what they are. They are moral-less people. I shouldn't be knocking them down, I'm as guilty as they are right to the hilt. I'm paying for it as they are.

"I used to be a pretty straight guy: didn't drink, didn't smoke, didn't take drugs, and I worked. There was no way I would ever consider going to crime. Then about five years ago I found out that I had been thrown in an orphanage and adopted when I was a baby — a piece of garbage that was thrown out at six weeks of age! That didn't sit well with me. My parents had never told me and my brothers and sisters never knew either. I was trying to be a part of this family all my life, but somewhere in my head I'd known. I was going through a trunk of stuff as a kid, maybe about seven or eight, and I seen these adoption papers. They were mine, but I put it in my head that they were my brother's. I didn't want to deal with the reality of. I buried it away until some person got mad at me and just laid it on me. It just freaked my mind out. It ate on me and ate on me.

"I first blamed my parents for not telling me, but that's all behind me. They are the greatest, the greatest, but initially I was very upset because I thought I was somebody I wasn't. I was living a lie and it played heavy on my head. I started into doctor prescription drugs and I stayed in my basement apartment — a total recluse. This really alarmed my parents of course. I did my poetry and my songs and I alienated myself from the rest of the world. I used to love life, everything was a beautiful colour to me. I loved it and then it got black. I started seeing the cracks in my world. I started seeing hunger and misery in the world. It finally got to the point where I was really fouled up in the head and I wanted to die. It hit me really hard, too hard. It shouldn't have hit me that hard. Now I realize that and I'm seeing a psychologist here in prison.

"I ran into Raymond quite by accident. He has a really heavy record and I knew him from high school. He's a dangerous person to a degree and he's attacked a policeman in court. He can be a very nasty guy. He said to me that he'd be a criminal all his life. That sort of made me sick, his whole demeanour, his whole person made me sick. I seen a person who cared nothing for other people. I seen something totally alien to me and it made me sick. And I actually got to despise the guy the last few months. I ran into him strictly by accident and we started talking about robbery. He was telling me a lot of bull and then I thought that was a good way to go out. You know, exit. I was thinking of doing myself in, but I couldn't do it because of my religious convictions. 'So let someone else do it!' I latched on to this idea — going out in style, in grandeur, like in the old western days. That was the basic reason for my involvement in bank robbery. I couldn't take my life so I wanted the police to shoot me. The money I didn't need. Through the drugs I developed this idea that it's okay if somebody else did it.

"But it didn't happen. When I walked out of the bank everything was totally silent. There was people everywhere, but everything was silent. I never expected it to get past one or two banks. Never, not in my wildest dreams. I was stoned out of my mind when I was involved in these things. No way I should have ever done 12 bank robberies. I'm still wondering how we could have done 12 bank robberies. We just kept going. As far as hurting other people goes, nobody was threatened or hurt. There was never a live gun carried because there's always a chance you might shoot somebody. There was no violence, no screaming or swearing at 'em or threatening. We'd try to keep people calm in the bank. 'Look, it's nothing against you good people, we're just fighting inflation.' I was in a fantasy world. I know I did it, but it was like a dream to me. It's still like a dream. It didn't seem real. The media made us look big, but we aren't big. We were a joke. We were robbing banks, but we're not bank robbers.

"There were times when I started to come around to a little sanity and I didn't want to go through with them. Several times I backed out so we'd drive off. It was getting on my partners' nerves and there'd be some arguing, angry arguments. I'd just say, 'Stick it in your ear.' But when it came time to do it, there'd be just the right precise moment. I'd pop enough pills and be able to go in there and do it. It just seemed that after I took a lot of pills I could walk into the bank. It's not a case of courage. I wasn't scared of death. It was a moral thing. My conscience was very strong and I knew I was doing wrong inside my head. Them pills had to kill my conscience and when I could kill the conscience I could walk in and do it.

"The police didn't have many witnesses. I was their main witness against myself. I walked into court and pleaded, no strings attached. I could have got less time if I had made a deal, but I didn't. I decided I would testify, which is something I didn't have to do. It's obvious that I wanted to get caught. I'm ashamed of what I've done. I'm not happy about it and I'm paying my time for it. I made it clear to my partners that I would not lie. I was unhappy with myself for being with these people. I seen what kind of people they were. Raymond was a very bad individual. As far as I'm concerned he shouldn't be running around the streets. There was no reason to make a mockery out of the court system. There was no reason to bring these young girl tellers up on the stand and make them go through what they've already been through again. So get up there and act like a man! Plead guilty. And if you don't want to plead guilty then I'll help you do it. They all pleaded guilty because I made it clear that had we went to trial I would have testified. I wasn't going to wash one hand clean and leave the other one dirty.

"I've come to my senses and I don't want to die. I went from a good guy to a bad guy. Now it's time to go to a good guy and maybe leave a little of myself behind somewhere. See, I believe that I'll be going with Him. Therefore, my ideology is taking me in a different direction. The supreme force stopped me and he has stayed with me all through my life. The best thing that ever happened to me was getting caught. Until I pleaded guilty I hadn't made made my amends to Him. I've changed and my head's on straight now. As has happened many times in my life I was saved by God. I'm not going to say what will happen when I go out, but I'm in His hands. Wherever he takes me, I go. I've basically committed one mistake and it's my last one. That's it. There's no excuse for it. I'll do my time and I'll never see a jail again. Never. And I'm through with drugs. Me and drugs, we had a one-time dance."

Author's Note: *This gang received a great deal of publicity and were operating in a specific area of the city. After placing the gang under surveillance for several weeks, the Hold-Up Squad arrested them as they emerged from a bank robbery. The officer in charge of the special task force describes the arrest as follows:*

They came out of the bank and scooted behind it to where they had parked the car. In the meantime we had set up so as to block their path with our own vehicles. When they turned the corner they were faced with two dozen policemen in helmets and bulletproof vests aiming everything from automatic rifles to shotguns at them. I hollered, "Drop your guns and hit the ground." Three of them hit the dirt, but he [the subject] just stood there with the pistol in his hand! "Drop the gun! Drop the gun! Drop the gun! Drop the goddam gun! Drop that fucking gun!" We're screaming at him and everyone's cocked his gun and he's just standing there holding the gun and looking at the ground. "Like what do you want to do man, die? Drop the goddam gun." Finally he dropped it. It was empty.

The postal carrier whose information led to the Swamp Gang's arrest received a $10,000 reward from the police and an additional $10,000 reward from the Canadian Bankers' Association.

Jimmy the Rat

Jimmy is an informant working with the F.B.I. They believe him to be responsible for several contract murders on behalf of organized crime. The interview took place in his apartment living room in the presence of his wife who periodically listened and went about her chores. A small man, 140 lbs, heavily tatood, one tooth missing, and approximately 30 years old, Jimmy was friendly and cooperative but seemed distressed discussing his cooperation with the police.

"I was convicted in 1976 and again in 1979 with the North End Gang. That was the name given by the media. In 1976 I got hooked up with a well known bank robber and he introduced me to the crime. He had 12 to 15 banks under his belt. I met him through a mutual friend and I was only 17 young at the time. He told me, 'It's really nothing.

Over 90 percent get away and if you're not caught with the money and guns, you're not going to get convicted.' The way he explained made sense. The money made even more sense. I was very scared and very uncertain as to what my role would be. Since there was only two of us, he would jump the counter and I would hold people at bay so no one leaves and people who enter stay. He knew what he was doing. We got $27,500 for that robbery. Not bad for a few minutes work. [Wife interrupts: Yes, but it's not worth it because it's really a high price to pay when you go off to prison. Then you're paying it back interest and all. Husband agrees.] I blew it foolishly. On all of them. I didn't try to invest — not even investing in drugs or a business. Easy come, easy go. Clothes, go out and have a good time. I was not into big drugs. I smoked a little pot.

"I was convicted on one of these scores, but my co-defendant was not. I didn't tell on him. I got away on all three, but I was young and sort of a braggart and I told a friend thinking I was telling him in confidence. I later found out that he had no value. He wanted to be a tough guy and the cops questioned him. He said, 'You know Jimmy robbed the bank and I know it and you ain't going to catch him.' I was only 17 and the police played psychological games on my head. 'You're going to get 20 years Jimmy. We can give you a break.' I ended up pleading guilty because my lawyer advised me to do so. They had a stack of statements against me from people I knew. My lawyer said he can get me a deal if I plead guilty. They let me say I robbed the bank, but I didn't have to say anything about the other guy. I would have like to have let the rats testify and have to live in shame. Let them testify in court where there will be some stand-up guys who will see them do it. They did it not to be Joe Citizen but out of jealousy or envy. These were friends that I had known most of my life through grammar school.

"I got two years on that and went to a federal prison. I was released to a halfway house and a friend introduced me to a friend of his who was into robbing banks in supermarkets. This friend I knew since I was three or four years old, we lived on the same block. He says, 'Jimmy, this guy is robbing banks and wants to talk to you.' I speak with the guy [See *Papa Was a Rolling Stone*] and he's about the same age as me — about 19 at the time. We did a couple of supermarket banks and I got 15 years. He testified against me and a dozen others. There were different guys doing banks in twos and threes. I was in a halfway house at the time and had been there 28 days before being busted. I was set up by a Lenny's older brother who had an arson charge pending.

"The media played a major, major, major role. They covered the trial and, prior to the trial, they gave it a lot of publicity. Granted, it was very heavy shit, but they added a few pounds to the bushel. Especially on me. I was on T.V. half a dozen times. The newspaper had an article, a whole page on me in the local news section. Prior to the trial the image they portrayed was that we terrorized the north end of the city. They emphasized the dramatic parts such as the fact that we counter vaulted. I remember we watched the 11 o'clock news and the newsman said, 'Three pistol packing punks went in the super-duper and not for groceries.' But they're like that.

"I was recently arrested along with another guy for an attempted murder, and the guy who was shot lived but couldn't identify who did it. My co-defendant told his wife to go bomb a witness's house and she did! She took a container of gasoline and attached a cloth, lit it, and threw it through the window. Then he had her say it was my wife and the police arrested my wife. I said, 'It's not true and I'm willing to sit down and spill my guts out.' The cops were happy about that. They wired me and I spoke to his wife. I said to her, 'My wife is pregnant. She can't do time. How the hell did you do it?' She says, 'I bought gas and took off my t-shirt and threw it through the window.'

"I have a wife and three gorgeous children and I'm happily married. My wife has stuck through this with me and trusted in me. After trusting in my people for so long and being betrayed I have finally found someone who had confidence and trust to help me. I can do the same for her. 'Two wrongs don't make a right' one criminal I know said to me. 'Okay, I'll do another decade in prison and lose my children! Forget that.' I already lost my daughter doing my first bit. I served nine years straight before I got out — 1976 to 1985. Her mother has her and I haven't seen her since she was a day or two old. I saw a picture of her two and a half years ago.

"After the incident with the bombing and I wore a bug to clear myself, I was very depressed. I got into drugs a little, but my wife and mother pulled me through that. I don't live in complete security out of fear of certain reprisals from these people. My co-accused Freddie is a dangerous guy — a miniature Rambo. When the police busted him he had grenades and a .44 Magnum. Before this occurred I was affiliated with the top-notch people in the city. When they found out I was working with the cops they became very nervous I would do it to everyone. I didn't, I only did it to people who did it to me — a payback. I went through a bad state of depression recently thinking that the few friends I had, I have no more. I have not had the opportunity to tell my side of the story without getting a bullet in my head.

"There are many precautions we have to take. We'll be moving from here soon to save some money. We can't move too far because I have a stepson and his father has visiting rights. I used to go to this park. Now we go to other parks not in the area these people frequent. We're dealing with some serious people. There was a handicapped person in the house where they threw the bomb. They could do it to me. Why not? My two sons have a cable T.V. in their bedroom so to avoid having them sitting near the front window. It's not that they're secluded in their bedroom, but I'm just playing it safe. I have a fear for the safety of my family. I believe that paranoia is something you think is out there but isn't. But when you know there's something out there, you know it's not paranoia. My wife and I have had a few arguments — let me take that back — we've had a few discussions on what we are supposed to do. I had no other alternative but to cooperate. What was I supposed to do? I've been married three years and I have a daughter of seven months and a 28-month-old son. I also have a stepson. A lot is on the blackboard as to what we want to do. I have family responsibilities now.

"I used to believe that you go to jail because you're a man and refuse to inform. You can flush that philosophy down the toilet. I held a lot of respect with the mob and I know my reputation is shot. I know you look at me with no teeth and arms full of tatoos and you ask, 'How could this guy have any weight?' But I did. This thing is on my mind every single day. The police are hanging back on that tape waiting to nab Freddie. I'm hoping that I won't be forced to testify. At the time I didn't like doing it, now I don't regret it in the least. He doesn't know about the tape. He knows one guy was arrested because of me, but that's because he falls in the same terms as before — do onto others as they do onto you. It seems that everywhere you turn there's somebody telling. A lot of people get screwed around by the police and I want to prove it's not always like that. If you shoot straight, they're not just there to put you in jail. They're there to help you too. At times I'm sceptical, but what choice do I have? None. I have to believe they'll keep their word. I don't feel the same about myself having done this."

CHAPTER NINE

In the Arms of the Law —

Encounters with the Police

- Mexican Standoff
- In the Arms of the Law
- Ambush
- The Turk and the Man from Glad
- One-Armed Bandit
- Go Boy and Surveillance Squad

The police refer to robbery as a "dumb" crime because the risks are great and the payoffs are small. The chance of getting caught on a single robbery may be low, but serial robberies increase the risks substantially. Because the amounts of money obtainable are modest, anyone who wishes to support himself or herself this way has to rob one bank after another. Given the fact that police and banks respond immediately to a bank robbery, the odds against anyone surviving in this career for long are great. This is evident by the fact that the Hold-Up Squad typically clears over 70 percent of all bank robberies.

The police, courts, and banking community take a view of bank robbery that differs markedly from the relatively benign definition of so many offenders. Although this crime causes no serious financial losses for the banking community, banks are concerned for the safety and well-being of their customers and employees. The police additionally worry about the welfare of police officers and bystanders who may interfere with or confront armed robbers. Police in major urban centres have investigated many instances in which robberies have resulted in injuries or deaths to victims, bystanders, the police, and the offenders themselves. People who rob banks are always presumed to be armed and dangerous and tellers are instructed to cooperate, hand over the money, and press the alarm only when it is safe to do so. The policy in some branches is to press the alarm only after the robber has left the bank to prevent a hostage-taking incident. The police similarly attempt to arrest the bandits only after they have left the bank premises.

Even unarmed bank robbers are regarded as a threat because of the trauma they inflict on victims. "Beggar bandits" who pass a note demanding money implicitly or explicitly threaten bank employees and are considered more heinous than fraud artists who nonetheless pose a more serious financial threat. The weighty definition of robbery explains the efforts that the banking community and the police put forth to catch, prosecute, and deter bank robbers as well as the heavy sentences imposed by the courts.

The most dangerous stage for the police occurs when they attempt arrest an armed robber. The risks involved in this confrontation are clearly illustrated in the first two case selections. In one incident an officer is shot while confronting an armed bandit inside the bank while, in another case, a plain-clothes detective subdues one culprit as his partner struggles for control of the other man's gun. Police response to armed robbery is often violent as well. In one case the Hold-Up Squad engages in a shoot-out with an armed gang killing one and wounding two others. In another case the offender alleges and describes the police use of force in their attempt to obtain a statement. The final two cases illustrate arrests made both reactively — through the police response to an alarm — and proactively — following the surveillance of a bank robbery crew.

Mexican Standoff describes an incident in which a young bank robber is confronted by a plain-clothes detective inside a bank. As they face one another with their guns drawn, the bandit makes the decision to fire. The incident described in *In the Arms of the Law* involves a confrontation with the police outside a bank as the robbers emerge. One bandit is subdued and while the other is told to drop the bag. He refuses and engages in a dramatic struggle with the arresting officer for the gun. *Ambush* is the story of an armed crew who had the misfortune of leaving the bank only to find the police waiting in ambush. The subject describes how one partner is killed and two others wounded in the shoot-out. The bank robbery crew of which this man was a part planned their getaways in detail but did not consider the possibility that the police would engage in a shoot-out. Their failure to anticipate a violent police response to their use of weapons, violence, and diversionary tactics is a deadly mistake. *The Turk and the Man From Glad* describes this subject's most recent robbery, his arrest inside a bus, and the rough treatment he alleges occurred at the hands of two Hold-Up Squad officers in their attempt to obtain a statement. *One Armed Bandit* and his partner plan their escape in the subway but find themselves trapped as the police halt the train and begin a search for the culprits. The two bandits sit helplessly in the unmoving subway car awaiting their arrest. *Go Boy and Surveillance Squad* describes an incident that took place in Roger Caron's bank robbery career — also briefly reported in his autobiography *Go Boy* (1978). Roger and his partner spend several weeks scouting out banks while being followed by a surveillance team of six officers. One side of the story is told by Roger and the other is described by the officer who headed the surveillance squad. The project ends dramatically when the police arrest the two bandits as they leave the bank.

Mexican Standoff

This individual describes an incident in his youth when, confronted by a police officer, he decides to shoot. He is the same person who years later hijacks a helicopter and robs two banks (see Flying Bandit in Chapter 7).

"The first time I ever fired a gun I shot a policeman. He was a detective and he was dressed in a suit. He had his gun out when he came into the bank. He looked to my left and to my right. He didn't recognize me as being the robber. I turned around to go out the door and I hear, 'Hold it right there kid.' I had a .44 Magnum holstered that he could see, but I also had a .25 automatic in my pocket. I turned around and pulled the .25 out of my pocket and I pointed it at him. I had it pointed at his face. We were a few feet apart. I could see the bullets in the barrel of his gun and he said, 'I mean it kid.' He was white.

"When I looked at this guy I could see that he had a wife and kids and I didn't want to pull the trigger. And then I realized that if I didn't pull the trigger, he was going to pull the trigger. So I just told myself, 'I'm going to take a dive.' This flashed through my head, 'I'm going to shoot him before I go down.' All this took place in a fraction of a second, but it seems like time stands still. We're just standing there facing each other in a Mexican standoff. I could almost feel his thinking. He could see I was young and he didn't want to kill a 16-year-old kid. That's why he didn't shoot me. And the funny thing was that I reciprocated to his thought and I was seeing him and his wife and his kids. I didn't want to kill him either.

"I pretended I was going to put my gun down and shot him in the solar plexus. At the same time I dived to the floor so he didn't shoot me by reflex. He just collapsed on the other side of the counter. I shot him because he would have had to shoot me. Maybe he wouldn't have tried to kill me, but he would have done the same thing if I hadn't done it. Luckily he didn't die.

"That cop I shot in the bank, I shot him when I was in reform school. I had just got out of a juvenile institution and I was carrying a chip on my shoulders. Prison is the first time a lot of guys are actually confronted with the reality of who you are. You have to stand up for yourself. You become a victim and you pick up the characteristics, the habitual thinking, the prejudices of the prison and of the prisoners. And when you leave you take that with you into the outside world. You can't take it off like a coat and hat and hang it up on a rack. It leads you into trouble. The world is not there to offer you any experiences to offset all those negative things you've picked up.

"Violence is learned. In prison you learn about force. They use force on you from the time they pick you up: they push you into a courtroom, they lock you in their cells, and they strip you naked. With the bitterness and the magnitude of the grievance that you have against society, this is the force that tells you to pull the trigger."

In the Arms of the Law

This 25-year-old offender is a small, boyish-looking man who is serving seven years for possession of a prohibited weapon and harbouring an escaped criminal. His criminal record begins in his early teens and includes theft, break and enter, weapons offences, escape, and drug charges.

"I beat that last charge. They can't bring this back on me so I don't mind talking about it. It was a touch-and-go situation. I thought I was gone for sure. As soon as I walked out of the bank I knew something was wrong 'cause two guys come right up to us. They're plain-clothes and one grabs my partner. I looked over and the other guy's coming up to me. So it gives you a second to prepare yourself. I'm thinking, 'Fuck, what do I do?' It's a big decision to make. It's one of the biggest decisions I ever made in my life. It was my life there and it was his life too. The main thing is not to take a fall. If you can get away, you gotta go for it. I've always taken that one extra shot at life and freedom. I make sure they gotta work to get me 'cause I ain't gonna walk out with my hands up.

"I looked over to my partner and the cop had him down on the ground with a gun to his head. The second cop walks up to me and puts a gun in my stomach. I had a bag of money in my hand and he says, 'Drop the bag!' I said, 'No.' The gun was dug right in my stomach and this guy was six foot something — big. I'm thinking, 'Well, I've got a choice. I go for it or drop the bag.' The first thing I thought of was this place, the joint. I said, 'Fuck that, either I get away or I go under.' So I dropped the bag and got his hand up in the air and we were wrestling for the gun. I'm on my toes because this guy was big. I said to myself, 'I can't let go of this thing now 'cause he might bring it down and — bang!' Then I seen a cop car coming and I knew that as soon as the cop showed up I'm fucked. They'd just jump me and I can't get away. He had both hands on that gun and he wasn't letting go. I didn't have a gun, my partner had it.

"I had one hand on the gun and grabbed hold of his pants with my other hand and threw him right into the bushes. I was gone like a bolt. I went right through traffic. My partner couldn't do nothing during all this. The cop that had my partner on the ground was gonna shoot me. My partner told me that he was getting up so the cop wouldn't shoot me and the cop turned around and put the gun back on him. He didn't talk. A few months later, they picked me up on some other charges and they found a picture of me and my partner. The cop that I wrestled with seen the picture and said, 'That's the guy that robbed that bank.'

"I still can't believe I beat that charge. In court the judge asked the cop, 'This small guy threw you?' I'm only 125 lbs and the cop was over 200 lbs. They had two cops testify against me and an old lady that said she seen us, and they all positively identified me. I had make-up on and a wig that fell off. They all identified me in court, but they all gave different descriptions before seeing me. They were off a lot. Weird thing. Like, if I were the judge I would have convicted me. I would have without a doubt. When the cop got on the stand he said, 'That's the guy right there that I wrestled with.' My lawyer said, 'How do you know for sure?' He said, 'I know 'cause I thought I was gonna die that night.' I said to myself, 'Yeah, right!' I was thinking the same thing. I got respect for him cause when everything was over he said, 'Okay, you beat the charge. We'll get you the next time.' I said, 'Listen, I'll give you credit. You never shot me in the back.' I shouldn't have said that."

Interview with his Partner who is Serving Ten Years

Age 25, this man has a lengthy criminal record that goes back to early adolescence. He has spent most of his teenage and adult life behind bars and shows no interest in a law-abiding life. In the incident described above he was apprehended but refused to inform on his partner despite the offer of a considerable reduction in his sentence.

"My partner broke loose and got away. He was picked up three months later and for some reason they found him not guilty. We had an agreement not to squeal. The cops offered me a three-year term if I'd name my partner. They were concerned that one officer almost got shot in the scuffle. They said the robber had his finger over the trigger and was pulling the gun towards him. I'm doing ten years when I could be doing three, but it's a code. You're not supposed to inform.

"I knew my partner since I was 13 or 14. He was into B & Es and I was into a bit of everything. I suggested we do some B & Es together and stole a car. We were only in grade nine and I was living with foster parents. We went away for the weekend and he told his parents that he was at my place and vice versa. We did this one place that had an alarm. He was the first one out and got caught. I walked out the front door and disappeared. Later I went back and picked up the car, which was full of stuff we had stolen. My name never came up and we've been close ever since."

Author's Note: A year after the interview, this man was released on parole, committed another robbery, and while awaiting trial in custody he was charged along with several inmates in the beating death of another prisoner.

Ambush

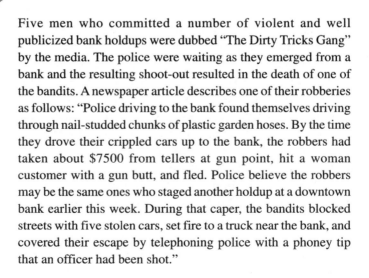

Five men who committed a number of violent and well publicized bank holdups were dubbed "The Dirty Tricks Gang" by the media. The police were waiting as they emerged from a bank and the resulting shoot-out resulted in the death of one of the bandits. A newspaper article describes one of their robberies as follows: "Police driving to the bank found themselves driving through nail-studded chunks of plastic garden hoses. By the time they drove their crippled cars up to the bank, the robbers had taken about $7500 from tellers at gun point, hit a woman customer with a gun butt, and fled. Police believe the robbers may be the same ones who staged another holdup at a downtown bank earlier this week. During that caper, the bandits blocked streets with five stolen cars, set fire to a truck near the bank, and covered their escape by telephoning police with a phoney tip that an officer had been shot."

"We were a quarter mile away from the bank when the cops pulled cars out in front of us and started shooting. They were behind trees, cars, buildings, fences, and up on the roofs. The idea was to get rid of us. They let off fire for what seemed like a hell of a long time. I don't know how long. It's hard seeing a friend of yours get blown away. The guy who got killed had his hands up in the air. He had no place to go. Half our guns didn't work anyway. They weren't for fighting or for blowing anyone away, they were there to scare. We didn't expect to run into an ambush or have to shoot anyone. We were prepared for resistance further down the line where we had some heavy artillery.

"Before doing the score we usually broke off. Two would walk one way, two would walk the other way and just float into the bank. The van would be right there beside the bank for the getaway. We always had a few stolen cars parked along the way as well. We had some junkie steal the car. We'd give them $50, tell them to wait in the parking lot. We blocked the cops right in so they couldn't get around. None of these junkies knew what was going down. We'd blow the horn at him as we passed by and he'd park the car across the road and fuck off.

"The way we did banks, one guy would stand at the door and three would go over the counter. I was one of the three. The one who stayed near the door had the gun and he would keep track of time. One guy would take the tills and I'd take the head teller into the vault with her keys and tell her to start opening these boxes. I'd empty them into the bag until I heard him yell, 'Okay, let's go!' It doesn't matter how much money is lying there, you depart as soon as 45 seconds came up. I'd back out the door and tell her to get on the floor. The fourth guy is another watchman making sure no one's pushing any buttons. The guy at the door makes sure no one sneaks out the door. Both these guys were big guys and made sure there weren't any heros.

"I guess when the police were following us they could have busted us anytime for weapons, but we made fools of them too many times [laughs]. They'd be pulling up and we'd walk right by and, 'Voom.' The press called us the 'Booby Trap Gang' and other names [laughs]. That was for the nails on the road, a van that exploded on fire, and a few other tricks we were alleged to have pulled. I guess the cops didn't like that. Everyone knew that if we kept it up we were going to get caught. It's as simple as that. But the funny part is that we always talked about, 'What if they pick one of us up?' The idea was to have nothing lying around, no guns, no disguises, and so on. We weren't expecting to get caught so dramatically. The press said, 'Booby Trap Gang has Shoot-Out with Police.' Shit man, they were doing all the shooting [laughs]. No shoot-out there.

"I don't remember the name of the bank where the ambush happened, but we were going to come out the back into the alley where our van was parked. It was a fake door with a wall built there [laughs] so we had to go out the front door and around the back. We took off down the back street and they pulled out a car and cut us off. We clipped this car, slammed on the brakes, and went off the road into this chain-link fence. First thing you know there's shots being fired. I was in the back of the van getting ready to throw out boards with spikes going through them. I had all sorts of gimmicks back there for the cops. When we hit the fence I just flew to the front. I wasn't knocked out, just dazed for a second. Then the guys are out the doors. They all bolted out at the same time.

"I could see through the window in the side of the van and I watched Steve stick up his hands and get blown away. I couldn't believe it. I thought to myself, 'Holy shit!' I looked to the other side and saw the other two guys go down and I thought, 'Holy shit! What did I get myself into?' I turned around quick and looked out the sliding doors and there was a cop looking right in at me. I didn't even have a gun, but he backed off. The guns were in the bag with the money. Then I heard him say, 'There's another one in the van,' and the van started popping with holes. Bang, bang, bang, bang, bang. I saw the walls of the van caving in.

"I wasn't sure where I was going to go. I wasn't going out the side door because he was out there. I didn't want to go out the back door because I'd run right into them. So I decided to go out the side door anyway and before he could get the gun off I was around the front of the van and running. I was moving at one hell of a speed. It was a dream world and everything was going too slow. I couldn't run fast enough [laughs]. Bullets were flying everywhere. I crossed the road, rolled on the ground, and dove underneath this car. I could feel the car bouncing. Poor guy who owned that car because they shot the hell out of that car. They didn't stop shooting until people started coming out of their buildings. They kept on shooting until someone yelled,

'Pedestrians. Hold your fire.' Then I peeked out and I see people coming out doors and looking out windows. If it wasn't for the people coming out of their buildings, they wouldn't have stopped. They wanted to finish the job — no paper work [laughs].

"At that time, on the ground, I thought I was dead for sure. I'm trying to think, 'What am I going to do? How the hell am I going to get out of this?' I'm trying to think how I can get away in this car, trying all the alternatives and just by-passing them. Nothing would click in. It just came down to the end where you're finished, 'Say your prayers' [laughs].

"They didn't come over for a long time. Steve was only a couple of feet from me and I was going to ask how he was and then I saw blood pouring from his mouth. I knew he was finished. He was lying there and he didn't have a stomach left. Then I was yelling out, 'Hey, I'm unarmed. I haven't got a gun.' I was screaming. I was laying on the ground for the longest time before I heard someone say, 'Don't you fucking move or I'll blow your head off.' Then I was being pulled out and I had this foot in the center of my back and a shotgun pointed at the back of my head. I figured for sure this guy was going to pull the trigger. He says, 'You even twitch and your head's coming off.' Then I was in the back of a car and I had on this phoney beard, which was making my face itchy. Because my hands were handcuffed behind my back I can't scratch it. I asked the cop if I could take the beard off and he says, 'Leave the fucking thing alone.' In court this cop said that I was running like a bat out of hell. I couldn't run fast enough [laughs].

"I thought about it a lot afterwards and I'm not angry. If you put me in the cop's shoes I'd do the same fucking thing. Sure, I'm not going to play games. If someone's going to rob a bank with a gun, they must be willing to shoot at someone. I wouldn't have thought, 'They have a couple of .38s, they're not really loaded because they don't want to hurt anybody.' Who would think that? [laughs]. When you come right down to it, yes we were prepared to shoot, but not there at that spot at that particular time."

Author's Note: This man received four years for his part in the robbery but had the term increased to six years when the prosecutor appealed.

Interview with his 22-year-old Partner

"This scar on my neck is a tracheotomy. I was shot in the back of the neck and the shotgun pellet is still there. I didn't feel nothing, not a thing. Down and out. I imagine the shot must have thrown me because I was bruised on my head. I don't know if my throat is ever going to heal. It hurts but I'm all right. I've got to get this pellet out of me. They told me it's a serious operation because if it moves one way they can take it out, but if it moves the other way I'm dead. So they left it in.

"The police were waiting for us outside the bank. Apparently I was under surveillance for the few days prior to the robbery. That came out in court. You don't expect something like that — an ambush. They waited until we went into the bank and it went down smooth. We came down this road and the shit hit the fan. It was survival from there on in. Come an ambush, I'm getting away. I'm not getting caught. I'm going to shoot my way out. I'm running man, and you ain't catching me and sending me to prison.

"When the van crashed I grabbed a bag of money, pulled out my gun, threw open the doors, and tried to make a run for it. If I made it, I was making it with some money. I didn't want to get caught. I'd been to jail before and there's too many lonely nights, man. They just shot us down; I jumped out and they just fucking opened fire on us. So I let off a shot and I started running. Once I got shot it was game over for me. It more or less wiped out my memory for that day. It took me a long time to remember it. I remember it now. I used to be a rambunctious kid — more or less wild. This has really settled my ass down [laughs] at a tender age. I still look at myself as young, but the judge made me aware that I was no longer young. He said, 'You're not young no more.' That's what he said, 'You know what you was doing. You know what you was getting into.' They didn't kill me so they tried to put me away for life. Everybody was fucking happy when I got ten years, everybody but me. My mother-fucking lawyer wanted to shake my hand, she thought ten years was a good sentence. 'Considering,' she says. It ain't her who is serving this sentence."

The Turk and the Man from Glad

Age 26, this offender is serving a seven-year term on four counts of robbery and an additional eight years for a single robbery committed while on parole. He has a lengthy juvenile record and has spent most of the past 12 years in institutions.

"I was with a friend and we go over to the place he used to live because he wants to see his old landlord. We stopped for a coffee and cigarettes at this plaza near his apartment building and there is a bank right on the corner. We went into his building and he gets an interview with his landlord and we go and meet his girlfriend upstairs and we are having coffee. So I tell him, 'Listen, I wouldn't mind popping this little bank on the corner while we are up in this area of the city.' He thought I was crazy, 'This isn't what you normally do is it?' I said 'Yeah.' So he said, 'All right.' He felt confident with me I guess. We said we were going out for cigarettes saying we'd be back in a few minutes. So we go to this coffee shop — mistake number one 'cause that was a witness in court — and we're talking. I said, 'I want you to come in,' because I wanted somebody standing behind me. 'I'll go in and stand in line and you come in 20 seconds later and stand behind me.' He said okay, so I walk into this bank and there is nobody in it, no business at all, and there are four tellers to choose from. I do a psychological test and I pick the one I feel will be the most cooperative. Go up and passed her the note and it went down just like it was out of the book.

"She read the note, looked at me, got her description like she was supposed to do, opened the drawer, put the money in the bag, closed it. I walked out. As I'm walking out, he comes walking in. He's too late, that is how quick it happened! So he looks at me and I look at him and the cameras are going off both ways. They are getting back, front, and side views of me. So off I go and he stays in the bank. He can't just turn around and go. He doesn't want to do that. He used to have a bank account there. So they locked the doors on him, 'There has been a robbery and you'll have to stay.'

"I duck down the back and come through the fence and up to this broad's place. Knock on the door, 'Come on in. Do you want a beer.' 'Thanks.' 'Where's Bob?' I said he met some buddy and he's down there chatting to him, he'll be back in a few minutes. So we're having a beer watching 'The Price is Right.' Then somebody says, 'Jesus Christ, you should see all the police outside.' 'Oh really.' So they go over to the balcony and are looking over and they kept watching. 'There's Bob. He's getting out of a police cruiser!'

"So I ran into the washroom and I pull the money out and wrap it up in this plastic and I sink it into the back of the toilet. I come back and sit down because I'm expecting the door to come off the hinges. I just saw two cops and him walking into the apartment and he's got tattoos and everything. They have interviewed him in the bank because he's the only customer: 'What did he look like? Would you recognize him again? Do you have a record? What are you doing here? You live in the east end, what are you doing in the west end?' 'I came to see my landlord.' So they check it out. They came to the building and they see the landlord who said, 'Oh yeah, he was here. I seen him today.'

"So the cops left and he leaves and phones me from the other side of the city. He says, 'Holy fuck, wait until you hear what happened to me.' I said, 'What is going on? I've got to get out of here.' He said, 'Don't worry, I've got a friend with a truck who will drive you out of there for $100.' 'No problem, if he gets me out of here I'll give him $200.' The guy was there in 20 minutes. 'Ding dong. Is Johnny there. Come on down.' 'Can I use your washroom?' I go in, grab the dough, come out and it is dripping down into my pants. 'See ya, thanks for the beer. Bye.' Out I go down to the truck — in between where the stick shift is — and they drive me out of the city. We buy a pound and have a few beers and I give my friend $500.

"He was supposed to report to the police station to look at mug shots and he didn't go. They have a description of me already. He comes to see me the next day and I asked if he was followed. He said, 'Well I never went home.' 'Good because they are probably watching your place. You have a criminal record and they figure we are frick and frack, maybe they got us made.' He says, 'Nah.' I said, 'Well we are getting out of the city.'

"We got the smoke and we roll it up into ounces and count all the money I have left, about $2000. We decided to go to the main bus terminal. I did that knowing that the bus terminal is not safe and they probably have snapshots of me because in most banks the camera starts clicking as soon as the teller presses the alarm. I knew this and I did it anyway. We had a few tokes of this gold Columbian and a few beers down at the bus terminal. 'This is how we'll do it. I'll put the dope in a locker. Now you go buy your ticket and come back. Then I'll go buy my ticket and that way we are not together.' 'Good plan.' Off he goes and comes back with a ticket. Off I go and come back with a ticket.

"Now I'm thinking banks, banks, banks. Never would I think a narcotics agent is watching me, it wouldn't dawn on me. Apparently they were watching for drugs coming or going out of the city. And they see this movement with the bag and they wonder, 'What are these guys up to?' So I get on the bus, my partner gets on the bus and sits back. He wants to smoke and I said, 'You can't smoke up front, go to the back.' So he goes and sits six seats back. Now a cop gets on the bus. I don't know he's a cop at the time — big boy with a ski jacket on — and he goes to the back. I said to my buddy, 'Why don't you put that cigarette out and come sit up here with me until we get going.' So he gets up and he moves. Now another one gets on and he's wearing a trenchcoat. He gets on, gets off again, gets on again, looks at us, gets off again. A bell goes off, 'They are looking for someone but it ain't me.' So I'm reading the paper looking for my robbery. I did that on a regular basis. I buy every paper available and I check just to see what some stooge, some foolish cop has told the reporter. If he tells the reporter too much, I learn about it. Here it is on the second page, 'Lone bandit robs bank and escapes with an undisclosed amount of cash. The suspect is being sought. No further leads whatever.' Wonderful.

"Now this guy gets on again but this time he walks to the partition where the step is. He puts his badge and gun over and says, 'Would you kindly put your hands on top of your heads. Stand up very slowly.' Now we're the only passengers on the bus. Isn't that funny. So I get up to get off the bus and here is the guy in the back seat with both hands holding a gun. Hum, these guys are serious. They don't know I don't have a gun. So we get off the bus and I have $2000 and he has $600 in his wad. We are sitting in the squad room now and I don't know that they are on to us for banks. I figure it is just a dope bust. I got enough cash on me to buy my way out, the fine, maybe get bail. The narc says they're booking us on the drug beef. They are weighing the pot on the triple scale. He says to me, 'We are also charging you with fraud.' Maybe they caught up to me with the cheques out west! 'What fraud?' 'Well it appears that your ounces are only 25 grams' and they start laughing. So they are joking around and loosening up a bit. Then the Hold-Up Squad comes in.

"A little fellow — a Turk — and a tall fellow with white hair — the Man from Glad. I've heard of them and I know what is going to happen. I'm just waiting for a little green room treatment. There is no question about it, there is a beating coming. I know fellows it has happened to. They grab my partner first and, like I said, I've only known him about a month now. They take him into a little room and they let him out again and then they go, 'All right Smith, in here.' They know my name! I had false I.D. and they haven't printed me yet. Into the room I go and I sit down and he pulls out a bag, 'So this is your dope?' I said, 'Yeah.' He said, 'Why are you selling dope?' I said, 'To get by.' He said, 'You got two thousand fucking dollars.' I said, 'Well you'd have $2000 too if you were running around the city with gold Columbian marijuana.' 'How much are you selling your ounces for?' He is doing a calculation. 'How much have you sold?' So I got through that all right. Then they play this little game with me for half an hour.

"I've never seen them before, but I know they're Hold-Up men. They were the ones who went up on that beef for cutting that kid's scrotum a few years ago. One is wearing snakeskin shoes and a diamond ring. We are just a couple of punks to them, so they play this little game. The Turk pulls out this manilla envelope. First he slides out this photostat copy with the bank's name written on the top of it — bad bills that were in the drawers the day of the robbery. Then he pulls out my money from a plastic bag and he puts on rubber gloves and he pulls the fucking bills out. 'Are you in the habit of selling marijuana to the bank of [names the bank]?' I go, 'I beg your pardon?' 'Well tell me where you got this money?' I said, 'Well it is from the ounces of course.' I just want to cop out to this dope if I can and get out of there. 'Were you up in this area yesterday? Did anybody buy dope off you up there?' 'As a matter of fact, no.'

"Now the Man from Glad with the silver white hair pulls out the envelope and there is a picture of me from fourteen different fucking angles. Every dimension possible, big 12 x 9 glossies. 'You got a brother?' This guy is enjoying himself. Oh yeah, they have lots of fun. They are fucking sadists, they are sadistic bastards. So I said, 'That ain't me.' Then they got rough. The Man from Glad left and the little Turk has me all by himself. He pulls his gun out and he pulls my hair back. I'm handcuffed, 'How would you like this up your fucking ass, you punk?' And he starts beating me around the room. Down with the pants around my ankles and now the Man from Glad comes in and holds my feet. 'Have you ever had children?' 'No.' 'Well you're not going to by the time we are finished with you.' He's got this little steel rod and he lifts my testicles and he's rubbing it up and down the bottom of my scrotum. He is scaring the shit out of me. I go, 'Look you guys got your pictures, you got your marked bills, bust me. Book me or fuck off, I don't have to take this shit. You can beat me from today till tomorrow, I don't know what the fuck you're talking about.'

"They didn't hurt me after they had my pants down. It was all a bluff, but it was very embarassing. But it scares you, you don't know if you're going to die in there. They can really inflict fear into a person. I read in the paper months later that some kid took these two guys to court alleging they had tortured him. He took them to court and he lost. It was their word against his. After that they beat it and went over to homicide, which is a good fucking place for them — working with dead people. Anyway it was an open and shut case. They had teller witnesses so I went down."

One-Armed Bandit

> This 35-year-old offender is serving three years for his involvement in one count of robbery with another subject — "That Wanderless Feeling" [Chapter 4] — whom he refers to as Tom. The respondent has a lengthy criminal record involving assault and a variety of theft and drug offences. He also admits to having a serious alcohol problem. He has only one arm having lost the other in a car accident years earlier while driving impaired.

"Tom is different than myself. He's quite confident. It's like he's going to make an ordinary withdrawal. He pretty well convinced me this would be no problem or else I wouldn't have done it. I'm just not the type of person to be involved in a bank robbery. You stand out too much as it is. Tom, he's never used a disguise. This really shocked me. That's why I said there's no way I'm going into a bank looking like this. I'd be easily identifiable with just one arm and even if I had my artificial arm on you could tell if you looked. And Tom looked just like me — long hair and a beard.

"I was in a bit of a jackpot. I owed money for a drug deal that went sour. I got money up front and the people I was dealing with were bikers. I took off from the halfway house with the intention of returning and getting the money back in the right hands after we robbed a bank. I'm on parole and I'm not supposed to go beyond a 25 mile radius, and I'm travelling 500 miles by bus without a travel permit. I planned on going back there and straightening out my affairs with these people, and I figured no one would be the wiser. I'd only be gone two days to get down there, two days to get back. I had an appointment with my parole officer in eight days time so I had lots of time.

"He'd checked out these banks five years previous to that 'cause he'd robbed them all. We were caught on the subway, right on the subway. It's really weird how it happened. When Tom came out of the bank he met me around back. Things did not go the way they were supposed to. The change of clothes should've happened right there, but the timing was really bad. Public transit workers were coming down an alley from the station. I was right in the middle waiting for Tom, and we'd seen people come so we couldn't start the exchange of clothing with people around. Tom's shirt came out and the money started coming out of the shirt. He had a little manila envelope that wasn't big enough to hold all the money so he filled his shirt with it. The money worked its way down the shirt when he was walking. He got to me, the transit fellas are walking down — myself and him hurrying. I can still see it all [laughing]. The money started coming out the back of his shirt. It's just like a T.V. program — a comedy — getting caught wasn't. Everything started fouling up. I just have the one arm, and with the hook, well.... The money was falling out of Tom's pocket and the transit workers were yelling at him saying, 'Sir, you're dropping money.' We couldn't leave the money there with them looking at us. We had to pretend that everything was on the up and up and pick it up.

"The style that Tom used was always the same: in, note, out, on the subway, gone. But the police aren't stupid, they know how banks are robbed and how the people get away. As soon as the police hear about the bank robbery — boom! — they send a car right to the station and another one to the bank. When Tom started spilling the money we were in a hurry to get it off the ground and get to the station before our time had run out. We were getting close to maybe the two-minute mark by then. I picked up a lot of the dollar bills and by this time the transit workers had gotten away from where we were. I figured I can stuff them in my pocket, which was a mistake because with just one arm I couldn't get the change out that I needed. I told Tom, 'Go ahead and leave me behind, I've got nothing to worry about, you have the money, go on.' Just in case anything screwed up we'd planned where we were going to meet later on.

"As long as he got away because I had nothing, I wasn't in the bank. They never saw me. But things didn't work good for me at all. Tom got to the subway and down. I had all these dollar bills on top of the change that's in the bottom of my pocket and had trouble getting it out of my pants. I wore jeans that were snug. I finally got it out, but the time went by and the police were on their way.

"It was the beginning of August and it was really warm that day, and I guess with the perspiration rolling off me the way it was I looked like I've been jogging all day. I find out later that as soon as I left the coin thing and hopped the escalator to the platforms the police pulled in. The fellah that accepted my coins where you buy your tickets looked at me and he looked out to the entrance of the subway station itself. The police pulled up to the subway station and this ticket-taker asked what was happening. The police told him that the bank on the corner had just been robbed and they were looking for a guy with long hair and a brown short beard. Tom had long hair and a brown short beard, but so did I. So the guy told the police, 'Well a guy went flying through here just seconds ago in a real big hurry fitting that description.' That's how we got caught.

"The drivers on the train are equipped with radios right in the train. So they just radioed from where I dropped my coins in at the booth there and said, 'After you have your doors shut, keep it there. The police will be down to check it out.'

"When I got to the bottom of the steps and on the platform, the eastbound train was just taking off so I assumed that Tom had got on the train and I was quite pleased with everything then. I figured he's gone, I'm safe. All I've got is maybe 50 bucks in my pocket in dollar bills. They don't usually bait smaller bills, they bait the big bills. So I wasn't really worried. I wasn't in the bank. I wasn't the guy. I never went anywhere near the bank at all. I didn't feel threatened after I saw that train leave. About 20 seconds after — of believing this — I feel a tap on my shoulder. I turn and it's Tom! He had just gotten to the bottom of the eastbound steps when the doors were shutting on his train. He missed it! He had to run back up the steps over to the westbound side and try to catch it. That's where I was. He just missed it by seconds. The doors had just shut. Our platform was fairly vacant. There was maybe one body and it was way at the other end. A couple workers, sanitation workers down there too. We did the change of clothing and I got his clothing into my plastic bag. Things really fouled up then. If anybody had been around and close to us, they could've saw we were nervous: 'Something is wrong here. These guys look paranoid.'

"We hear the train approaching and it seems like it's taking forever to get there. Oh God, panic, paranoia! You have to wait. There's nowhere you can go unless you wanna run into the train tunnel and then you're liable to get run over by the bloody thing. This is not planned so you don't do that. Tom says, 'Jesus Christ, this is really fucking up.' And I said, 'Yeah, looks like it.' And the train came. It seemed like it was going slower than normally it would be, and maybe this is just all in my mind because the time factor is getting close to the three minutes being over. The cops are gonna be here. They know the routines. It got there and finally the doors opened. When it does get there normally the doors open right away as soon as it stops and people get off. It didn't and I wondered about this, but when it did open we were right on. Tom went on first and went to one end of the car. I got on second and went to the other end, like we weren't together type of thing. He had the money, I had the bag with the jean jacket in it — fatal mistake. I should've gotten rid of it in the garbage dispenser there.

"God, then we sat down. The car was packed, packed. That was good in a way simply because we could get ourselves lost a little bit. Then the doors shut. Seconds ticked away and nothing was happening. The first minute went by and I'm listening to peoples' conversation in the train knowing why the train wasn't going. The one fellah across from me and his friend were saying, 'Ah, they're probably getting high in the tunnel at the end of the car. The driver's doing this and the driver's doing that.' I was saying to myself, 'No, he's not, he's waiting because he was told to stop and not to move.' So I jammed the bag underneath the seat. There's a bit of a ledge so I tried to push it under a bit without causing a lot of suspicion. We were really sweating and everybody else was calm, cool — we stood out. Not only did we look like two bikers — long beards, long hair, and the way we were dressed — we didn't even look like we should be on the subway. I don't even take the subway when I'm in the city.

"It was about three minutes before the police arrived. I looked to the left and I saw all these uniforms coming, guns out 'cause the note had said, 'Armed with a gun.' They came in numbers and they came with guns out. There were nine to twelve I'd say. When you see guns like that you know they mean business. You either gotta run or give up when they spy you. There's no way I'm getting shot for three thousand bucks. They walk on, they go to Tom's end of the train and they see him. He's trying to be as cool as possible, but it's just not working. They know. It's a guy with long hair and a beard and he looked rough. They asked him off the train. I didn't actually hear the words that were spoken as they were quite a ways away. For some reason I figured, 'Well, they're not going to come for me because they only believe there's one guy.' But just to cover their ass, in case that they were grabbing the wrong guy, they saw me at the other end, looking rough, and they took me off also. No guns pointed at me — the guys with the guns stood on the ramp. They never came in because there's innocent people in there and if any gun play were to go down inside somebody else may get shot. The police are cautious that way. They don't want to hurt anybody that's not involved. They're good that way. I have a lot of respect for the cops, without them the world would be pretty crazy.

"The police officer that asked me to step off the train, before he did, he asked me if the bag on the floor belonged to me. I said, 'No, it didn't.' The first thing he did was turn to the girl sitting just over to the left of me and said, 'Does this bag belong to this man? Did you see this man with this bag?' She said, 'I don't want to get involved.' He picked the bag up and said, 'I believe this is your bag, so I'll take it with me.' They took us out in two different cars and they found the money on Tom. He's caught cold. Now me, I had these brand new crisp dollar bills in my pocket, jammed in there, and even though it wasn't big money it was brand new bills and why would I be carrying all new bills? Why would I be carrying a jean jacket in a plastic bag? They had an open-and-shut case. They didn't have to beat us up to get any information out of us or anything like that. They treated us fine. We're waiting for the Hold-Up Squad to come; they were a little more demanding, wanting to know where we were at this date and time. Luckily I still had my ticket stub from the bus, I still had it so that proved I just got off and, luckily, it was a long weekend and no banks had been open that weekend. So they couldn't get us for anything. We just got into town. That was the only bank that had been robbed that day.

"We pretended we didn't know each other for quite a while. Once they ran the check they found out that we were both on parole from out West, both from the same penitentiary. They put us together just like that. It was very simple for them; they didn't have to do a month's investigating.

"I've never done banks before. I would never go into the bank because of the way I look and everything. I just did it as a friendly gesture 'cause he was helping me get money to pay back those people I was involved with over drugs. I wanted to contribute a little. Over the years Tom and I talked about the banks he had got away with and it all sounded so simple."

Go Boy and Surveillance Squad

Roger Caron is one of Canada's most famous bank robbers. His fame comes not from bank robbery nor from his many escapes from federal penitentiaries, rather it comes from his literary successes. Beginning with *Go Boy*, his award-winning autobiography, followed by *Bingo*, an account of the violent 1971 Kingston Penitentiary riot, and now with *Jojo*, a crime fiction novel, Roger has established himself as the most successful practitioner of "Con-lit" in Canada. From the age of 16 he had never been free longer than a few weeks or months at a time. For 24 years Roger spent every birthday and every Christmas incarcerated in federal penitentiaries. Then for 12 years he enjoyed his freedom and made a living as a writer. Recently, however, at age 55, Roger Caron was convicted of a number of armed robberies in Ottawa and sent to prison once more. He blames his downfall on the fact that he developed a cocaine habit in his attempt to deal with Parkinson's disease.

The interview with Roger is followed by an interview with the head of a special O.P.P. task force surveillance squad that arrested Roger and his partner in the act of robbing a bank.

"We used to rob banks gangster style. You go into the bank, jump the counter and give an Apache yell, 'Everybody freeze! Back away from the tills. Back away from the phones. Lay down on the floor.' People go numb in a bank. Some tellers are really dumb and you have to shout at them. The first few seconds there is a lot of shouting. You want them to freeze so they can't think. If they can't think, they can't function so they follow orders. The idea is to terrorize them so they don't push the alarms and then when they're on the floor to pacify them, 'Don't worry, we're not going to hurt you. We just want the bank's money. Just do what you're told and everything will be all right.' Even today I will look at a bank the way a guy looks at a girl, 'Boy, that's an attractive bank. Boy, in the old days I would have gone crazy over that bank.'

"The most dangerous elements in bank robbery are the unknowns — the flukes that you can't control. For instance, a cruiser drives by as you're running out with the loot. Bank robbers jumping into a car look like bank robbers jumping into a car. Everybody is piling into the car in a big hurry. There is an atmosphere about it. If you're robbing a lot of banks, you are almost inevitably heading for a downfall. Mathematically the odds are against you. The odds are great that some fluke will sink you. It's like parachuting, the more jumps you do, the more likely you are to get injured. Sooner or later something will malfunction.

"I never liked robbing banks. As a kid I did, but even then I didn't. There was a lot of dread and a lot of danger and a lot of fear. As you get older you start realizing the danger even more and it's the last thing in the world you want to think about. So you subconsciously put it off until your funds are so low that you have to do it. And the more you do it, the better you become. You experience fear, but that fear becomes cold, controlled fear. I'd be uptight and sweating until the moment of truth. My moment of truth was when I was about to pull into the driveway of the bank. I'd drive by and look to see if there were any strange cars or strange people parked nearby. What invariably happens is that you're ready to go but you can't for one reason or another. You're cruising by the bank to see if someone is parked in your spot or if there's a policeman cashing a cheque. I'm not going to rob a bank while someone is sitting in his car with nothing better to do than watch people go into and out of the bank. I'm not going to go into the bank and let him see me pull my hood down.

"When it looked right we'd go in. I never drove — the guy who is the muscle never drives. I'd tap the driver on the shoulder and say, 'We go.' That was my by-word. The moment I'd say, 'We go,' a whole transformation would come over me. I would be fearful and jumpy until then, but now I knew that fear could destroy me, doubt could destroy me. It was no longer a time for pessimism, it was a time to think positive. You can't let doubt enter your mind. And no fear. You say to your partner, 'We go,' and the transformation comes over you and you're a light beam. You focus on that bank. You've got a one-track mind and you go right to the bank. From now on every second counts. There's no backing out now. It's go all the way. If anyone gets in your way, if a policeman comes between you and the money, then look out. It's me or him and one of us is going down. It's survival. It's the final moment of truth.

"And for God's sake, let no one try to be a hero or they'll get what they have coming to them. It's cut and dried. Don't be a hero. We're not after your money, we don't want to hurt you, just give us space, give us room, we've got enough problems without you guys interfering. So please, no heroes. If you're going to be a hero, we're in an awful big hurry, our life is at stake here and you're going to get wiped. Bank robbers get indignant, 'Who is this son-of-a-bitch who suddenly deputized himself? If he wants to be a headline grabbing hero, then he's going to get what he deserves.'

"You balance the risk against the gain. It's a gamble. If you're caught, you're caught. If you're not, you're not. And if you're shot, you're shot. For any one score the odds are in your favour. When you're planning to rob a bank you know that there's the possibility that you are going to die brutally or that you are going to be wounded, captured, and sent away for life. It's not a game. You say to yourself, 'Please, I hope everything goes well. I know I'm dumb, I should go out and get a job, but I'm not. I'm robbing banks. I've made up my mind and I'm willing to gamble my life that I can get away. I just hope there are no police in there.' In your heart you know that you can't bat 1000. Every time you do a job you are that much closer to a fall. It just takes one bad day and you'll regret it for the rest of your life. It's not baseball — three strikes and you're out.

"I never really thought of myself as a thief. Bank robbery was glamorous to me and I wasn't stealing from a person. I saw myself as an outlaw. An outlaw has his own ethics on what is right and wrong. A thief is just a thief. I would look down on petty thieves. Old time bank robbers are basically honest guys, you can trust them. They steal from institutions, but they wouldn't rob a guy on the street. You could invite a bank robber to your home and not have to worry about him stealing from you. I can rob a bank, but I couldn't keep the extra change that some store clerk might give me by accident. I'd think about keeping it, but I couldn't. My conscience would bother me. Today it's mostly drugs. I'm discouraged about bank robbery today.

"Back in 1972, Rollie and I were planning a score. We would check out banks three, four, six times over several weeks. After you've robbed a bank and you rush out you never know what's going to be there. We didn't know it, but we were under surveillance by an O.P.P. squad formed just to nab us. We were looking at this bank and it was a Friday night and only three banks in the city were open. The police have a tailor-made situation and they only have to sit and wait. I'm a real suspicious guy. I would say to myself, 'If I was a policeman, where would I set an ambush on this bank?' My partner was ready to go in, but I wouldn't go. I would drive a wider and wider and wider circle. I kept expanding my arch until I spotted them. They were parked behind a nursing home. I spotted one and once I spotted one I spotted the others right after. They admitted to me later that they were waiting with high-powered rifles on the rooftops and they had me in their sights. This was the city police force. Meantime, this O.P.P. special squad was also following us around in six unmarked police cars.

"The city police were on a stakeout and this special task force was on our tail. I hadn't made up my mind which bank I was going to do and I scouted them all. They saw me checking out many banks and they didn't know which bank would be the one I was going to knock off. They knew I was very alert. We were looking everywhere, but we couldn't spot them. When we finally decided on a score and came out of the bank they hit us from three different directions. They smashed one car into us and I opened the car door on the passenger side and was about to put my foot on the pavement. As I levelled my gun over the window a second car hit us on the side. I was aiming at the car that had hit us from the front. I looked into his eyes and I had an automatic pistol and I had him. I tried to shoot, but as I held my gun up the second car hit us on the side and knocked me down onto the seat and the gun went flying. I wasn't expecting it. I was lucky I didn't lose a foot. If the second car had hit a second later, I would have had my foot on the ground. He would have slammed the car into the door and it would have cut my foot off. That saved the cop. If I had had a shotgun or a machine-gun, I would have fired through the window.

"I could never understand why they didn't shoot. I think it's because I didn't have a gun in my hand and my partner didn't have a gun in his hand. They made a mistake; they should have shot. One guy jumped onto the hood and was laying across it with a shotgun pointed at the windshield. I was reaching for the gun that went flying when the third car hit and knocked me off balance again. By that time I was looking into the barrel of a shotgun — I finally got the message. He should have shot me by all rights. I think he didn't quite have it in him. He was very verbal. The guy who was on the hood was very verbal and usually guys who talk the most do the least. I don't think that anybody, just anybody can kill. They should have killed me."

Surveillance Squad

The following are excerpts from an interview with the officer in charge of the special O.P.P. task force surveillance squad that arrested Roger and his partner after they emerged from having robbed a bank. This story provides a different perspective on the incident described by Roger in his interview.

"This was the first time our force had formed a surveillance squad and it was meant for the higher echelon of criminals. This is back in 1972. We trained for awhile and then we went out on the road. It was believed that Rollie had done one prior to March, but we couldn't prove it. Both he and Roger were known bank robbers. We found out where Rollie lived and we decided to do a project on them. We had six men on our surveillance team and two technical guys who looked after the wires. We had their phones tapped, but they didn't say much on the phone. We tailed them from March 5th until we busted them on the 21st and they had no idea we had ever tailed them. It's hard to do. Rollie lived in an apartment and Roger lived in a townhouse. We decided to key on Rollie because his residence was easier to observe. They would meet for breakfast anytime after 10:00 A.M. and then case banks. They'd drive around, have lunch, work out in the afternoon at a health club, then drive around and case some more banks.

"Initially we lost them a lot until we got used to them. We didn't know the city that well at first so it was better to lose them than to be spotted. After that we didn't lose them very often. Roger was very surveillance conscious. We began by watching Roger's townhouse, but we saw him with binoculars a couple of times! Oh yes, he used to case the area looking for anybody sitting around. We would have been spotted after awhile so we laid back. That's why he was so surprised when we nabbed him. He said to us, 'I should have seen you guys. I don't believe it.'

"They went through subdivisions looking for tails and they were always recording licence plate numbers at the police station. They were cautious about what they said when they talked to each other on the phone. They knew what they were doing. Since we were from out of town we stayed in the same hotel and we'd be up a little after 7:00 A.M. and have breakfast as a group. We stayed together and lived together. The odd weekend we went home because there were no banks open. They cased some on Friday nights so we stayed a few Friday nights. We'd watch Rollie's place from around 8:00 A.M. and if his rental vehicle was in the driveway, we assumed he that he was at the apartment. He'd come out and get in the car and we'd follow him wherever he went.

"The only way to get these guys is to get them right in the act. We watched them do it; you can't get them any better than that. If we had grabbed them, we would have had them for nothing. The way they were going we never knew when they were going to do it. This happened so fast. Bang, they did it. They would have shot us if they had the chance. Our strategy was to smash them when they emerged from the bank. My boss didn't like that idea initially, but I said, 'Would you sooner have a high-speed chase or a hostage situation?' I told him that we had one thing going for us and that was surprise. They didn't know we were on them. They were going to be flabbergasted and they were.

"Before that, they were looking at doing another bank on a Friday night. It was loaded with money and we knew that Roger loved it. He wanted to do that one and we were ready. They were around that bank 20 times a day for three days. Rollie was in four or five times just changing money and having a look. Then they got spooked. We let the city police know we were there and that we had everything under control. We told them to keep their men back and if we got them, we'd turn everything over to them. But Roger checked the perimeter and he saw two guys in a detective car drinking coffee and went close enough to hear their police radio. That blew the whole thing.

"They were all set to do it. In fact that night we watched them steal a truck. They planned the escape route and had left their cool car, the rental car, sitting a half minute away. They were there to do it, but before Roger would do it he'd go through the whole thing again. Then he spotted the detectives. Roger called them 'skunks.' We thought initially he had spotted one of our guys, but then they talked on the phone about the 'two skunks in the D-car.' We were on a real high because we knew they were about to strike. Then it was a downer because they didn't do it. We had put in days following them and got up to that high where we thought they were going to go. We were with them and we knew they had that stolen truck. And then they cancel out! It's hard coming down. We were on a low. Christ, all that work gone.

"Then we almost missed them. After the weekend, we'd drive back Sunday night or Monday morning because they didn't leave until after 10:00 A.M. As long as we were there before 10:00, we could pick them up. We got a call that something was up and we drove like madmen to get down there at 9:15 A.M. We got to Rollie's apartment and his car was gone! He had never left at that time before. He never left the house before ten and here it is 9:15 and he's not there! Everybody fanned out to the places they usually went to and I found them in a restaurant not too far from the house. They were having breakfast. We knew something was up because they had a car from a guy who had reported it stolen. He must have known what was going on and reported it stolen after they went to do the bank.

"Surprise was our biggest advantage. We knew these guys were professionals and wouldn't be spending much time in the bank. From my observations from a snowbank with binoculars I saw them pull the car up and leave it running. It was cold enough that you could see the exhaust. They got out of the car and they had on touques — balaclavas. As soon as they got to the front steps they pulled the balaclavas down over their heads. Roger had never gone into a bank before. It had to be. They had two cars. They left the cool car a short distance away and had done a lot of spinning looking for tails. They went through a subdivision and we stayed off them.

"As soon as they walked into the bank I picked up the radio and said, 'They're in the bank. Count to ten and start closing in.' I jumped into my mustang and pulled out in front of an air force officer. I was driving very slowly and I stopped at the green light. He was blowing his horn probably wondering what is wrong with this guy. Then we saw them run out of the bank. Roger had the gun. He ran around the passenger side and his partner opened the driver's door. He threw the satchel with the money inside the car. They were both wearing balaclavas. They got in the car and pulled their balaclavas up. They just started to move when I pulled across the curb and hit them broadside. Roger's eyes were that big [indicating with his hands]. They were both laughing because they thought it was a successful bank job. When I hit them I was going about 15, 20, 25 miles an hour — enough to bounce them back. I gave it a good shot as I went over the curb. Roger had the gun on the dash and I had a shotgun in the car and my sidearm. When I hit their car his gun fell to the floor. My door jammed and I couldn't get the shotgun out and I couldn't get my sidearm. We were looking each other in the eyes, just the hood of the car separating us, and he was reaching for the gun. I knew what for, but I couldn't get mine.

"Just then J.C. hit them the other way and they were done. Roger would have shot me if he had got to that gun. There's no doubt he was going to do that. By the time I got the door open it was over. There was a car behind, another one of our guys with a shotgun, another one with a rifle. It happened in seconds, it was so fast. I came out of the car and we put them up against the bank and Roger said, 'You bastards are real cool. I knew we shouldn't have done this. You're something else.' And then he said, 'We have only one gun, it's in the car.' All Rollie would say is, 'Take this stupid thing off my head,' referring to the balaclava. Roger asked me afterwards, 'Who are you guys?'

"Meanwhile the air force officer saw everything. He went into a restaurant to phone the police and said, 'I can't believe what's happening. There's a Mustang. He's drunk. He pulled out and passed me and then he slowed down. He's gone off and hit a car broadside and they're out of the car with guns and now they're going to kill each other.' There was one cruiser in the area when the bank alarm did go off and he came over with his gun out and he was shaking like a leaf.

"Roger still can't get over that we didn't waste him. He told me that several times. I told him that we didn't have any reason. We had them. It would have been like shooting fish in a barrel. If they had fired a shot, it might have been different. We knew they were runners so we put the cuffs on their feet so they couldn't run. Their records included 'Escape,' 'Escape,' 'Escape.' They were put in two separate jails because they were escape artists, but they both escaped! I couldn't believe it when I heard that Roger had escaped. We were working on another case and we heard it on the news. 'Jesus Christ!' And then Rollie escapes too! Jesus, they both do it! They were recaptured and each got 12 years. Roger and I kept in touch, I even dropped in and saw him in prison. He was not like others you deal with. He was looked at by other criminals as top dog because he never squealed on anybody. He kept telling me that he was going to make something of himself and his book. I didn't believe him. He wrote me a long long letter asking me to go to bat for him on parole — no way. There's no way I'd take the chance because I figured that Roger, sure he had changed, but if he ended up with a crisis and something didn't go right there would be no doubt in my mind that he'd be right back into it. I feel he's done well and he deserves a lot of credit, but if that book had failed he would have either killed himself or gone right back to robbing banks. We treated Roger fairly and he recognizes that."

CHAPTER TEN

Deals and Appeals —

Sentencing and the Courts

- •Lifer
- •Framed
- •Deal Making Time
- •Blind and Disabled
- •I Need Help not Prison

Most bank robbery cases are resolved through guilty pleas and many of these are arrived at through pre-trial negotiations between the defendant and his counsel on one side and the police and prosecuting attorney on the other. The bargain is often struck between the defence attorney, who initiates the proceedings, and the investigating officers who then seek the consent of prosecuting attorneys. A plea bargain typically involves an agreement by the defendant to plead guilty to certain offences in exchange for other offences being dropped or lowered. The prosecutor may also agree to the defence's request that the proposal submitted to the judge concerning sentencing be within a certain range. Judges may not be informed of plea bargains nor are they bound by them in determining sentence. However, they know this is a standard practice and typically go along with an agreement worked out by the defense and prosecution. A plea bargain in which the accused pleads guilty and receives an adequate sentence is also a measure of competence for detectives. It saves court time and indicates that the evidence is strong and the case well prepared — since a weak case is more likely to be challenged in court or result in an unsatisfactory sentence. The police, therefore, seek an admission of guilt from suspects in order to strengthen their case, deter courtroom trials, and plea bargain with the defence from a position of strength. Defendants and their attorneys are more likely to negotiate if the prosecuting case is strong. One of the more damaging pieces of evidence against a suspect is a statement admitting guilt, particularly if it is corroborated by other evidence. In such cases the defence's only chance is to challenge the validity of the statement in court, but that is fraught with problems and unlikely to succeed. A more plausible course of action is to plead guilty in exchange for a reduction in charges and/or an agreement regarding sentence. In robbery cases it appears that the police and prosecution do not offer lenient sentences in their pre-trial negotiations. Their strategy instead is to threaten the offender with an extreme sentence and reduce it somewhat in exchange for the plea (Desroches, 1995:251-252).

Because the criminal justice system defines robbery as a violent crime, the penalties are great. First offenders are typically sentenced to penitentiary for a minimum four or five years and repeat offenders often receive ten years to life imprisonment. The average sentence of the 80 men in this study was 9.37 years in federal penitentiaries. The harsh sentence reflects not only the seriousness of the crime but the fact that most had lengthy criminal records (73/80) and many (51/80) were on probation, parole, or had escaped from custody when they committed their recent crime(s).

One of the main principles of sentencing in robbery cases is deterrence. Deterrence theory suggests that the severity of the sanctions imposed by the courts will prevent crime and is based on several assumptions that are questionable and difficult to prove. For one thing it assumes that sentences will become known to would-be offenders through word of mouth or the media. It also assumes that offenders will consider the possibility that if they commit the same crime, they too will receive a harsh sentence. It further suggests that offenders will act rationally and be deterred from crime due to fear of imprisonment. Clearly, it is quite likely that knowledge of severe sentences never reaches that group of young men who are most prone to crime. It is also likely that even if it does, they will not be deterred since research (Desroches, 1995; Feeney, 1986; Katz, 1991) indicates that offenders believe they will not get caught. Social control theory further suggests that persons who lack social bonds, commitments, and investments in the social order will evaluate the situation as one in which they have little to lose and will also be undeterred. In short although criminals use a degree of rationality in the commission of their offences, they are not totally objective nor is the possibility of a harsh sentence in the distant future the only variable or the most significant factor in the decision to engage in illicit activities. From the interviews, it seems that the bank robbers are unaware of the odds, the risks, and the penalties in their endeavour. Nor does the formal policy of heavy sentencing appear to be a topic of discussion on the street level where offenders live and move about. In addition most fail to realize that robbery has another hazard — the fierce and sometimes deadly response of the police.

The heavy sentences commonly prescribed are often unexpected and criticized by bank robbers who continue to define their crimes less seriously than official authority. *Lifer* is an interview with a 34-year-old man serving ten life sentences. This is the third time he has been imprisoned for bank robbery and his criminal record goes back to his adolescence. He appears to have a somewhat tenuous grip on reality and fails to accept the significance or seriousness of his actions. His history clearly outlines a man whose path has seldom steered away from crime. His story can also be looked at in part from a social control theory perspective as he constantly refers to his lack of community and his desire to find a place within society where he can fit in. *Framed* is a man who claims to be innocent of the crime. He was initially uncooperative in the interview because of anger over his conviction and sentence. He became interested in newspaper articles of his case and then began to describe the incident that led to his arrest. He provides a very unconvincing explanation of how he came to be in possession of stolen money. *Deal Making Time* describes a case in which an armed parolee is suspected of several robberies. He is uncooperative and is treated harshly by the police who threaten him with a 12-year sentence. The offender eventually agrees to plea bargain and recieves a six-year prison term. *Blind and Disabled* is a partially disabled individual who impulsively robs a bank in order to continue a drinking binge. He later turns himself into the police and is sentenced to probation and community service. *I Need Help Not Prison* also gives himself up to the police in order to seek psychiatric help but bitterly finds himself in a federal penitentiary. His letter to the parole board is reproduced.

Author's Note: *Offenders pay close attention to what the judge says about their crimes and his or her reasons behind the sentence. Even though they disagree with the harsh sentences, convicts appear to hold judges in high esteem and view them as impartial.*

Lifer

> Age 34, this offender is serving his third penitentiary sentence for bank robbery. He is the first person to receive a life sentence for robbery in Canada. The penitentiary system classifies him as a security risk because of three prison escapes.

"I was charged with ten bank robberies and they gave me ten life sentences concurrent. It was a non-violent crime. I mean I can understand their animosity towards me, and I can understand the sense of justice and the things that have to be taught to other would-be bank robbers in a community, a sentence's gotta be just. It doesn't matter how many times you do something, it's gotta weigh itself out and this doesn't. I treated everybody with roses, smiles, and kisses and I get life imprisonment. Just mellow, cool and mellow. Like in six weeks I committed 19 robberies. I wasn't rushing, I was just mellow. So they slapped the book on me. I have something before this; I got seven bank robberies and eight bank robberies previous on my record. They certainly want to make an example because you've done this before and you haven't learned your lesson.

"I've done ten years inside. Like how do you learn your lesson from this hole, from life? There's no holistic medicines within prison, there's hardly any type of nourishment for rehabilitation where a person is taken and brought forth and looked at for his individual problems and these are worked on. We don't have those types of programs where a person could be healed by his own choices, by his ability to take possession of his negative energy and let go of it and put that positive energy to better use. I've tried to go straight and commit no crimes. I did really bad communicating with people because I didn't have no previous experience in being away from the community and I couldn't adapt well to people once again. And people couldn't adapt to me. There was this aura, this feeling about me that wasn't coming across too well. There was something missing about me. The whole thing about belonging to a community just wasn't there for me although I tried. I joined churches and I go to different places to look for sharing. The sense of belonging for some reason wasn't there. Coming from a place of such complexity as a prison to a place of serenity such as a church and nice people, it caused me to be more anxious than serene. It's such a mystery with me. I feel bad about being here again. I'd like to answer that because I think it's very important. I think it was disassociation from the normal wholeness of an individual — the fullness of an individual. My body, my mind, and my soul just wasn't together, wasn't in unison, sort of flowing out of me. And being unemployed and hearing people's snivelling words around Christmas time. Crying on welfare and feeling sorry for themselves and just bad about life in general. They're caught up in this little trap, travelled this welfare trip and they can't get out of it. They're drinking away their money and didn't have enough money for food.

"So when you're caught in this complexity, it's hard to know how you're gonna react to it. I had maybe ten beers that day — just drinking draught in a hotel. It was apparently the money of this guy's girl. I didn't know that. So the next thing I knew we were at his place and she was screaming at him for spending her money. I said, 'Listen, don't worry about it. I got some money at home. I'll lend it to you for Christmas time. Pay me whenever you can.' So I went out and I robbed a bank. I did it that moment. I took a taxi about eight blocks and said, 'Stop over here.' Went in and robbed the bank.

"I hung out at bars or clubs; it's the best place to meet people. You gotta have a mutual something happening between you — not magic. You don't know people so they gotta be into something. So they like booze, okay, so we drink. They like coke, I'm willing to check it out. A couple of weeks when I'm down to eight robberies I just realized, 'What am I doing?' I left town for two weeks and did the nine robberies in that other city. It was taking a lot out of me. With the use of cocaine, that takes a lot of energy. When I came back on the train I was totally wasted. I was ready to settle down. I was at any given time going to go straight, but there was no offers to go straight. I don't know where to go straight. I went to places where I thought I might get away from society — isolate me in such a way I will be well hidden and I would be into a new form of life. Out of crime completely, but I was on drugs and I didn't know if these ideas were like a 'drug bug,' just thinking too much about my life. But still it was me. It was my thoughts even though they came from a drug-oriented mind. Still they were good ideas. Then I got caught. They had this place staked out and these two detectives had guns pointed at me outside the bank. At the time I was a parole violator because I haven't reported. I knew I was wanted — what is the point in wearing a disguise?

"The reason I robbed banks is because they're unmerciful. I always felt like Stephen Leacock about banks. I've always admired his story about the banker who was an aristocrat and this small little fellow who was just so tiny, and this guy, this banker was so huge. Everything was so complex to this little guy. This little guy always entrusted his money to the big guy and it was a kingdom, sort of, of just people living off people — sleazy. I seen that for 20 years in Canada and unfortunately that's the way I feel about banks. I don't hate people who work in banks, I'm not talking about people, it's the institution itself. When we're pressed or when we're depressed, when we're a farm or a small businessman or just a person taking out a loan, why do we have to pay so much for a loan? Why do people have to make so much money? Why at the end of the year do banks have to make sixty million dollars? Why do their executives have to make two hundred thousand dollars a year? Why do us small guys gotta pay off to them our livelihoods, our blood, our sweat and tears so we can have a few joys in life, a few little precious things that they have implanted in our minds in the first place? It's not right what they do. Abuse, abuse, the whole monetary system is really flaky.

"I got ripped off. The bankers came and repossessed my car, mine and my wife's car. They just came and took it from the street. Didn't knock on the door or anything. I thought the car got stolen. It was my responsibility to pay the bills for the car and I was one month behind and I wasn't working. Anyways, it took me three days to find the car then, when I did, they were selling my car — like for a ridiculous amount of money. It's a monopoly. They repossess my car and sell it to their friend or whoever. They stole my car and they sent me a bill.

They sold it for $500 and the car was worth $4000. Like it's your own pride and joy, you take care of it, you put oil into it. It's your car. The bank sends me the bill for the rest of the money I owe on the car. It's an invisible brutality they invoke on you. It was like a kick in the face when you're down. Doing a really dirty trick, dirtiest trick in the world. A man works his guts out, saves, scrimps, and tries to put his life together. The bank sent me this bill and we argued about this bill. Eventually I paid for the bill myself with the money that I robbed from the bank. I had to pay for it because it was in my wife's name and they would have been docking her pay. They got the money from the dealer and they got the money from me even though I had to go out and rob them for it. They're always backed up so why not give the poor sucker a break? I don't know why I want to justify anything with banks.

"I was influenced by the older, legendary folk stories about bank robberies. There's a good image of bank robbery if it's done non-violently — each man for his own cause. To me, it's gotta be non-violent, it's gotta be cool and sharp and get away with no harm done to anybody. The colourful images that were portrayed or implanted in my innocent mind. And newspaper articles, when you're young and sitting around looking for jobs you read about bank robbery. And when I was 16 they put me in detention with a bank robber. He had a lot of bullet holes in him and he told me about robbing banks and about his lifestyle. I think that the crimes that I later committed were indirectly sort of from those three areas. From this individual, from the news media, and most of all from the hassles with the bank. I would say 40 percent hastles, 30 percent the news media, and 15 percent myself.

"At the sentencing my lawyer didn't have much to say on my behalf because we weren't getting along. The lawyer didn't even talk five minutes in court for me. There was like four postponements and 22 months to go to trial. Five minutes of your time after 22 months, hey, come on fella! I could have fuckin' pleaded guilty fuckin' twenty months ago to this fuckin' thing and got the fuckin' life myself! I don't want you saying a word on my behalf 'cause you don't know what you're saying. You don't know me and you never got to know me, never cared to know me, never part of me. And the police, they were trying for glory by arresting me and giving me ten life sentences and by having their names put in the paper.

"My parole officer told me 20 months before I got sentenced that the police were going for a life sentence. I stole money and maybe I deserve a life sentence, I don't know. Maybe I do, but I just don't know how to interpret life sentences — ten life sentences is ridiculous. I have a problem dealing with that right now. I really didn't think about the seriousness, the nature, the responsibility of conducting my life in a rightful manner. 'It's against the law to commit crime.' 'Well you knew that all the time fella!' 'No I didn't. I didn't want to know that.' 'How come you didn't want to know that?' So you question yourself till your mind comes to that wholeness. It's because there's so much confusion in life, so many complexities, highs and lows; and somehow you're entwined and entangled within this whole like in a spider web. Floating in the universe, you lose all this energy to other people. I just wanted to get something more out of life. I like to think my other life hasn't begun yet. I like to think that one of these days I'm going to overcome some of the difficulties I have been dealing with and become a positive force. Whether it's in the correctional field, theology, or just working in a back room typing. I don't want to stay in prison, I got enough of prison for me and two other guys. I have this blessing of knowing that somehow things will work out."

Author's Note: Stephen Leacock, the humourist, whose story apparently inspired this man to embark upon a bank robbery career, is widely studied in Canadian schools. His most famous book, Sunshine Sketches of a Little Town *(1912), contains a story on bank robbery entitled* The Mariposa Bank Mystery. *Leacock also wrote other short stories dealing with the public's fascination with crime and his own experiences with banks.*

This offender escaped two years after this interview, committed several bank robberies, and was re-incarcerated.

Framed

This interview was arranged after another inmate failed to appear. The subject was not fully informed about the purpose of the interview and was initially uncooperative stating that he was appealing his conviction for bank robbery. He was quite upset about his trial and conviction, refused to sit for the interview, and expressed great anger claiming that he had been framed. He eventually became interested in talking when I pulled out several newspaper clippings of his case. He showed me clippings he had saved and asked if he could have a copy of the ones I had. I agreed and he began to answer my questions finally taking a seat. Age 39, he admitted to previous convictions for bank robbery but vehemently denied the present one claiming that he had been framed.

"What appears to have occurred is that a man robbed the bank and was chased by a male teller. Two other young men witnessed the chase and joined in out of curiosity. The chase went in and out of alleys and along streets, up and down snowbanks, across streets, and ended with me being arrested when I tried to take a cab a few blocks away. The main witness at the trial was one of the men who gave pursuit and he said that he saw the robber throw money out onto the street as he ran. At one point the teller stopped to gather the money and at another point his friend grew tired and gave up the chase. He stated that he saw the man hide behind some parked cars and later emerge and hop into a taxi. In court he testified that he saw me go down an alley and come out later with different clothing after presumably throwing off a balaclava and a leather jacket.

"I was in the area and I found this bag of money on the street. The robber must have thrown it away. I picked it up and hailed a cab when this guy approached the driver and told him that I had just robbed a bank. The cabbie refused to budge so I got out and hailed another cab and this guy told him not to move. Finally the police arrived and I was arrested with marked money from the bank. They searched the area but failed to find the robber's mask and jacket.

"I was trying to hail a cab because I didn't want to get mugged or robbed of the money. How many citizens are going to stick around and hand over money that they've found on the street? You'd be stupid. Anyway, because I was on parole and living in a halfway house for ex-cons, the police didn't believe my story and I was arrested. I had a jury trial and was identified by the witness who had chased the robber to the taxi. The witness stated that he had not seen the robber's face in the pursuit and had lost sight of him briefly when the robber hid. He waited and then spotted me walking down a street and entering a cab. I had to take the stand to testify on my own behalf and this allowed the prosecution to introduce evidence that I had two previous convictions for bank robberies. The judge later made numerous references to my criminal record in his address to the jury but hardly said anything about the present offence. There was all kinds of evidence that the police held back including a photograph of the robber in the bank, which would have proved my innocence. The prosecution had no witnesses who could identify me, no fingerprints, and could not produce the gun or coat the robber used.

"The police took the stand and said that the gun and the coat were probably thrown and picked up by someone in the vicinity. My lawyer asked the police if I appeared to be out of breath and they said no. I wasn't out of breath despite the fact that I was alleged to have been involved in a lengthy chase! Also, the testimony of the witness had changed from his initial statement and he was coached by the police. He took the stand and lied in order to obtain the $1000 reward offered by 'Crime Stoppers.' Police always have unsolved robberies which they try to solve by framing others. They even tried to pin a second bank robbery on me but later dropped the charge when they found out that I had only been out of prison for eight days."

Author's Note: The subject refused to answer any questions about his previous convictions stating angrily, "I don't want to talk about them!" During the interview he left briefly to retrieve some documents from his cell. He produced partial trial transcripts and several newspaper articles dealing with his arrest and conviction. One article described how a bank robber was chased through the streets by a bank employee and a customer. Two other men joined the chase as the robber threw the money into the air as he fled.

The article stated:

> *It was later learned that immediately after the robbery, the suspect had removed his coat containing some of the money and stuffed it under a parked car but it was never found.*

Another newspaper article stated:

> *ROBBER LEAVES COURT IN RAGE. Furious bank robber was taken back to jail after being convicted. "That's*

your kind of justice! I expected that all along," he screamed. The article also stated that the man had been sentenced to ten years for robbing a bank while on parole at the time. He had been living in a hostel and had been released only eight days earlier. "Ten years for nothing," he yelled in court.

A third newspaper article dealing with his sentence was entitled, "Angry Judge Criticizes 'Bleeding Hearts.'" The subject had crossed the word "Angry" and scribbled in "Mad Judge." He also showed me another article that had quoted him as saying, "Yeah, but I'm not guilty," and claims to have said, "Bullshit, but I'm not guilty." He claimed to have told the jury that he was not looking for sympathy but just a fair trial. His appeal of his conviction was later dismissed.

Deal Making Time

This 32-year-old offender was on parole at the time of his latest offence. He was suspected of a recent bank holdup and placed under police surveillance. When he robbed again, the Hold-Up Squad was waiting outside the bank.

"I was convicted of four banks a couple of years ago. On this trip they gave me six years just for one. I got an early release from prison on parole to a halfway house. There was a bank robbery, and the way the robbery was pulled off fit the description of the way I was doing them two years earlier. They put me under surveillance and I made this robbery and they got me. They were fucking dead sure it was me who did the other one too.

"The police are just fucking pricks. Especially the Hold-Up Squad. They're notorious. They're fuckin goofs, assholes. I told 'em that. They bring me in and there's these cops from another city and they were fucking telling me that I did this one too. They say I did and I say I didn't. So everytime I say, 'No, I didn't,' well I get a kidney shot, gut shot, a kick in the balls. Like they had me handcuffed behind my back. Like they were just being fuckin goofs. They can kick the shit out of me all they want but I don't give a fuck, you know. Doesn't bother me, go ahead.

"If I'm sitting in a chair and I'm fucking handcuffed, okay, I know I'm getting a beating, it goes without saying. I know it's coming. This kind of shit, getting beaten, you just take that for granted that it's the way it goes. That's the bottom line. You know it's expected. I knew it was coming. I don't like it, but I mean it's there. As soon as you hit the room, about the same size as this, there's three of them in there and you know that it's coming. I know it's coming. I don't like it. I don't look forward to it, but it's there. It's just a fact of life. That's just the kind of shit these assholes do just to show their authority. There's no reason to. I mean, the justice system is a farce — it sucks. There's no justice system, okay. There's no such thing as innocent until proven guilty. Like before all this I never spent a fuckin day in jail in my entire life. I've got a record, but it was for possession of marijuana. Like minor, petty, just shit. You think I can get bail on these bank robbery charges? On my first fucking bank robbery I had fucking $250,000 to put up for bail and they wouldn't give me bail. Like that's one quarter of a million dollars! It's a long sad story.

"Then it was the deal making time. We were going through the courts and they had me on the one, but the others, well everything fit. They knew I did them. I know that they know that. They charged me with all of them, but they can't prove that I did them. But they knew that I did them. So I can go into court and plead guilty to one and not guilty to all the rest and they're going to fucking nail me with large time for that one. Or else we make a deal. Talk and plead guilty to them all so they can clean up their fuckin books. They were asking for 12 years — ridiculous numbers. So they said, 'You come in and plead guilty to them all and we'll give you six years.' After all was said and done and I'd been charged and the bit in the torture chamber and the cell with no bed and the court and detention centre and all the shit they were hanging over my head, I made a deal."

Blind and Disabled

Age 26, this man received a suspended sentence for one bank robbery. The police file contained the following: Suspect and another man [unknown] entered bank and the suspect approached a teller and stated, "I've got a weapon. Don't make a disturbance. Hand over all your money." Suspect then left with the money. Suspect is legally blind and physically disabled.

I called his home and spoke with his mother who was polite but cautious concerning my project. She stated that her son is a remarkable young man and the bank robbery seemed to be a turning point in his life, "He has gone from strength to strength." She explained that in addition to being legally blind (having ten percent vision in the right eye and no sight in the left), her son is physically handicapped, walks with a cane, and uses a battery powered cart to get about. The interview took place in the man's downtown apartment — small and crowded with several desks, three filing cabinets, a computer terminal, and stereo equipment.

His apartment door was opened when I arrived and I waited until he finished his telephone call before I entered. "Sorry to hold you up," he said laughing and shaping his hand like a gun and pointing it at me.

"The decision to rob that bank was made in a split second. It was at the end of a long weekend and I was with this friend and he was a rounder type — a rather aggressive and rangy sort of fellow — a lot of fun actually. I ran into him on the Friday night and we bought a few pops and drank all weekend. We boozed here and we boozed there and we boozed everywhere. On the Monday morning there were only six beers left and I drank four of them. I said to him, 'Holy shit, I'm flat broke. I don't get paid for two weeks and all the money's gone.' I said, 'I don't know what we're gonna do. I might have some money in another bank account, we should go and check it out.' I hadn't used that account for three years.

"Initially it had been my intention to go and panhandle. As a disabled individual I can ply upon the sympathy of others and make not a bad buck doing it. I lived five years on the street supporting myself panhandling. But we had decided that that wasn't a productive endeavour given the time constraints and the degree of our hangovers. So we went to the bank and he was at or about the centre of the bank and I went up to the teller. Because of my balance difficulties and because of my visual difficulties, I have a tendency of standing right next to the teller's wicket even if there's somebody there. I just stand to the side and I try to be unobtrusive and not too outrageous. This customer finished and he had a horrendous stack of bills, which he was pouring into the old wicket. I don't know what the hell hit me, but when I got to the teller I simply looked right at her and demanded that she hand over the money.

"She handed me a stack of bills four or five inches thick. I said, 'Come on,' to my buddy, 'Joe, let's go.' I used his nickname and he and I went out the door of the bank and I proceeded to hail a cab. Because of my low vision and my hurry to get out of there I was whacking my cane on the hood of occupied cabs. He had to make me stop. Finally we got a cab to take us this restaurant. All of a sudden I start to get paranoid and I said, 'Holy shit, what have I done here? I got to get off the street man. This Hold-Up Squad is murder. What if that cab driver has something to say?' So we pile into another cab and grab a couple of cases of beer and come back to this place. My friend had no idea what I had done. When we hit the street I just said, 'Holy fuck, guess what? I just robbed the joint. I just robbed the jug. Let's go.' So we got back here and he was getting a little antsy. He wanted to get away from me cause I was bit wild. The last days of my drinking I was quite wild. Aggressive, I mean really aggressive. Alcohol just seemed to have that effect, verbally aggressive, argumentive. He wanted some money so an argument ensued over how much money I was going to give him and I said, 'Hell, you weren't involved in any of the planning. You weren't involved in anything at all, here's $150 bucks. Get lost.'

"He wanted half and I said, 'Forget it Jack!' Away he went with his $150 and I had a buddy who was staying here and helping to pay the rent and stuff. He was a boozer too and he and I got into the booze and I passed out. Then about seven or eight o'clock at night I woke up and realized what I had done: 'Oh my God!' I called my mother and I remember distinctively having to tell her about eight times before she finally got the message that I was serious and this wasn't a drunken hoax. Then it was the hyper search for a solicitor and she found one and called me back. She said, 'I'm coming to get you. Just stay in the apartment and I'll come in and get you.' I've often thought, 'Jesus, if I hadn't turned myself in, I wonder if I ever would have been caught?' She came and got me about ten o'clock at night. The degree of her fear was such that she had me lie down in the back seat of the car. I got really concerned. I was crying and everything else.

"The lawyer went through the usual interview and there was no issue as to guilt. My interest was just getting the damn thing over with. I had no desire to join the boys behind the bars. Rather in than behind, thank you. The only concern the police had was that I was refusing to identify the person I was with. I made it plain right from the outset that that individual had no knowledge of my intention — as I didn't until immediately before the fact. There were a couple of cops around who played the heavy and you just don't react to them. It's the same thing if you're in a bar and some 6'2" gazoonie is mouthing off at you, if you want your teeth rattled then you talk to him, but if you don't, then you don't.

"I was put in the holding cells and they're not the quietest of places. You've got people in there withdrawing from drugs, psychiatric cases, and half of a domestic screaming his head off. That coupled with the metal — everything is metal — and the noise is unbearable. I ran into two guys I knew from the street — real rangy bastards — and they said, 'My God, what are you doing here?' I said, 'I robbed a bank.' They wouldn't believe me. I said, 'Hang out in the bail court and you'll find out.' We get into bail court and the prosecutor was saying, 'Jesus, Your Honour, there's gotta be a psychiatric matter here.' Mom's up there saying, 'No way, no way. The guy's a drinker and has a serious alcohol problem and rah, rah, rah, rah, rah.' She took the stand and the end result was, 'Released on your own recognizance to the care of your mother.' My first reaction going through my mind was, 'Why you bastards! My mother [hearty laugh]. It's going to be the A.A. routine and all the rest of the bullshit.

"It was one hell of a long time before I got out of that bail court. They take me to the justice of the peace and he reads me the riot act and about my responsibilities and how serious it is and how dangerous I am and all the rest of this crap. 'You're going to be out on the street and it's only through the grace of God that you're so privileged to be one of society, and only marginally so, because you better be back here next week or you're dead meat.' Mom is right there to take all this in and when I get out my first intention is to get rid of her. I needed a drink real bad. I told her that I was going to stop drinking and I'd be looking into some means of getting some help 'cause clearly it was a problem. I got rid of her and went home and there weren't any beers in the fridge because my old pal had guzzled them all. I sent him down to the beer store and he crawled back with a 24 and about 19 bottles smashed. But at least I got some booze into me.

"Then there's a very authoritative knock at the door and it's the coppers! They want to come in and talk to me and they're saying, 'Look, we've found out who your buddy is.' You know how they play the game. They like to lead you to believe that they have information that you know damn well they don't have because they couldn't have it. Turns out they did have it. They said, 'We want to search your place.' I said, 'Come on in. Help yourself.' They came in and they sat around and they started quizzing me about my buddy. The idea of searching totally escaped their mind. I figured play ball with them and they probably aren't going to go after me 'cause they probably think it's a joke anyway. They questioned me about my buddy — they really wanted him, they wanted him badly. They were adamant that he put me up to it, so they were quite voracious about it, oh yeah. Finally they left. I had saved a little money from the robbery and I spent it in the next two weeks. I ran into my buddy, Joe, and we went out and got pissed a few times. He was very concerneed about my ability to keep my mouth shut. I had to repeatedly tell him. At one point I just told him, 'Fuck off. If I'm gonna rat on you, you wouldn't be here man. So, shut your mouth.' Joe got grabbed two months later and charged with being an accessory to and after the fact. It took me quite some time to convince him that it wasn't me that had turned him in. The prosecutor made the argument that Joe was a real rotten son-of-a-bitch and he took advantage of disabled people. I testified that the man had no knowledge respecting my intentions to do anything and he was acquitted.

"I drank for a month after I got out on bail and then I went through an alcohol program and stayed sober for a couple of months then I went and got stiffed. At one stage I was convinced I was going away. I was gonna lose the apartment and lose everything else. I got really depressed and attempted suicide. I just wanted to say to hell with it. I woke up in the cardiac unit of the hospital. This was about seven or eight months after my arrest. You go through a period where you're waiting for trial and the fucking thing is just hanging there and hanging there. You're just waiting and you can't really do anything else. You don't know what you're gonna do. You don't know what's gonna happen. Your life is stalled. It's in abeyance and you're at the whim of almost anybody. So I started to make the tour of the detox centres, get stiffed, go into a detox centre for a few days, eat well, and so on and so forth. I would say that a good percentage is 'poor me-isms' and the other 70 percent is denial scenario. There is no way you have an alcohol problem. You're either a world-killer or a 'poor me-ism' type.

"I had adopted the most irritating practice of calling my mother between two and four in the morning. At one point she finally got disgusted and said, 'I've really had enough talking to you when you're drunk. Don't call me until you start to do something about your alcohol.' I used to call her up and harass the shit out of her and tell her to pull my bail. Really just drive her around the bend. She refused to do it — never did, never did [laughs], poor mom.

"I pled guilty and the prosecution argued before the judge that there was a substantial increase in bank robberies and that a first conviction for robbery generally resulted in a sentence of two to three years! My whole defence was solely comprised of character witnesses. My mother took the stand, four character witnesses testified, and I had another 15-20 letters presented to the court as well. The argument being that mitigating circumstances, in the case being alcoholism, and that there is no prior history of any criminal wrongdoing. 'Honest to God Your Honour, absolutely no intentions of ever doing it again.' My lawyer argued that this is a very special case. It was an outrageous demand to expect that the accused should be locked up for three years. The judge said, 'I am suspending your sentence for a period of three years.' He put me on probation and I had to do 200 hours of community service work.

"I did the community service work within two and a half months of being sentenced. Eventually, I joined Alcoholics Anonymous and I have not seen the need to drink or do drugs since. I didn't go to Alcoholic's Anonymous because I was out on a Sunday afternoon for a stroll and decided I'd drop in on an A.A. meeting. People don't go to A.A. for that reason. People go to Alcoholic's Anonymous because they know they're desperate. I think this robbery thing and my arrest and trial have really turned things around. I used to drink myself out of jobs. I got back my old job part-time and I'm doing some volunteer work. I get by working part-time and I have disability pension that keeps my head above water."

I Need Help not Prison

This inmate is serving two years and nine months. He is 46 years old, robbed four banks, handed tellers a note, and turned himself in because he was remorseful. He has previously served time for manslaughter.

"I gave myself up and asked to be sent to the psychiatric hospital because I couldn't understand why I robbed banks. 'Cause that's not me, I'm not a thief. Most of the stuff I've done all my life is always on impulse and I never seem to plan anything. If I could only control my impulses.

"I have been in trouble with the law before. One of the worst was when I was charged and convicted of manslaughter for killing my wife. I got five years for that. We had family problems. I was drinking, I was drunk. I don't remember anything about that night. I only remember up to a certain hour and after that everything went blank. They told me that I stabbed her four times.

"Once I was sentenced to 18 months. I was charged with wounding with intent to kill, but it was dropped down to causing bodily harm. I was in a poolroom shooting pool and this guy came in and he had been drinking himself. I owed him $1.80 from before and I'm shooting this old guy, Billy. I'd spotted him 25 points for five bucks and there was three balls left on the table — blue, pink, and black. This guy comes in and starts demanding his money and I says, 'Look, as soon as I finish this game I'll pay ya.' Just as I wound up, he hit my pool cue and made me scratch. He says, 'No, I want my money now.' He was twice as big as I am and has shoulders yay wide. I got mad, turned around, and hit him over the head with the pool cue. That was it.

"A lot of people think that I'm a violent person because I got assault charges and I did kill my wife, even though I don't remember. And the parole board has a rule and the rule is: if you have any crimes with violence or threats of violence, you cannot get this or you cannot get that. When you're eligible for parole they say, 'Forget about getting it' because of that rule. The thing is there was no violence in the bank robberies. In the note there was a threat of violence if you interpret it that way, but I pointed out to them that I gave myself up. That shows there was no threat of violence. I asked myself, 'What the hell am I doing?' Robbing those banks got me scared. What happens if I run up against a little old woman who's got a bad heart and I give her a note and she has a heart attack?

"I go up front of the parole board next month. What I want to do is get out of here and go to the psychiatric hospital. What really bothers me is I gave myself up so I could get help and they sent me to prison. They're not giving me the help I want. They figure it's better just to contain the problem instead of solving it. They're just interested in keeping me in. They say to me, 'Well, we gotta do what's best for society.' I can't win. If I'd have known this was gonna happen, I'd have never have given myself up because I know, even though I didn't like doing it, they would never have caught me. I come before the parole board next month. I brought a copy of my letter to the parole board.

National Parole Board

Dear Sir or Madam,

I felt I had to write this letter to supply the board with information that may enhance my chances for day parole which is before you now.

Last year I committed a serious offence. I robbed four banks and got away with it. If I didn't give myself up, I know that I wouldn't be here today. My lawyer and the investigating officer said that if he didn't give himself up that they doubted that I would have been caught. Also I never kept the money for myself. I gave it to people who I knew really needed it. I didn't want it. So please ask yourself this. Why? If he meant to commit these crimes and get away with it why did he give himself up? If not for personal gain why? I really can't answer that. It was like a compulsion. I didn't want to do it and I knew it was wrong, but I couldn't stop myself. I don't expect you to

---

understand something like this, but neither do I. I got scared and afraid if I continued someone may be hurt. Not from me, but be frightened enough to keel over. They may of had a bad heart or anything like that and that scared me. I'm not a criminal of that kind. Yes, I have a record that you say is bad, but I am not a thief. I gave myself up in hopes of getting the help I needed, which I couldn't afford to pay for myself. I was not aware at the time that there was government funding for this type of treatment.

When I told the police I had done these banks, they took me to them to see if the tellers could give a positive identification. I had asked them if I could see the tellers personally so I could apologize too them for giving them such a terrible scare, which they did and I thanked them for it. When I talked to my lawyer, he felt that what happened had something to do with my having killed my wife. I really don't know and that is what I have to find out. In court, the judge remanded me for a 30-day observation at the psychiatric hospital. It is very hard for me to communicate with people so not very much was accomplished. There wasn't enough time. In the report though, the doctor stated that they would gladly institute treatment upon my release, which, I think, you have a copy of a letter confirming that.

The judge commended me for what I wanted to do but said, however, he had to impose a penitentiary sentence but he would also send a letter recommending psychiatric treatment. He gave me a sentence of two years nine months for each charge to run concurrent. My lawyer says that is the lowest that this judge has given out on a charge like this. I truly thank him for it. He must have believed me and I feel if he could he would have suspended sentence in order for me to get the treatment started now, but he couldn't.

Please don't get me wrong. I know that what I did was very serious and wrong, but I am sorry for what I did and I seriously dislike myself for doing it. No matter how I feel I can't change it. Only get things done so it won't happen again. For awhile there things were coming together beautifully. I hadn't been drinking for almost two years. Then things started to come apart and boom. Here I am. I don't expect you to believe me, but I am telling the truth. I have a chance now to get my life and head straightened out, which may not be there a year or two from now. You have a letter from the psychiatrist saying they would give me the help I need and you also have a letter from a college saying I can retake my courses if I can get out. I gave myself up asking for the kind of help I think I seriously need. In so doing I put my trust and faith in the authorities and society. I hope I haven't made a mistake putting my trust in the authorities. If you think it is in the best interest of society to just contain the problem and not help get rid of it, so be it.

Don't get me wrong, I'm not angry with anyone. I will just feel sorry. Sorry for people who can't tell the difference when a person commits a crime and a person who is a criminal and commits a crime. Well I have said what I felt I had too. The decision is yours. Help or not to help, that is the question. I hope my trust was not misplaced.

Sincerely yours

REFERENCES

Anglin, M.D., and G. Speckart. 1986. "Narcotics Use, Property Crime, and Dealing: Structural Dynamics Across the Addiction Career." *Journal of Quantitative Criminology* 2:355-375.

_____. 1988. "Narcotics Use and Crime: A Multisample, Multimethod Analysis." *Criminology* 26:197-233.

Ball, J.C. 1986. "The Hyper-Criminal Opiate Addict". In *Crime Rates Among Drug Abusing Offenders*, B.D. Johnson and E. Wish eds. National Institute of Justice, New York: Narcotic and Drug Research Inc.

Ball, J.C., J.W. Shaffer, and D.N. Nurco. 1983. "The Day-to-Day Criminality of Heroin Addicts in Baltimore: A Study in the Continuity of Offence Rates." *Drug and Alcohol Dependence* 12:119-142.

Ballard, M. 1992. "Bank Robbery 1991." *Canadian Banker* May-June: 28-30.

_____. 1993. "The Bad Guys Take a Break." *Canadian Banker* May-June: 40-41.

_____. 1994. "Holdup Review 1993." *Canadian Banker's Association*. Unpublished.

Bassiouni, M. 1981. "Terrorism, Law Enforcement, and the Mass Media: Perspectives, Problems, Proposals." *Journal of Criminal Law and Criminology* 72:1-51.

Berkowitz, L. 1984. "Some Effects of Thoughts on Anti- and Prosocial Influences of Media Events: A Cognitive-Neoassociation Analysis." *Psychological Bulletin* 95:410-417.

Blackwell, J.C. and P.G. Erikson. 1988. *Illicit Drugs In Canada: A Risky Business*. Scarborough: Nelson Publishers.

Blumstein, A., J. Cohen and D. P. Farrington. 1988. "Criminal Career Research: Its Value for Criminology." *Criminology* 26:1-35.

Camp, G. M. 1968. *Nothing to Lose: A Study of Bank Robbery in America*. Ann Arbor, Michigan: University Microfilms.

Caron, R. 1978. *Go Boy*. Toronto: McGraw-Hill Ryerson Limited.

_____. 1985. *Bingo*. Toronto: Methuen.

Chaiken, J. M., and M. R. Chaiken 1990. "Drugs and Predatory Crime." Pp. 203-239, in M. Tonry and J. Q. Wilson (eds.), *Drugs and Crime*. Chicago: The University of Chicago Press.

_____. 1989. *Redefining the Criminal Career: Priority Prosecution of High-Rate Dangerous Offenders*. Washington, D.C.: National Institute of Justice.

_____. 1982. *Varieties of Criminal Behavior*. Santa Monica, Calif: Rand Corporation.

Chambers, C.D., W.R. Cuskey, and A.D. Moffett. 1970. "Demographic Factors in Opiate Addiction Among Mexican Americans." *Public Health Reports* 85:523-531.

Ciale, J., and J.P. Leroux. 1983. *Armed Robbery in Ottawa: A Descriptive Case Study for Prevention*. Department of Criminology: University of Ottawa.

Clarke, R. and D. Cornish. 1985. "Modelling Offender's Decisions: A Framework for Research and Policy." In M. Tonry and N. Morris (eds.), *Crime and Justice: An Annual Review of Research*. Volume 6:147-85. Chicago: University of Chicago Press.

Cloward, R. 1959. "Illegitimate Means, Anomie, and Deviant Behavior." *American Sociological Review* 24:164-76.

Cloward, R. and L. Ohlin. 1960. *Delinquency and Opportunity*. Glencoe, IL: The Free Press.

Cohen, A. 1955. *Delinquent Boys: The Culture of the Gang*. New York: The Free Press of Glencoe.

_____. 1965. "The Sociology of the Deviant Act: Anomie Theory and Beyond." *American Sociological Review* 30:5-14.

Cohen, L. E. and M. Felson 1979. "Social Change and Crime Rate Trends: A Routine Activity Approach." *American Sociological Review* 44:588-608.

Collins, J.J., R. L. Hubbard, J. V. Rachal. 1985. "Expensive Drug Use and Illegal Income: A Test Of Explanatory Hypotheses." *Criminology* 23:743-763.

Comstock G. 1980. *Television in America*. Newbury Park, California: Sage.

Conklin, J. E. 1972. *Robbery and the Criminal Justice System*. New York: J. B. Lippincott Company

Cornish, D. B and R. V. Clarke (eds.). 1986. *The Reasoning Criminal*. New York: Springer-Verlag.

Cornish, D. B. and R. V. Clarke. 1986. "Introduction." Pp. 1-16, in D. B. Cornish and R. V. Clarke (eds.), *The Reasoning Criminal: Rational Choice Perspectives on Offending*. New York: Springer-Verlag.

Cressey, D. 1971. *Other People's Money: A Study in the Social Psychology of Embezzlement* (2nd. ed.). Belmont, CA: Wadsworth.

Desroches, F. J. 1995. *Force and Fear: Robbery in Canada*. Toronto: Nelson Canada.

_____. 1974. "The April 1971 Kingston Penitentiary Riot." *Canadian Journal of Criminology and Corrections* 16:317-331.

_____. 1981. "The Treatment of Hostages in Prison Riots: Some Hypotheses." *Canadian Journal of Criminology* 23:439-450.

Durkheim, E. [1893] 1933. *The Division of Labor in Society*. New York: The Free Press.

_____. [1899] 1951. *Suicide*. New York: The Free Press.

Fagan J. and J.G. Weis. 1990. *Drug Use and Delinquency among Inner City Youths*. New York: Springer-Verlag.

Faupel, C. E., and C. B. Klockars. 1987. "Drug-Crime Connections: Elaborations from the Life Histories of Hard-Core Heroin Addicts." *Social Problems* 34:54-68.

Feeney, F. 1986. "Robbers as Decision-Makers." Pp. 53-71, in D. B. Cornish and R. V. Clarke (eds.), *The Reasoning Criminal: Rational Choice Perspectives on Offending*. New York: Springer-Verlag.

Gabor, T., M. Baril, M. Cusson, D. Elie, M. Leblanc, A. Normadeau. 1987. *Armed Robbery: Cops, Robbers, and Victims*. Springfield, IL: Charles C. Thomas, Publisher.

Gandossy, R.P., J.R. Williams, J. Cohen, and H.J. Harwood. 1980. *Drugs and Crime: A Survey and Analysis of the Literature*. Washington, D.C.: Government Printing Office.

Gibbons, D. C. 1992. *Society, Crime, and Criminal Behavior*. Sixth Edition. Englewood Cliffs, NJ: Prentice-Hall.

Glaser, D. 1956. "Criminality Theories and Behavioral Images." *American Journal of Sociology* 61:433-44.

Goldman, F. 1976. "Drug Markets and Addict Consumption Behavior." In *Drug Use and Crime*. Report on the Panel on Drug Abuse and Criminal Behavior. Research Triangle Park, NC: Research Triangle Institute.

Gottfredson, M. and T. Hirschi. 1986. "The True Value Of Lambda Would Appear To Be Zero: An Essay On Career Criminals, Criminal Careers, Selective Incapacitation, Cohort Studies, And Related Topics." *Criminology* 24:213-233.

Greenberg, D. F. 1991. "Modeling Criminal Careers." *Criminology* 29:17-44.

Greenberg, S.W. and F. Adler. 1974. "Crime and Addiction: An Emperical Analysis of the Literature, 1920-1973." *Contemporary Drug Problems* 3:221-269.

Hanson, B., G. Beschner, J.M. Walters, and E. Bovelle. 1985. *Life With Heroin: Voices from the Inner City*. Lexington, MA: Lexington Books.

Haran, James F. and John M. Martin. 1977. "The Imprisonment of Bank Robbers: The Issue of Deterrence." *Federal Probation* 41:27-30.

_____. 1984 "The Armed Urban Bank Robber: A Profile." *Federal Probation* 48:47-53.

Hirschi, T. 1986. "On the Compatibility of Rational Choice and Social Control Theories of Crime." Pp. 105-118, in D. B. Cornish and R. V. Clarke (eds.), *The Reasoning Criminal: Rational Choice Perspectives on Offending*. New York: Springer-Verlag.

Hirschi, T. 1969. *Causes of Delinquency*. Berkeley: University of California Press.

Johnson, B., P. Goldsein, E. Preble, J. Schmeidler, D. Lipton, B. Spunt, and T. Miller. 1985. *Taking Care of Business: The Economics of Crime by Heroin Abusers*. Lexington MA: Lexington Books

Katz, J. 1991. "The Motivation of the Persistent Robber." In M. Tonry (ed.), *Crime and Justice: A Review of Research*. Volume 14:277-306. Chicago: The University of Chicago Press.

Linden, R. 1992 "Social Control Theory." Pp. 315-348, in R. Linden (ed.), *Criminology*. Toronto: Harcourt Brace Jovanovich.

Livingstone, N. 1982. *The War Against Terrorism*. Lexington, MA: D.C. Heath.

Mande, M.J. and K. English. 1988. *Individual Crime Rates of Colorado Prisoners*. Denver: Colorado Department of Public Safety, Division of Criminal Justice.

Matza, D. 1964. *Delinquency and Drift*. New York: John Wiley and Sons.

McGlothlin, W.H., M.D. Anglin, and B.D. Wison. 1978. "Narcotic Addiction and Crime." *Criminology* 16:293-315.

Merton, R. K. 1938. "Social Structure and Anomie." *American Sociological Review* 3:672-682.

_____. 1968 *Social Theory and Social Structure* (2nd. ed.) New York: Free Press.

Pease, S. and C. Love. 1984. "The Copy-Cat Crime Phenomenon." Pp. 199-211, in R. Surette (ed.), *Justice and the Media*. Springfield, IL: Charles C. Thomas, Publisher.

Petersilia, J. 1980. "Criminal Career Research: A Review of Recent Evidence." In N. Morris and M. Tonry (eds.) *Crime and Justice: An Annual Review of Research*. Volume 2:321-379. Chicago: The University of Chicago Press.

Petersilia, J., P.W. Greenwood, and M. Lavin. 1978. *Criminal Careers of Habitual Felons*. Washington, D.C.: U.S. Government Printing Office.

Peterson, M.A. and H.B. Braiker. 1980. *Doing Crime: A Survey of California Prison Inmates*. Santa Monica, CA: Rand.

Plair, W. and L. Jackson. 1970. *Narcotic Use and Crime. A Report on Interviews With 50 Addicts Under Treatment*. Research Report 33. Washington, D.C.: Department of Corrections.

Reid, S. 1986. *Jackrabbit Parole*. McClelland and Stewart-Bantam Limited.

Schmid A., and J. de Graaf. 1982. *Violence as Communication*. Newbury Park, CA: Sage

Shaw, C. R., and H. D. McKay. [1942] 1972. *Juvenile Delinquency in Urban Areas*. Chicago: The University of Chicago Press.

Simcha-Fagan, O. and J.E. Schwartz. 1986. "Neighborhood and Delinquency: An Assessment of Contextual Effects." *Criminology* 24: 667-695.

Simon, H.A. 1957. *Models of Man.* New York: Wiley.

Speckart, G. and M.D. Anglin. 1986. "Narcotics Use and Crime: A Causal Modeling Approach." *Journal of Quantitative Criminology* 2: 3-28.

Stanton, J.M. 1969. *Lawbreaking and Drug Dependence.* Albany: New York State Division of Parole.

Surette, Ray. 1992. *Media, Crime, and Criminal Justice: Images and Realities.* Pacific Grove, CA: Brooks / Cole Publishing Company.

_____. 1990. "Media Trials and Echo Effects." Pp. 177-192, in R. Surette (ed.), *Media and Criminal Justice Policy.* Springfield, IL: Charles C. Thomas, Publisher.

Sutherland, E. H. 1947. *The Principles of Criminology* (4th. ed.). Philadelphia: J.B. Lippincott.

Sutherland, E. H. and D. R. Cressey. 1978. *Criminology* (10th ed.). Philadelphia: J.B. Lippincott.

Sykes, G. M. and D. Matza. 1957 "Techniques of Neutralization: A Theory of Delinquency." *American Sociological Review* 22:664-670.

Thornberry, T. P. 1987 "Toward an Interactional Theory of Delinquency." *Criminology* 25:863-891.

Toby, J. 1957. "Social Disorganization and Stake in Conformity: Complementary Factors in the Predatory Behavior of Hoodlums." *Journal of Criminal Law, Criminology, and Police Science* 48:12-17.

Voss, H.L., and R.C. Stephens. 1973. "Criminality History of Narcotic Addicts." *Drug Forum* 2:191-202.

White, H.R., R.J. Pandina, and R LaGrange. 1987. "Longitudinal Predictors of Serious Substance Use and Delinquency." *Criminology* 25:715-740.

Williams, T.M., and W. Kornblum. 1985. *Growing Up Poor.* Lexington, MA: Lexington Books.